THE CATHOLIC UNIVERSITY OF AMERICA
CANON LAW STUDIES
No. 202

Adverse Possession, Prescription and Limitation of Actions. The Canonical "Praescriptio"

A COMMENTARY ON CANON 1508

BY

THOMAS O. MARTIN, PH.D., S.T.D., J.C.L.
Priest of the Diocese of Grand Rapids

A DISSERTATION

Submitted to the Faculty of the School of Canon Law of the Catholic University of America in Partial Fulfillment of the Requirements for the Degree of Doctor of Canon Law

THE CATHOLIC UNIVERSITY OF AMERICA PRESS
WASHINGTON, D. C.
1944

Nihil Obstat:

Hieronymus D. Hannan, S.T.D., LL.B., J.C.D.,

Censor Deputatus.

Washingtonii, die 9 Maii, 1944

Imprimatur:

✠ Franciscus J. Haas, D.D., LL.D.,

Episcopus Grandormensis.

Grandormii, die 20 Maii, 1944.

Printed by

The Paulist Press

New York, N. Y.

 51

TABLE OF CONTENTS

CHAPTER III

FOREWORD

It is the purpose of this dissertation to give to the Canonists in the United States a brief view of the American Law on Adverse Possession, Prescription, and Limitation of Actions, since all these institutes are covered by the canonical "*Praescriptio*" which, according to canon 1508, is now to be regulated in the canonical courts of this country by our civil law except for the points expressly excepted in the Code of Canon Law.

It will be noted in this study that authors who have written on the Canon Law are used very sparingly. The reason for this is that writing on the Continent with a continental background they are not, generally regarded, familiar with the law of England and of the United States of America, as is indicated by the footnotes in their works. This unfamiliarity has at times led them to state that "*praescriptio*" does not exist in our law, or does not exist in our law as to movable goods, which, of course, is false; or to give an entirely inadequate impression of the time required for "*praescriptio*" here.

To obtain a better understanding of the practical application of the canonical institute of "*praescriptio*" one may find useful the cases cited from the Sacred Roman Rota, even though the rule "*stare decisis*" does not hold under the Canon Law, because this method of treatment accords better with the method of citing cases in the American Law to state the law of the various jurisdictions. The cases from the American Law have been kept to a minimum lest the bulk of this work become too unwieldy.

The American Law on these institutes is so vast that of necessity much has been omitted. It is therefore suggested that a court of Canon Law would do well, in the event that a case involving these matters is brought before it, to make use of the advice and counsel of some one skilled in the law of the particular state in which the court has jurisdiction, that so advised and counseled it may be able to follow the law of that state as the Code requires.

The writer wishes to take this opportunity to render public thanks to those who have made possible the course of studies in the School of Canon Law of The Catholic University of America and all those who by their assistance, advice, and counsel have aided in the preparation of this work, especially the Faculty of the aforesaid School of Canon Law.

CHAPTER I

GENERAL NOTIONS

Article 1. Nature of the Institute

1. *"Praescriptio,"* as the name implies, was a notation by the pretor at the top of a bill of a complaint, e. g., *"Si in ea re decem anni non decurrerint,"* which indicates its place originally as a remedy.[1] The idea of limiting the time within which actions might be brought for the recovery of property, real or personal, which is very ancient in the Roman Law,[2] was, when the Canon Law began to develop for itself, taken over for several reasons: (a) it served to prevent questions of ownership of property from being confused and uncertain for a long time; [3] (b) it ended suits more readily, where otherwise they would be practically immortal; (c) it removed the fear of possessors that they might lose their property, as a result of which fear no one would cultivate his fields or, if he did, would do so carelessly,

[1] Cf. Hostiensis, Cardinalis (Henricus de Segusio), *Summa Aurea* (Lugduni, 1568), f. 163v, *"Ex quo vidimus de exceptionibus in genere, dicamus in specie et sic apponamus rubricam de praescriptionibus . . ."* hereinafter cited Hostiensis; Ernricus Pirhing, S.J., *Jus Canonicum* (ed. noviss. 5 vols. in 4, Dilingae, 1722), lib. II, tit. 26, n. 1, " . . . *quia vero praescriptio est quaedam species exceptionis peremptoriae* . . . ," hereinafter cited Pirhing; Anacletus Reiffenstuel, O.F.M., *Ius Canonicum Universum,* (ed. noviss. 6 vols. in 5, Romae 1831-1834), lib. II, tit. 26, n. 3, hereinafter cited Reiffenstuel; Franciscus Schmalzgrueber, S.J., *Ius Ecclesiasticum Universum* (5 vols. in 12, Romae, 1843-1845), Part. III, tit. 26, *princ.*, hereinafter cited Schmalzgrueber; Franciscus Xaverius Wernz, S.J., *Ius Decretalium* (2. ed., 6 vols. in 10 toms., Romae et Prati, 1905-1913), tom. III, tit. 11, n. 293, hereinafter cited Wernz; and modern commentators generally.

[2] Cf. Gaius, *Institutiones* (ed. Johannes Baviera in *Fontes Iuris Romani Antejustiniani,* Florentiae, 1909), (2.44), hereinafter cited Gaius; *Corpus Iuris Civilis* (ed. stereotypa quinta decima, Vol. I, *Institutiones,* recognovit Paulus Krueger, *Digesta,* recognovit Theodorus Mommsen, retractavit Paulus Krueger, Berolini: apud Weidmannos, 1928), I (2.6), hereinafter cited I and D.

[3] Gaius (2.44); I (2.6).

since he might be working for some one else; (d) it stirred men from their lethargy so that they would protect their rights and take more care of their property when they saw that they would lose their right of ownership as punishment for their negligence.[4]

2. The English common Law at first allowed a plaintiff to summon a defendant at any time which suited the plaintiff's convenience.[5] It was found, however, as at Rome, that such a privilege for the plaintiff produced great inconvenience, and at times even great injustice to the defendant, because the plaintiff could, and at times did, wait until witnesses were dead or papers destroyed, and then proceeded to enforce claims to which at an earlier date a successful defense could have been made. As a result titles were rendered uncertain, the tenure of property was less secure, and litigation was fostered. The doctrine of fines which appears early in the history of the common law, the purpose of which was to put an end to controversies, grew out of the efforts to obviate the aforesaid evils, and there were frequent statutes, though their scope was limited, to this same end. It was not, however, until 1623 that stat. 21 James I, c. 16, entitled, "An act for Limitation of Actions, and for Avoiding of Suits in Law," known ever since as the *Statute of Limitations,* declared in comprehensive fashion the law on this subject. The law therein contained is substantially that which exists at the present day in England, whence our ancestors brought it to this country. It has passed, with modifications, into the statute-books of every state in the Union except Louisiana, whose laws of limitation are essentially the prescriptions of the Civil Law, drawn from the *Partidas,* or Spanish Code.[6]

3. The periods of time vary according to the variation in economic conditions in various epochs, but the fundamental purposes

[4] Schmalzgrueber, Part. III, tit. 26, n. 4; Pirhing, lib. II, tit. 26, n. 4; Reiffenstuel, lib. II, tit. 26, n. 18 sqq.; Wernz, tom. III, tit. 11, n. 294; and modern authors generally.

[5] 13 East. 449.

[6] Bouvier's *Law Dictionary* (Rawle's third revision, 2 vols., Kansas City, Missouri, and St. Paul, Minnesota, 1914), 2 Bouvier 1998, hereinafter cited Bouvier; cf. generally for American Law 2 Bouvier 1998-2021, 37 C.J. 666-1260.

of the limitation of actions remain those stated above, whether in regard to the Roman and Canon Law, or in regard to the English and American Law. The Civil and Canon Laws for centuries followed the time limits established by Justinian, i. e., three years for movables, ten years for realty if plaintiff and defendant had both lived in the same province for that length of time, twenty years if plaintiff had not been living in the same province with the defendant (possessor). If plaintiff had lived partly in the same province with the defendant and partly outside of that province the years spent outside were doubled in computation, e. g., if he lived five years in the province and then moved out he was allowed ten more years, making a total of fifteen before the adverse possession or prescription was considered complete. Thirty years was considered sufficiently long to cut off all actions, though at Rome in the sixteenth century this was reduced to sixteen years. Whether the adverse possession was begun in good faith, as was required in the case of the ten- and twenty-year periods, or not was, under the Civil Law, immaterial if the adverse possession had lasted thirty years. In the case of Churches, however, the forty-year period was established to afford them greater protection in matters of property.

4. The Code of Canon Law speaks of "*praescriptio*" as a means of acquiring property or rights and of freeing one's self from an obligation.[7] The distinction of the American Law, after the English, between adverse possession or prescription continued for the established period of time as a means of acquiring title, and limitation of actions as a defense to an action, seems, however, to be clearer, since it stresses the fact that it is not merely the running of the period of time but the possession of the property or right adverse to the interests of the true owner which is to be considered in the two former institutes, leaving the third, limitation of actions, what it is primarily, i. e., a matter of procedural law affecting one's right to sue.[8]

[7] *Codex Iuris Canonici Pii X Pontificis Maximi iussu digestus Benedicti Papae XV auctoritate promulgatus*, Romae: Typis Polyglottis Vaticanis, 1917. Reimpressio, 1930, hereinafter cited, canon 1508.

[8] Cf. Battle v. Shivers, 39 Ga. 405; Baker v. Kelley, 11 Minn. 480; U. S. Bank v. Biddle, 2 Pars. Eq. Cas. (Pa.) 31.

Adverse Possession in the American Law is the enjoyment of land, or such estate as lies in grant, under such circumstances as indicate that such enjoyment has been commenced and continued under an assertion or color of right on the part of the possessor.[9] A prescriptive title rests upon a different principle from that of a title arising under the statute of limitations. Prescription operates as evidence of a grant and confers a positive title.[10] The statute of limitations operates not so much to confer positive title on the occupant, as to bar the remedy. Hence it is said to be properly called a negative prescription.[11] It applies only when there has been a disseisin or some actionable invasion of the real owner's possession.[12]

Prescription in the American Law is a mode of acquiring title to incorporeal hereditaments by immemorial or long-continued enjoyment.[13] An incorporeal hereditament is said to be anything, the subject of property, which is inheritable and not tangible or visible,[14] a right issuing out of a thing corporate (whether real or personal) or concerning or annexed to or exercisable within the same.[15] From what has been said thus far, one can see that while one may hold realty or personalty adversely, one cannot properly be said to "prescribe" them.

Article 2. Persons Involved

5. It is clear that suit will not be brought except against a person already in possession to oust him, and in such case he will be the one to use the defense of title by adverse possession or of prescription of the right; or against a defendant in a personal action

[9] 3 East 394; Wallace v. Duffield, 2 S. & R. (Pa.) 527, 7 Am. Dec. 660; French v. Pearce, 8 Conn. 440, 21 Am. Dec. 680.

[10] William Cruise, *A Digest of the Law of Real Property* (rev. H. Hopeley: Boston, 1849-50, 7 vols. in 3), tit. 21, ch. 1, § 4.

[11] *Ibid.*

[12] Clawson v. Primrose, 4 Del. Ch. 670 n.

[13] 2 Bouvier 2671.

[14] 2 Richard Wooddeson, *Lectures on the Laws of England* (Notes by W. R. Williams, Philadelphia, 1842), Lect. 4.

[15] 2 Blackstone's *Commentaries on the Law* (ed. Bernard C. Gavit, Washington Law Book Co., Washington, D. C., 1941), 20; Walker v. Daly, 80 Wis. 222, 49 N.W. 812.

who will use the defense of limitation. If the one in possession desires to assert his right to the property he will merely state that he is now and has been for a long time in possession thereof and that he believes himself the true owner. Thus he is not likely to consider it necessary to claim "adverse" possession, unless he needs to remove a cloud which now appears on his title to the property. Were the possessor to bring an action to be declared owner merely because he had held the property for the stated number of years, one might suspect that there was bad faith involved and that he had been merely waiting for the statutory period to lapse in order to proclaim himself owner, when he had known all along, or at least suspected, that he was not really entitled to the property in question.

6. Anyone capable of holding property may under certain conditions hold it adversely to the interests of another whether the one holding be a natural physical person, or a corporation.[16] Likewise the one whose property is adversely held may be either a natural physical person, or a corporation, according to the conditions required by law.[17]

Article 3. When an Action Is "Brought"

7. Since the gist of the limitation of actions is that if the action is not brought within the specified time it cannot under the law be brought at all, it is necessary to consider what constitutes the bringing of an action or the commencement of process. The Canon Law states specifically that when process has been duly served or the parties have of their own accord come into court the *"praescriptio"* is interrupted,[18] and this is the law of some of the United States. The Canon Law, however, considers the laws of the country in which

[16] Cf. Rufinus, *Summa Decretorum* (ed. Singer, Paderborn, 1902), hereinafter cited Rufinus, p. 358; Bernardi Papiensis *Summa Decretalium* (ed. Laspeyres, Ratisbonae, 1860), lib. II, tit. 18, n. 8, hereinafter cited Bernardus Papiensis, *Summa;* Hostiensis, f. 163v; Pirhing, lib. II, tit. 26, n. 9; Sancti Raymundi de Peñafort *Summa* (Veronae, 1744), lib. II, tit. 5, q. 9, hereinafter cited S. Raymundus, *Summa;* Schmalzgrueber, Part. III, tit. 26, n. 17; Wernz, tom. III, tit. 11, n. 296; and modern commentators generally.

[17] Cf. authors mentioned in the preceding note.

[18] Canon 1725, 4°.

the canonical court is sitting as binding in the matter of *"praescriptio,"* [19] and in the American Law it is quite uniformly held that the bringing of an action or the commencement of process is the delivery or transmission by mail in due course of the writ or process to the sheriff, in good faith, for service.[20] The American Law, therefore, considers a suit begun when the summons is delivered to the officer who in Canon Law would be known as the *"cursor,"* [21] hence the running of the limitation stops sooner in the United States than elsewhere under the Canon Law, except in those states which require actual service to stop the running. The date of the writ is *prima facie* evidence of the time of its issuance,[22] but is by no means conclusive.[23] The exception mentioned as to some states is likewise to be found in Federal procedure where the suit is not "brought" or "commenced" to stop the running of the statute, until there is a *bona fide* attempt to serve the process.[24] It seems, however, that since the court of Canon Law sits within the territory of the state, and canon 1508 mentions "territory," the rule in the particular state must be followed in this regard.

8. In some cases failure of the action suspends the running of the limitation. Examples of such cases are: 1—if a summons seasonably issued fails of a sufficient service or return by any unavoidable accident, or by any default or neglect of the officer to whom it is committed, or is abated, or the action is otherwise avoided by the death of any party thereto, or for any matter of form, or judgment for plaintiff is arrested or reversed, the plaintiff may, either by virtue of a statutory provision, or by reason of an implied exception to the general rule, commence a new action within a reasonable time; and that reasonable time is usually fixed by the statutes at one year, and by the courts in the absence of statutory provision at the same

[19] Canon 1508.

[20] Jackson v. Brooks, 14 Wend. (N.Y.) 649.

[21] Canons 1591, § 1; 1717, § 1.

[22] Gardner v. Webber, 17 Pick. (Mass.) 407; Johnson v. Farwell, 7 Greenl. (Me.) 370, 22 Am. Dec. 203.

[23] 2 Burr. 950; Badger v. Phinney, 15 Mass. 364, 8 Am. Dec. 105.

[24] U. S. v. Lumber Co., 80 Fed. 309; cf. canon 1721.

period; [25] 2—if a petition when amended contains only a restatement of the case as contained in the original; [26] 3—if a petition stricken out because it does not contain the formal allegations required is subsequently amended; [27] 4—if the action was dismissed merely because of the clerk's omission seasonably to enter it on the docket; [28] 5—if a petition is dismissed [29] for want of jurisdiction where it was brought in the wrong county; [30] 6—if an action to recover for personal injuries is dismissed for failure to file a declaration.[31] In these cases, then, the "*praescriptio*" at Canon Law will be interrupted.

9. In other cases failure of the action does not stop the running of the limitation. Examples of such cases are: 1—if the attorney made a mistake as to time of the sitting of the court, and consequently failed to enter suit, the interruption is not allowed; [32] 2—if a non-suit is entered; [33] 3—if there are two defendants, and by reason of failure of service upon one an alias writ is taken out, this is no continuance, but a new action; [34] 4—if the amending bill introduces new parties; [35] 5—if suit is brought at law after being dismissed from chancery for want of jurisdiction, the time having run; [36]

[25] 1 Ld. Raym. 434; Downing v. Lindsay, 2 Pa. 382; Huntington v. Brinckerhoff, 10 Wend. (N.Y.) 278. Irregularity of the mail is an inevitable accident within the meaning of the statute, Jewett v. Greene, 8 Greenl. (Me.) 447; and so is failure of service by reason of removal of the defendant, without the knowledge of the plaintiff, from the county in which he had resided and to which the writ was seasonably sent, Bullock v. Dean, 12 Metc. (Mass.) 15.

[26] Chicago & A. R. Co. v. Henneberry, 42 Ill. App. 126.

[27] Howard v. Windom, 86 Tex. 560, 26 S.W. 483.

[28] Allen v. Sawtelle, 7 Gray (Mass.) 165, considered mere matter of form there.

[29] Not so in Maine, cf. Donnell v. Gatchell, 38 Me. 217.

[30] Woods v. Houghton, 1 Gray (Mass.) 580.

[31] La Follette Coal, Iron & R. Co. v. Minton, 117 Tenn. 415, 101 S.W. 178, 11 L.R.A. (N.S.) 478.

[32] Packard v. Swallow, 29 Me. 458.

[33] Harris v. Dennis, 1 S. & R. (Pa.) 236; Ivins v. Schooley, 18 N.J.L. 269; Swan v. Littlefield, 6 Cush. (Mass.) 417; some states hold otherwise, Long v. Orrell, 35 N.C. 123; Haymaker v. Haymaker, 4 Ohio St. 272.

[34] Magaw v. Clark, 6 Watts (Pa.) 528.

[35] Miller v. McIntyre, 6 Pet. (U.S.) 61, 8 L. Ed. 320.

[36] 1 Vern. 74; Barker v. Millard, 16 Wend. (N.Y.) 572.

6—if the original petition stated no cause of action whatever, and the amendment is filed after the statute has run.[37]

Article 4. What Law Governs

10. Considered in its remedial aspect *"praescriptio"* will not come under consideration until it is raised as a pleading in defense to an action instituted in some court. It will then be considered according to the rules of that court rather than according to the law of the place where the contract is made or the wrong done. If the statute has run against a claim in one state, the remedy is gone, but the right is not extinguished; and therefore the right may be enforced in another state where the remedy is still open, the time limited by the statute not having expired,[38] provided, of course, that there is some title whereby the judge in the other state is competent to sit in judgment on the case in question.[39] Conversely, if the statute of the place of the contract is still unexpired, nevertheless, an action brought in another place is governed by the *lex fori* and may be barred.[40]

11. Statutes giving title by adverse possession are to be distinguished from statutes of limitation. Adverse possession gives title; lapse of time bars the remedy only. A right acquired by adverse possession in the place where the adverse possession is had is good elsewhere.[41]

12. Some states have statutes providing that an action will be considered barred in that jurisdiction whenever it is so barred by the law of the state where the cause of action accrued. Such a statute has reference only to the primary and original jurisdiction in which

[37] Missouri, K. & T. R. Co. v. Bagley, 65 Kan. 188, 69 Pac. 189, 3 L.R.A. (N.S.) 259.

[38] 15 East. 439; Flowers v. Foreman, 23 How. (U.S.) 132, 16 L. Ed. 405; Putnam v. Dike, 13 Gray (Mass.) 535.

[39] Cf. canons 1559-1568.

[40] Nask v. Tupper, 1 Cai. (N.Y.) 402, 2 Am. Dec. 197; 5 Cl. & F. 1; Thomas v. Clarkson, 125 Ga. 72, 54 S.E. 77, 6 L.R.A. (N.S.) 658.

[41] Shelby v. Guy, 11 Wheat. (U.S.) 361, 6 L. Ed. 495; Townsend v. Jemison, 9 How. (U.S.) 407, 13 L. Ed. 194; Joseph Story, *Conflict of Laws* (5. ed., Boston, 1857), p. 582.

the action arose, and does not contemplate other jurisdictions in which a cause of action may arise because a defendant takes up his domicil therein.[42] Where, therefore, the action in the original jurisdiction is not barred, but is barred by the statute of another state of which the defendant is a resident, the original action is not barred in a third state which has a comity statute.[43]

Article 5. When "*Praescriptio*" Does Not Operate

13. Those whose relationship to the true owner is such, namely, that as a result of it they cannot properly assert a right to the property in opposition to his, cannot plead the limitation of actions. Thus a cleric, no matter how long he possesses a thing as remuneration from the church, cannot by adverse possession acquire it as his own property.[44]

14. A tenant, at Canon Law, could not acquire by adverse possession against his landlord.[45] It is likewise the American Law that the possession of the tenant is the possession of his landlord, and cannot be adverse unless he distinctly renounces his landlord's title,[46] and one who holds personalty by consent of the true owner is not entitled to have the statute run in his favor until denial of the true

[42] McKee v. Dodd, 152 Cal. 637, 93 Pac. 854, 14 L.R.A. (N.S.) 780, 125 Am. St. Rep. 82.

[43] Doughty v. Funk, 15 Okl. 643, 84 Pac. 484, 4 L.R.A. (N.S.) 1029.

[44] C. 11, C. XVI, q. 3; *Decisiones Sacrae Rotae Romanae coram R.P.D. Marcello Crescentio* (5 vols., Romae, 1763), tom. 4, dec. 156, n. 7, hereinafter cited *S.R.R. coram Crescentio; Sacrae Rotae Romanae Decisiones Recentiores* (Part. I, Francofurti, 1623; Part. 2, Aurelii, 1623; Part. 3-19, Romae, 1645-1703), hereinafter cited by place, type of case, name of judge and date, as follows: *S.R.R. in causa Barchinonen., Congruae, coram Taia* (1673)—*Decisiones Recentiores,* Part. 18, tom. 1, dec. 81, n. 44. Under American Law he is a tenant.

[45] *Glossa* in c. 11, C. XVI, q. 3 ad v. *In ius proprium;* cf. also in c. 12, X, *de praescriptionibus,* II, 26, ad v. *Non obstante.*

[46] 2 Campb. 11; Willison v. Watkins, 3 Pet. (U.S.) 43, 7 L. Ed. 596; Shepley v. Lytle, 6 Watts (Pa.) 500; Alderson v. Marshall, 7 Mont. 288, 16 Pac. 576; Brunson v. Morgan, 84 Ala. 598, 4 South. 589; Bedlow v. Dry-Dock Co., 112 N.Y. 263, 19 N.E. 800, 2 L.R.A. 629; Parish Board of School Directors v. Edrington, 40 La. Ann. 633, 4 South. 574.

owner's claim,[47] while mere non-payment of rent during the time limited, there having been no demand, does not prejudice the landlord's right to enter and demand it, even though the lease contains a clause giving the right of entry in case of non-payment of rent.[48] Payment of rent is conclusive evidence that the occupation of the party paying was permissive and not adverse.[49]

15. A licensee[50] is likewise incapable of acquiring by adverse possession both under the law of the *Corpus Iuris Canonici*,[51] and under the present Code, that which he holds, since in the American Law, if the possession is permissive it is not adverse.[52]

16. An agent, at Canon Law, holding in the name of another is not permitted to acquire by adverse possession the thing held, since he necessarily would be in bad faith.[53] The American Law, too, holds that the relation of the agent to his principal is a fiduciary one, so that he cannot plead limitation of the action against such principal until there is a breach of his trust or duty.[54] The possession of the agent is, after all, only the possession of his principal.[55]

The limitation runs then at American Law when: 1—a breach known to the principal occurs;[56] 2—a demand has been made on the agent to perform his duty and he has neglected or refused to comply;[57] 3—the conduct of the agent amounts to a declaration

[47] Lucas v. Daniels, 34 Ala. 188; Joseph Kinnicut Angell, *Limitations* (4. ed. by John Wilder May, Boston, 1861), § 304, n.; Baker v. Chase, 55 N.H. 61.

[48] Jackson v. Davis, 5 Cow. (N.Y.) 123, 15 Am. Dec. 451; 7 East. 299.

[49] 3 B. & C. 135.

[50] *Praecario possidens.*

[51] *Glossa* in c. 11, C. XVI, q. 3 ad v. *In ius proprium* and in c. 12, X, *de praescriptionibus,* II, 26 ad v. *Non obstante;* cf. also Schmalzgrueber, Part. III, tit. 26, n. 18.

[52] 2 Jac. & W. 1.

[53] C. 17, X, *de praescriptionibus,* II, 26; *Glossa* in c. 11, C. XVI, q. 3 ad v. *In ius proprium* and in c. 12, X, *de praescriptionibus,* II, 26 ad v. *Non obstante*; Schmalzgrueber, Part. III, tit. 26, n. 18.

[54] McHarry v. Irvin's Ex'r, 85 Ky. 322, 3 S.W. 374, 4 S.W. 800.

[55] Lantry v. Parker, 37 Neb. 353, 55 N.W. 962. Cf. Stanley v. Schwalby, 147 U.S. 508, 13 Sup. Ct. 418, 37 L. Ed. 259.

[56] Green v. Johnson, 3 Gill & J. (Md.) 389; Appeal of Hart, 32 Conn. 520.

[57] Downey v. Garard, 24 Pa. 52.

that he will not perform; [58] 4—the agent has disabled himself from performing; [59] 5—an untrue account is rendered by a collection agent; [60] 6—the agent has collected the money, if custom of trade or a law requires no demand, otherwise on the lapse of a reasonable time after notice to the principal of the collection.[61] In these cases, it will be noted, the principal is not without information of the agent's repudiation of the relationship. It is true that the Canon Law considered an agent holding against his principal to be in bad faith, but with the repudiation of the relationship known to the principal it seems that the relationship which prevented the adverse holding is terminated, and since the principal has knowledge of the fact he is bound to act within the required time even at Canon Law, since otherwise the agent would always be open to suit, which is contrary to the purpose of "*praescriptio*." [62]

If, on the other hand, the agent is really a trustee, e. g., if he is entrusted with money or property with power of investment, management, and general control, the limitation does not run under the American Law.[63]

17. A life-tenant is also, according to the Canon Law, precluded from acquiring by adverse possession the property by him held for life so as to turn it into a fee.[64] In this regard the American Law holds that the possession of a life tenant and of those claiming under him, or subject to his control, is not adverse to those entitled in remainder.[65] It is also said that the statute does not begin to run until a cause of action accrues,[66] so limitations do not begin to run against

[58] Farmers' and Mechanics' Bank of Georgetown v. Bank, 10 Gill & J. (Md.) 422.

[59] Cf. preceding note.

[60] Clark v. Moody, 17 Mass. 145.

[61] Lyle v. Murray, 4 Sandf. (N.Y.) 590.

[62] Cf. *supra*, nn. 1-2.

[63] Bacon v. Rives, 106 U.S. 99, 1 Sup. Ct. 3, 27 L. Ed. 69.

[64] *Glossa* in c. 11, C. XVI, q. 3 ad v. *In ius proprium* and in c. 12, X, *de praescriptionibus*, II, 26 ad v. *Non obstante*. Cf. also Schmalzgrueber, Part. III, tit. 26, n. 18.

[65] Austin v. Brown, 37 W. Va. 634, 17 S.E. 207.

[66] Aachen, etc., F. Ins. Co. v. Morton, 156 Fed. 654, 84 C.C.A. 366, 15 L.R.A. (N.S.) 156, 13 Ann. Cas. 692.

a remainderman suing a life beneficiary as trustee to determine the rights of the parties in trust property until the death of the life-tenant.[67]

18. A partner, no matter how long he possesses real estate paid for with partnership funds and conveyed to him, cannot bar the other partner, under the American Law.[68] There must be some action by one partner against the others, e. g., a demand for an accounting and settlement, to terminate the fiduciary relation before the limitation will run.[69] The relation between copartners does not, however, create such a trust as will exempt a bill for an account and settlement from the operation of the statute of limitations.[70]

19. A trustee, because of his relationship, cannot plead limitation of the action against his cestui que trust, provided the trust is technical, i. e., direct, express,[71] continuing, exclusively within the jurisdiction of a court of equity,[72] and subsisting; [73] because possession of the trustee is possession of the cestui and the trustee holds according to the cestui's title,[74] so while this condition exists no cause of action has accrued.[75] Laches on the part of the cestui or such lapse of time as gives rise to a presumption of discharge or extinguishment of the trust will, however, bar the cestui.[76]

Examples of trusts exempt from the limitation are: 1—those

[67] Putnam v. Lincoln Safe Deposit Co., 118 App. Div. 468, 104 N.Y. 4 (mod. 49 Misc. 578, 100 N.Y. 101, and rev. on other grounds 191 N.Y. 166, 83 N.E. 789); Pritchard v. Williams, 175 N.C. 319, 95 S.E. 570.

[68] Riddle v. Whitehill, 135 U. S. 621, 10 Sup. Ct. 924, 34 L. Ed. 282.

[69] Baker v. Brown, 151 N.C. 12, 65 S.E. 520.

[70] Williams v. Walker, 148 Ark. 49, 229 S.W. 28.

[71] Wallace v. Mize, 153 Ga. 374, 112 S.E. 724. But the rule is subject to exceptions.

[72] Finney v. Cochran, 1 Watts & S. 112, 37 Am. Dec. 450.

[73] Order of St. Benedict v. Steinhauser, 234 U.S. 640, 34 Sup. Ct. 932, 58 L. Ed. 1512, 52 L.R.A. (N.S.) 459, Ann. Cas. 1917 A 463 (rev. 194 Fed. 289, 114 C.C.A. 249 [rev. 179 Fed. 137]).

[74] Cf. preceding note.

[75] Wilmerding v. Russ, 33 Conn. 67; Stanton v. Helm, 87 Miss. 287, 39 South. 457; Cooper v. Cooper, 61 Miss. 676.

[76] Speidel v. Henrici, 120 U.S. 377, 7 Sup. Ct. 610, 30 L. Ed. 718; Etting v. Marx, 4 Fed. 673, 4 Hughes 312.

which Chancellor Kent called[77] "those technical and continuing trusts which are not at all cognizable at law, but fall within the proper, peculiar and exclusive jurisdiction" of courts of equity; 2—those which involve a deposit in a bank in trust for a person other than the depositor;[78] 3—those which arise when the purchase price is paid by joint purchasers and title is taken in the name of one;[79] 4—those which arise from the fact that one has given a certificate that one holds money to abide settlement of disputes as to its ownership;[80] 5—those which are executed, not executory;[81] 6—those which are "resulting," e. g., when one party pays the purchase price and title is taken in the name of another;[82] 7—those which are voluntarily recognized by the trustee;[83] 8—those which are imposed on executors, administrators, guardians, assignees of insolvents, etc., unless statutes provide otherwise;[84] 9—those which are imposed on directors in relation to the corporation in most jurisdictions;[85] 10—those which are imposed on a corporation in regard to stock in relation to the stockholders;[86] 11—those which are imposed on a fraudulent grantee as to the heirs of the grantor;[87] 12—those which are imposed on municipal corporations or public officers receiving money;[88] 13—those which are imposed on one who knowingly participates in the trustee's breach of trust;[89] 14—those which are im-

[77] Kane v. Bloodgood, 7 Johns. Ch. (N.Y.) 90, 11 Am. Dec. 417.

[78] Mabie v. Bailey, 95 N.Y. 80, 21 N.E. 714.

[79] Faylor v. Faylor, 136 Cal. 92, 68 Pac. 482.

[80] Peterson v. Taylor, 4 Cal. Unrep. Cas. 49, 33 Pac. 436.

[81] Harrigan v. Smith, (N.J.Ch.), 4 Atl. 13; Laguerenne v. Farrar, 25 Tex. Civ. A. 404, 61 S.W. 953.

[82] Martin v. Martin, 186 Ky. 782, 217 S.W. 1026.

[83] St. Paul's Church v. Attorney General, 164 Mass. 188, 41 N.E. 231.

[84] Joseph Story, *Equity Jurisprudence* (12. ed. by Jairus W. Perry, Boston, 1877), § 608; 2 Sch. & L. 607; Appeal of Norris, 71 Pa. 106.

[85] Ellis v. Ward, (Ill.), 20 N.E. 671.

[86] Mountain Water Works Constr. Co. v. Holme, 49 Col. 412, 113 Pac. 501; Yeaman v. Galveston City Co., 106 Tex. 389, 167 S.W. 710, Ann. Cas. 1917 E 191.

[87] Bumpass v. McGehee, 247 Fed. 306, 159 C.C.A. 400.

[88] New Orleans v. Fisher, 91 Fed. 574, 34 C.C.A. 15.

[89] Bunnell v. Stoddard, 4 Fed. Cas. No. 2,135.

posed on a husband holding for his wife, or vice versa; [90] 15—those which are imposed on a vendor as to land sold and still held by him or upon a vendee as to purchase money not yet paid by him.[91]

Examples, on the other hand, of cases in which the limitation runs are: 1—when the trust terminates, e. g., by its own limitation or settlement of the parties; [92] 2—when the trust is repudiated and adverse possession known to the cestui is asserted; [93] 3—when there is an adequate concurrent remedy at law; [94] 4—when the statute expressly covers a resulting trust as to realty,[95] provided the beneficiary knows of the existence of the trust; [96] 5—when the trust is only implied or constructive; [97] 6—when the trust affects directors in regard to the corporation, in some jurisdictions; [98] 7—when a third party having notice of the trust is held to be merely a constructive trustee; [99] 8—when on breach of the trust the cestui elects to consider the trust at an end; [100] 9—when to a demand by the cestui for an accounting the trustee opposes an unqualified refusal.[101] It seems that the Canon Law can consider that "*praescriptio*" runs in these cases, since the plaintiff has knowledge of the situation, and to refuse to allow it would be to avoid obtaining the end for which "*praescriptio*" was introduced.

20. A guardian, under the American Law, is in a relationship of express trust to his ward so the limitation does not run on an action of the ward against him as long as the trust is acknowledged,[102] or until the guardian accounts or repudiates his trust.[103] A guardian

[90] Comstock's Appeal, 55 Conn. 214, 10 Atl. 559.

[91] Chicago, etc., R. Co. v. Hay, 119 Ill. 493, 10 N.E. 29.

[92] Order of St. Benedict v. Steinhauser, 234 U.S. 640, 34 Sup. Ct. 932, 58 L. Ed. 1512, 52 L.R.A. (N.S.) 459, Ann. Cas. 1917 A 463.

[93] Cf. preceding note.

[94] Miles v. Vivian, 79 Fed. 848, 25 C.C.A. 208.

[95] Kingston v. Kingston Coal Co., 265 Pa. 232, 108 Atl. 718.

[96] Cliff v. Cliff, 23 Col. A. 183, 128 Pac. 860.

[97] Speidel v. Henrici, 120 U.S. 377, 7 Sup. Ct. 610, 30 L. Ed. 718.

[98] Cooper v. Hill, 94 Fed. 582, 36 C.C.A. 402.

[99] Hart v. Citizens' Natl. Bank, 105 Kan. 434, 185 Pac. 1, 3, 7 A.L.R. 933.

[100] Bunnell v. Stoddard, 4 Fed. Cas. No. 2,135.

[101] Philippi v. Philippe, 115 U.S. 151, 5 Sup. Ct. 1181, 29 L. Ed. 336.

[102] Hook v. Leland Bank, (Miss.), 98 South. 594.

[103] Mitchell v. Mitchell, 170 App. Div. 452, 156 N.Y. 76.

for a lunatic can claim the limitation only from the lunatic's death against his distributees' right to call for an account.[104] A guardian for an imbecile performing continuous active duties in control of the property and in supporting the imbecile could not plead limitation of the action against the imbecile suing to compel an accounting.[105]

With these general notions in mind as to the nature of the institute, the persons involved, the time when an action is considered "brought," the law which governs, and the cases in which the institute is inoperative, one may now pass to a consideration of the Canon Law of Adverse Possession and of Prescription, leaving for later chapters the consideration of the Canon Law of Limitation of Actions.

104 Lowder v. Hathcock, 150 N.C. 438, 64 S.E. 194.

105 Snodgrass v. Snodgrass, 176 Ala. 282, 58 South. 199.

CHAPTER II

THE CANON LAW OF ADVERSE POSSESSION AND PRESCRIPTION

Article 1. General Rule

21. The Code of Canon Law provides[1] with respect to "*praescriptio*" that with certain specified exceptions the Church accepts for ecclesiastical property what is provided in the civil legislation of the respective nation, whether it be considered as a mode of acquiring property or rights or as a mode of freeing oneself from an obligation. This is similar to the provision of the American Law that a court of the United States, whether sitting in law or in equity, must give effect to the statutes of limitations of the state where it sits.[2]

22. The present provision of the Code of Canon Law is by no means a novelty. Anyone who reads the *Corpus Iuris Canonici,* the Glossators, the writers on Canon Law, and the decisions of the Sacred Roman Rota will realize that in the period before the Code the Church with regard to this institute merely took over and adapted to its own uses the provisions of the Roman Law.[3] Nothing could be a clearer indication of the canonization of the Civil Law in this regard than the way in which the canonists before the Code determined the periods of time which limited actions. These were all taken from the Roman Law, with the exception of a few set by statutes, such as those of the City of Rome and of the City of Bologna. Furthermore, in discussing the import of the law the Glossators used Roman Law, following the lead of Gratian,[4] in their

[1] Canon 1508.

[2] Dupree v. Mansur, 214 U.S. 161, 29 Sup. Ct. 548, 53 L. Ed. 950.

[3] Cf., e.g., cc. 2, 6, 9, 12, 13, 16, 17, C. XVI, q. 3 and c. 4, C. XVI, q. 4, as well as cc. 3, 14, 20, X, *de praescriptionibus,* II, 26.

[4] Dictum post (hereinafter d. p.) c. 15, dictum ante (hereinafter d. a.) and p. c. 16, C. XVI, q. 3.

comments.[5] Other writers on Canon Law, like Hostiensis (+1271),[6] also used Roman Law to a great extent to explain the institute of "*praescriptio*" in the Canon Law.

23. Since even a brief presentation of the American Law, which is adopted into the Canon Law for the dioceses in the United States and its possessions, requires a more detailed treatment, it will be reserved for later chapters. For the present it will be more opportune to consider the exceptions provided by the Canon Law, i. e., points in which the American Law is not accepted by the canons if it is in conflict with the Canon Law.

ARTICLE 2. EXCEPTIONS

24. The exceptions concern things which are not subject to "*praescriptio,*" and those which are subject to it with certain limitations. Those which are subject to it with limitations are either such as can be possessed by private persons or such as cannot be possessed by private persons. The exceptions further consider the space of time required in the case of possessions of the Holy See and that required in the case of possessions of other moral persons (corporations) in the Church.

a. Things Completely Exempted

25. The things which are not subject to "*praescriptio*"[7] are: 1—things which are of divine law, either natural or positive; 2—

[5] In c. 1, C. XVI, q. 3 ad v. *Iura* and ad v. *Dubitatio*; in c. 4, *ibid.* ad v. *Legis*; in c. 7, *ibid.* ad v. *Offerre*; in c. 8, *ibid.* ad v. *Annos triginta*; in c. 10, *ibid.* ad v. *Auctoritate, Si Sacerdotes* and *Moriendo*; in c. 11, *ibid.* ad v. *In ius proprium*; in c. 13, *ibid.* ad v. *Postliminio*; in c. 15, *ibid.* ad v. *Pertineant*; in d. a. c. 16, C. XVI, q. 3 ad v. *Creditores, Commodum, Interrupta, Triginta,* and *Continuare*; in d. p. c. 16, *ibid.* ad v. *Longi temporis*; in c. 17, *ibid.* ad v. *Usucapione,* and in c. 2, C. XVI, q. 4, ad v. *Inconcussam.* In c. 2, X, *de praescriptionibus,* II, 26 ad v. *Futuris*; in c. 3, *h. t.* ad v. *Sincere*; in c. 4, *h. t.* ad v. *Se posse tueri*; in c. 5, *h. t.* ad v. *Noverit*; in c. 12, *h. t.* ad v. *Suae dioecesis* and *Non obstante*; in c. 13, *h. t.* ad v. *Principaliter*; in c. 15, *h. t.* ad v. *Interruptionem* and *Imponentes*; in c. 17, *h. t.* ad v. *Bona fides* and *Iustus titulus*; in c. 18, *h. t.* ad v. *Interruptio*; in c. 20, *h. t.* ad v. *Bona fide, Quam civilis* and *Nulla temporis.*

[6] *Summa Aurea.*

[7] Canon 1509.

things which can be obtained only by apostolic privilege;[8] 3—spiritual rights, which laymen are not capable of holding, when there is question of "*praescriptio*" in favor of a layman; 4—limits, certain and in no wise doubtful, of ecclesiastical provinces, dioceses, parishes, vicariates and prefectures apostolic, abbacies or prelacies *nullius;* 5—stipends and obligations of Masses; 6—ecclesiastical benefices to which one has no title; 7—right of visitation and obedience so that subjects could not be visited by or subordinated to any prelate; 8—payment of the *cathedraticum.*

26. These exceptions are the same as they were in the law before the Code. Hence to illustrate their meaning one need only look at the doctrine concerning them which existed before the present Code came into effect.[9]

27. It is naturally held in the Canon Law that things established by divine law, either natural or positive, are not subject to "*praescriptio,*" since this, being of human institution, cannot prejudice what God has established.[10] Thus, for example, it was held that a cleric cannot by custom acquire the right to exercise powers reserved to the Order of Bishop,[11] and marital rights cannot be acquired by possession.[12]

28. Although things which can be obtained only by apostolic privilege, i. e., by grant of the Holy See, are not subject to "*praescriptio,*" [13] it was held before the Code that a presumption of concession might be raised by long possession and user of such a privilege,[14] and this, it seems, is still the law.

[8] I. e., by grant of the Holy See.

[9] Canon 6, 2°.

[10] E. g., the Ten Commandments; cf. also canons 27; 100, § 1; 107; 108, § 3; 109; 196; 219; 329, § 1; 727, § 1; 731, §1; 948; 1012, § 1; 1038, § 1; 1060; 1071; 1322; 1529.

[11] C. 4, X, *de consuetudine,* I, 4, which, according to the *Abbas Siculus,* is a noteworthy case.

[12] *Glossa* in c. 11, C. XVI, q. 3 ad v. *In ius proprium.*

[13] This specific provision seems to derogate from the general rule of canon 63, § 1, that "*praescriptio*" is one of four ways in which a privilege may be acquired.

[14] This is still the law in canon 63, § 2, as it was in the case cited *S.R.R. in causa Nonantulana seu Nullius, Bonorum, coram Mantica* (1597)—*Decisiones Recentiores,* Part. 2, dec. 11, n. 2.

29. As to prescription of spiritual rights by laymen, they were not permitted[15] to withdraw from the possession of the Church its property by force or by any arguments. Gratian added that laymen could not acquire tithes or first-offerings either with or without title, no matter for how long a time the adverse possession might continue.[16] The *Glossa,* likewise,[17] stated that laymen have no right to tithes and cannot acquire such a right by adverse possession[18] and that they cannot by prescription acquire spiritual things from which divine law excludes them, e. g., jurisdiction.[19]

30. Perhaps one of the most ancient applications of the denial of adverse possession in Canon Law has to do with the limits of ecclesiastical circumscriptions of territory. This was to prevent disruption of the territorial arrangement of the Church.[20] The *Glossa*[21] mentioned that boundaries are not affected by adverse possession, and it[22] was solicitous to note that, if a bishop was given a possibility[23] of acquiring by adverse possession the boundaries of another diocese, this was to be explained by the favor

[15] C. 8, C. XVI, q. 3.

[16] D. a. and p. c. 16, C. XVI, q. 3, § 6; cf. also c. 7, X, *de praescriptionibus,* II, 26.

[17] In c. 7, X, *de praescriptionibus,* II, 26 ad v. *Detinere.*

[18] Cf. also *Glossa* in c. 11, C. XVI, q. 3 ad v. *In ius proprium* and *Glossa* in c. 1, *de praescriptionibus,* II, 13, in VI°, ad v. *Titulum*; Schmalzgrueber, Part. III, tit. 26, nn. 18, 51; Reiffenstuel, lib. II, tit. 26, n. 32.

[19] Cf. c. 7, X, *de praescriptionibus,* II, 26; Franciscus Xaverius Wernz, S.J.-Petrus Vidal, S.J., *Ius Canonicum ad Codicis Normam Exactum* (7 toms. in 9 vols., Romae: Apud Aedes Universitatis Gregorianae, 1923-1938), Tom. IV, Vol. 2, p. 307, hereinafter cited Wernz-Vidal; Arthurus Vermeersch, S.J.-Joseph Creusen, S.J., *Epitome Iuris Canonici* (5. ed., 3 vols., Mechliniae-Romae: Dessain, 1934-1937), tom. II, p. 579, hereinafter cited Vermeersch-Creusen; Dominicus M. Pruemmer, O.Pr., *Manuale Iuris Canonici* (5. ed., Friburgi Brisgoviae: Herder, 1927), p. 537, hereinafter cited Pruemmer.

[20] C. 6, C. XVI, q. 3; Rufinus, *Summa,* pp. 360-361; S. Raymundus, *Summa,* lib. II, tit. 5, q. 9, § *Que possint praescribi.*

[21] In c. 12, X, *de praescriptionibus,* II, 26, ad v. *Non obstante.*

[22] In c. 15, C. XVI, q. 3, ad v. *Pertineant.*

[23] C. 1, X, *de praescriptionibus,* II, 26.

given to the spread and preservation of the Faith, so that the one acquiring was dispensed from the general prohibition.[24]

31. Dioceses, it had been said,[25] could be acquired by bishops after thirty years, later forty, of adverse possession,[26] but this was limited[27] by the requirement that the dioceses of the bishops in question be within the same province, so that the boundary lines of these, at least, were safeguarded. With the passing of time the same care was used to preserve the boundaries of dioceses, and finally those of parishes.

32. Gratian[28] observed that, though Pope Gelasius I in 494 or 495 had declared that adverse possession would not be allowed to destroy a diocese which had once been set up, this was to be understood to apply if such adverse possession had taken place without any title but by mere usurpation, whereas if it had been begun on the authority of a judicial decree, or through a long continued custom, it could be sustained. He further explained[29] the decision of Gelasius as meaning that the adverse possession of ten or twenty years known to the Roman Law would not suffice in the case of churches. If, however, a territory had not been given definite boundaries adverse possession would run.[30]

33. The Glossators do not seem to treat the question of how adverse possession was possible against the diocese itself when it was not allowed against the boundaries. This, perhaps, was due to the system of land tenure in medieval times when an imperial monastery might exist within the limits of the Papal States, and papal monasteries might exist within the limits of the imperial domains. The situation was too common to cause comment. Furthermore, as long as the boundaries remained the same, the question of sovereignty over the territory was easily settled.

34. Under the Code it is settled that, once the boundaries are

[24] D. a. c. 15, C. XVI, q. 3.
[25] C. 2, C. XVI, q. 3.
[26] Cf. Rufinus, *Summa,* p. 360.
[27] C. 4, C. XVI, q. 3.
[28] D. a. c. 8, C. XVI, q. 3.
[29] D. p. c. 15, C. XVI, q. 3.
[30] C. 7, C. XVI, q. 3.

established, whether they be of provinces, dioceses, parishes, vicariates and prefectures apostolic or abbacies and prelacies *nullius*,[31] adverse possession will not run against them; [32] still one diocese may even now own property within the territory of another.[33]

35. The rule that stipends and burdens of Masses are not subject to limitation of actions to enforce them is made to insure the fulfillment of the obligation attaching to stipends. This rule repeats previous decisions of the Sacred Congregation of the Council.[34]

36. It is not surprising to find, too, that an ecclesiastical benefice cannot be acquired simply by long occupation, since it is an old rule of the Canon Law [35] that one cannot acquire an ecclesiastical benefice without canonical institution therein. Authors [36] taught that ecclesiastical benefices were not subject to the law of adverse possession if one had no title, because they could be obtained only by canonical institution on the authority of a superior. The present Code likewise states [37] that an ecclesiastical benefice cannot be obtained by adverse possession when the one holding has no title.

It is interesting, however, to note in passing that canon 1446 provides that if a cleric who possesses a benefice proves that he has been in peaceful possession of the said benefice for a whole period of three years and in good faith, even if with invalid title, provided

[31] Vicariates and prefectures apostolic as well as abbacies and prelacies *nullius*, being considered like dioceses in that only the supreme authority in the Church can erect them, circumscribe them differently, divide, unite, or suppress them (canon 215, § 1), it is logical that they should be included here.

[32] Canon 1509, 4°.

[33] E. g., a villa. Cf. *The Canon Law Digest* (2 vols. by T. Lincoln Bouscaren, S.J., Milwaukee: Bruce, 1934-1943), II, 425-426, sub can. 1357.

[34] S.C.C., *in Theanen.*, 17 iun. 1899—*Codicis Iuris Canonici Fontes, cura Eñi Petri Card. Gasparri editi* (9 vols., Romae: Typis Polyglottis Vaticanis, 1925-1939. Vols. VII-IX *ed. cura et studio Eñi Iustiniani Card. Serédi.*), n. 4309, hereinafter cited, *Fontes*, and S.C.C., *in Theanen.*, 27 apr. 1901—*Fontes*, n. 4312; cf. canons 828; 829; 839; 1551.

[35] "*Beneficium ecclesiasticum non potest licite sine institutione canonica obtineri.*—Reg. 1, R. J. in VI°.

[36] E. g., Schmalzgrueber, Part. III, tit. 26, n. 29; Reiffenstuel, lib. II, tit. 26, n. 35.

[37] Canon 1509, 6°.

there be no simony, he obtains the benefice by legitimate "*praescriptio.*" It was held [38] before the Code that this was not properly to be designated as "*praescriptio,*" but rather was an application of the "three year rule," though it was true that it was also said that benefices might be acquired by "*praescriptio,*" provided it was proved conclusively.[39]

37. That limitations would not run to free a subject from his duty to provide for a superior making a visitation, was mentioned in the *Glossa,*[40] which likewise taught that it would not run to free a subject from his duty of obedience.[41] This was deduced from the cases decided by Innocent III (1198-1216) and cited in the Decretals of Gregory IX.[42] Under the Code, since "*praescriptio*" will not run to emancipate a subject from the condition of being a subject,[43] it seems this previous law as to the duty of providing for a superior making his visitation, which is so closely connected with the condition of being a subject, likewise remains in force.

38. Canonists have taught, however, that a subject could acquire freedom, e. g., a Prince as regards being subject to the Emperor, though a Christian could not as regards being subject to the Pope,[44] and that an inferior could acquire against his sovereign certain rights, e. g., to declare persons legitimate, create notaries, coin money, levy taxes to wage war, i. e., those rights which were considered merely special signs of dignity.[45] Likewise, an inferior prelate, e. g., an abbot, or an archdeacon, could, under the law of

[38] *S.R.R. coram Crescentio* (1767), tom. 4, dec. 156, n. 7.

[39] *Sacrae Rotae Romanae Decisiones coram R.P.D. Cyriaco Lancetta* (7 vols., Romae, 1735), hereinafter cited by place, type of case, name of judge and date as follows: *S.R.R. in causa Hipporegien., Beneficii, coram Lancetta* (1704), tom. 2, dec. 328, n. 5.

[40] In c. 11, X, *de praescriptionibus,* II, 26, ad v. *In talibus.*

[41] In c. 12, X, *de praescriptionibus,* II, 26, ad v. *Non obstante.*

[42] Cc. 12, 16, X, *de praescriptionibus,* II, 26; cf. also S. Raymundus, *Summa,* lib. II, tit. 5, q. 9, § *Que possint praescribi*; Schmalzgrueber, Part. III, tit. 26, n. 51; *S.R.R. in causa Tirasonen., Iurisdictionis, coram Viceconite* (1663)—*Decisiones Recentiores,* Part. 14, dec. 115, nn. 21-22.

[43] Canon 1509, 7°.

[44] Schmalzgrueber, Part. III, tit. 26, n. 32.

[45] Schmalzgrueber, Part. III, tit. 26, n. 31.

the *Corpus Iuris Canonici,* acquire against a bishop certain episcopal rights.[46] Under the Code, however, the office of archdeacon has disappeared, so there can be question only of the "abbot," i. e., of an exempt religious superior who seems able according to the tradition of the law to acquire such episcopal rights as are consonant with his sacerdotal character, except that boundaries cannot thus be changed and that the erection of exempt houses requires the intervention of the Apostolic See.[47]

39. The matter of payment of the *cathedraticum,* since it is a nominal payment indicating the subjection of the one paying to the bishop to whom it is paid, is of course closely linked with the foregoing disposition that one cannot by passage of time cease to be subject to some higher ecclesiastical authority, from which it follows that one cannot be freed from the obligation to pay the *cathedraticum* indicative of such subjection.

These, then, are the things which under the Canon Law are not subject to adverse possession and prescription, with the result that there is no limitation of actions to enforce a right to these things. One may pass now to a consideration of things which solely with certain limitations are subject to adverse possession and prescription.

b. Things Partially Exempted

40. The "sacred things" mentioned in canon 1510 were described by Schmalzgrueber[48] as those which had been properly and solemnly dedicated to God, such as chalices, vestments, sacred ornaments, altars, temples, chapels, cemeteries, monasteries, and other holy and religious places which he said, without explaining how or by whom, could not be held unless the consecration had been taken away,[49] though he probably meant by lay persons.

41. Though in some cases these sacred things may be owned by a private person, e. g., a chalice, in other cases, e. g., a church,

[46] Schmalzgrueber, Part. III, tit. 26, n. 52.

[47] Cf. canon 497, § 1.

[48] Part. III, tit. 26, n. 25; cf. also Pirhing, lib. II, tit. 26, n. 12; Reiffenstuel, lib. II, tit. 26, n. 32; Wernz, tom. III, tit. 11, n. 299, canon 1496, § 2.

[49] Cf. *Glossa* in c. 12, X, *de praescriptionibus,* II, 26, ad v. *Non obstante.*

they are not usually owned nowadays [50] by any but an ecclesiastical moral person (corporation). Canon Law is clear as to the possibility of adverse possession and prescription in either case for it provides: [51] that sacred things which are owned by private persons can be acquired by private persons through adverse possession or prescription, though such persons cannot use them for profane purposes; if, however, they have lost their consecration or benediction, they can be acquired freely for uses even profane, but not sordid; on the other hand, sacred things which are owned not by private persons, but by an ecclesiastical moral person (corporation), can be acquired by another ecclesiastical moral person (corporation) through adverse possession or prescription, though they cannot be acquired by a private person. This means that sacred things which are the property of a corporation in the Church can be acquired only by another corporation in the Church, while those which are the property of a private person can be acquired by a private person or by a corporation, since nothing is said to prohibit such acquisition by the corporation.

c. Special Periods of Time

42. In a letter written in the year 590 [52] Gregory I decided that forty years of adverse possession by the monastery in question would suffice even if some things belonged to the Roman Church.[53] In 593, however, the same Pontiff [54] announced the principle that his silence, which he had observed in preference to occasioning scandal through the notoriety of a court action, should not be considered as estopping his successors in the Roman See from taking suitable action to regain property belonging to the Roman Church.[55]

43. That adverse possession and prescription could be exercised

[50] *Ius patronatus* is to be eliminated, according to canon 1450, § 1.

[51] Canon 1510.

[52] Jaffé, *Regesta Pontificum Romanorum* (2. ed., 2 vols. in 1, curaverunt S. Loewenfeld, F. Kaltenbrunner, P. Ewald, Lipsiae, 1885-1888), n. 1076, hereinafter cited J.L., J.K., or J.E., in designation of the responsible editors.

[53] C. 2, C. XVI, q. 3.

[54] J.E., n. 1262.

[55] C. 2, X, *de praescriptionibus,* II, 26.

against the Roman Church was also admitted by John VIII (872-882) in a letter to Louis the German, King of the East Franks, in the year 873,[56] though he stated clearly that such possession had to run for a period of one hundred years.[57] The *Glossa,* however, which mentioned the same rule,[58] remarked that adverse possession did not really run against the Roman Church, i. e., as to its jurisdiction, since it had fullness of power in all churches.[59]

44. Innocent III (1198-1216) likewise held that possession for one hundred years would be good against the Roman Church.[60] Boniface VIII (1294-1303),[61] while reaffirming the principle that a period of one hundred years must be completed for adverse possession to be effective against the Roman See, allowed children of heretical parents, who in life had been supposed Catholic, to acquire their parents' goods by a forty-year period of adverse possession as against the rights of the Roman See to which such goods were by law forfeit, provided, of course, that such children were themselves Catholics. This remained the law even in later times.[62]

45. By a special constitution of Benedict XIV (1740-1758),[63] the Vatican Basilica was granted the privilege that against its rights and property only a period of one hundred years of adverse possession or prescription should be good. The same period of one hun-

[56] J.E., n. 2970.

[57] C. 17, C. XVI, q. 3; cf. *Corpus Iuris Civilis* (ed. stereotypa quinta, Vol. III, *Novellae,* recognovit Rudolfus Schoell, absolvit Guglielmus Kroll, Berolini: apud Weidmannos, 1928), Novella 9, hereinafter cited Nov.

[58] In c. 17, C. XVI, q. 3, ad v. *Quas actiones.*

[59] In c. 20, C. XVI, q. 4, ad v. *Ecclesia.*

[60] C. 13, X, *de praescriptionibus,* II, 26.

[61] C. 2, *de praescriptionibus,* II, 13 in VI°.

[62] Cf. Schmalzgrueber, Part. III, tit. 26, n. 101; *Sacrae Rotae Romanae Decisiones Novissimae* (in *Decisiones Recentiores,* Part. 5, tomm. 1-2, Romae, 1642), hereinafter cited by place, type of case, name of judge and date as follows: *S.R.R. in causa Ferrarien. seu Comaclen., Bonorum de Nasellis, coram Coccino* (1627)—*Decisiones Novissimae,* tom. 1, dec. 81, n. 29—*Decisiones Recentiores,* Part. 5, tom. 1; *Decisiones Sacrae Rotae Romanae coram R. P. D. Iacobo Emerix de Matthys* (3 vols., Romae, 1701), hereinafter cited by place, type of case, name of judge and date as follows: *S.R.R. in causa Faventina, Successionis, coram Emerix* (1688), tom. 2, dec. 822, n. 2.

[63] *"Ad honorandam,"* 27 mart. 1752, § 30—*Fontes,* n. 420.

dred years was required against the Regular Orders, by concession of Leo X (1513-1521) and Pius IV (1559-1565), because these were immediately subject to the Holy See,[64] and against the Cistercian monasteries of St. Bernard's Reform.[65] Since these were privileges and there was an old rule of Canon Law to the effect that it is fitting that privileges granted by the prince should remain,[66] and since the reason for the privilege is the same today and there is no clear indication of any revocation thereof, it may be said to remain in force. The Rota held further that because of the communication of privileges between religious orders it was not lost even by very long non-user.[67]

46. When it was said that a period of one hundred years was required against the Holy See,[68] this, according to the old law, was understood to refer to the feudal possessions of the Holy See, not the possessions of private persons connected with the Roman Church,[69] and as to its property, not as to its universal jurisdiction.[70]

47. The requirement of one hundred years as against the Roman See in Canon Law is similar to the provision of the American Law that statutes of limitation do not, on principles of public policy, run against a state or the United States, unless it is expressly so provided in the statute itself,[71] and that no laches is to be imputed to

[64] Schmalzgrueber, Part. III, tit. 26, n. 101; *S.R.R. in causa Turritana, Conservatoriae, coram Albergato* (1688)—*Decisiones Recentiores,* Part 15, dec. 285, n. 17. For the Order of St. Benedict the period was sixty years.

[65] Schmalzgrueber, Part. III, tit. 26, n. 101.

[66] *"Decet concessum a principe beneficium esse mansurum"*—Reg. 16, R.J. in VI°; cf. canons 4; 70 sqq.

[67] Cf. *S.R.R. in causa Ianuen., Privilegiorum, coram Corrado* (1649)—*Decisiones Recentiores,* Part. 10, dec. 337, nn. 21-22.

[68] Canon 1511, § 1; cf. *S.R.R. in causa Ferrarien. seu Comaclen., Bonorum de Nasellis, coram Coccino* (1627)—*Decisiones Novissimae,* tom. 1, dec. 81, n. 29—*Decisiones Recentiores,* Part. 5, tom. 1; *S.R.R. in causa Faventina, Successionis, coram Emerix* (1688), tom. 2, dec. 822, n. 2.

[69] *S.R.R. in causa Faventina, Successionis, coram Emerix* (1688), tom. 2, dec. 822, n. 4.

[70] Schmalzgrueber, Part. III, tit. 26, n. 101.

[71] U.S. v. Insley, 130 U.S. 263, 9 Sup. Ct. 485, 32 L. Ed. 968; Stanley v. Schwalby, 147 U.S. 508, 13 Sup. Ct. 418, 37 L. Ed. 259.

the government.[72] The Canon Law is, however, more liberal than the American Law in that it allows adverse possession after one hundred years.

There is a further similarity between the two laws in the matter of private persons seeking private rights in the name of the governing body. The American Law holds that the state's immunity to the limitation of the statute has no application when a party seeks his private rights in the name of the state,[73] or when a foreign government sues for the benefit of an individual,[74] or when the sovereign becomes a party in a private enterprise, as, for instance, a stockholder in a bank.[75]

48. The present Code establishes a period of thirty years as a limitation on actions by an ecclesiastical corporation, other than those mentioned above,[76] to recover in an ecclesiastical court its property held adversely.[77] This period has in the past suffered various vicissitudes. The Roman Law, as Justinian (527-565) revised it, had provided for a ten-year limitation if both parties had lived all that time within the same province; twenty years if not both of them had lived in the same province,[78] and if the plaintiff had lived partly in the same province and partly outside of it, then the years that he had lived outside the province were to be doubled in the computing of the period required to make the limitation complete.[79] Justinian had also provided a limitation of one hundred

[72] U.S. v. Hoar, 2 Mas. 312, Fed. Cas. No. 15,373; People v. Gilbert, 18 Johns. (N.Y.), 228.

[73] Moody v. Fleming, 4 Ga. 115, 48 Am. Dec. 210; but cf. Glover v. Wilson, 6 Pa. 290; U.S. v. Beebe, 127 U.S. 338, 8 Sup. Ct. 1083, 32 L. Ed. 121; U.S. v. R. Co., 142 U.S. 510, 12 Sup. Ct. 308, 35 L. Ed. 1099; cf. supra n. 46, note 69.

[74] French Republic v. Spring Co., 191 U.S. 427, 24 Sup. Ct. 145, 48 L. Ed. 247.

[75] U.S. v. Buford, 3 Pet. (U.S.) 30, 7 L. Ed. 585; Bank of the U.S. v. McKenzie, 2 Brock. 393, Fed. Cas. No. 927; cf. in general Stanley v. Schwalby, 147 U.S. 508, 13 Sup. Ct. 418, 37 L. Ed. 259.

[76] N. 45.

[77] Canon 1511, § 2.

[78] *Corpus Iuris Civilis* (ed. stereotypa nona, Vol. II, *Codex Iustinianus*, recognovit et retractavit Paulus Krueger, Berolini: apud Weidmannos, 1915), *Codex Iustinianus*, hereinafter cited C. (7.33) 12.

[79] Nov. 119, c. 8.

years in the case that the Roman Church was a plaintiff.[80] For other churches a limit of forty years was set.[81]

49. Gratian, in giving consideration to canons which had been enacted before the time of Justinian, mentioned the thirty-year period.[82] The *Glossa* spoke of the thirty-year period,[83] but showed likewise the change from that older law to the newer one which required forty years. From the manner of speaking of the *Corpus Iuris Canonici*,[84] it appears that forty years was the usual period for adverse possession against churches and monasteries in the Middle Ages. Various decisions also held that forty years was the period required in church matters.[85] It was said to be sufficient as against the church and churchmen and between churches.[86] It was even said that if the possession for forty years was with title it would be held equivalent to immemorial possession.[87]

[80] Nov. 9.

[81] Nov. 131, c. 6.

[82] D. a. c. 16, C. XVI, q. 3; likewise d. p. c. 16 and d. a. c. 17, *ibid.*

[83] In c. 1, C. XVI, q. 3, *princ.*, and ad v. *Triginta*, and in c. 8, *ibid.*, ad v. *Annos triginta;* in c. 10, *ibid.*, ad v. *Item si de rebus* and *Tricennalis;* in c. 15, *ibid.*, ad v. *Potuerit;* in d. a. c. 16, *ibid.*, ad v. *Triginta*, and ad v. *Longi temporis;* and in d. a. c. 17, *ibid.*, ad v. *Quas actiones.*

[84] C. 16, C. XVI, q. 3; cc. 2, 3, C. XVI, q. 4; d. a. c. 16, C. XVI, q. 3; d. p. c. 16, C. XVI, q. 3; d. a. c. 2, C. XVI, q. 4; cc. 4, 5, 6, 8, 9, X, *de praescriptionibus*, II, 26.

[85] *S.R.R. in causa Romana, Castri Orciani, coram Emerix* (1676)—*Decisiones Recentiores*, Part. 18, tom. 2, dec. 628, n. 27; *S.R.R. in causa Romana, Castri Orciani, coram Albergato* (1676)—*Decisiones Recentiores*, Part. 18, tom. 2, dec. 629, n. 21; *S.R.R. in causa Praten., Iuris conferendi, coram Pauluccio* (1678)—*Decisiones Recentiores*, Part. 19, tom. 1, dec. 251, n. 38.

[86] *S.R.R. in causa Lucana, Bonorum, coram Lugdunen.* (1609)—*Decisiones Recentiores*, Part. 1, dec. 208, n. 1, through many decisions to *S.R.R. in causa Praten., Iuris conferendi, coram Pauluccio* (1678)—*Decisiones Recentiores*, Part. 19, tom. 1, dec. 251, n. 38; *Sacrae Rotae Romanae Decisiones Nuperrimae* (11 vols. in 10, Romae, 1751-1792), hereinafter cited by place, type of case, name of judge, date, and source as follows: *S.R.R. in causa Vercellen., annexae praestationis, coram De la Tremoille* (1701)—*Decisiones Nuperrimae*, tom. 7, dec. 161, n. 11; S.C.C., 16 febr. 1889—*ASS*, XXII (1889-1890), 20.

[87] *S.R.R. in causa Feltren., Praebendae, coram Coccino* (1605)—*Decisiones Recentiores*, Part. 1, dec. 91, n. 1; *S.R.R. in causa Pampilonen., Decimarum, coram Emerix* (1681), tom. 1, dec. 473, n. 3; *Decisiones Sacrae Rotae Romanae coram R.P.D. Ansaldo de Ansaldis* (2. ed., 8 vols., Romae, 1711), hereinafter

50. Nevertheless, the period of thirty years was held as the ordinary period for adverse possession and prescription as to the property and rights of a church in a decision of the Sacred Congregation of Bishops and Regulars,[88] which paved the way for the present canon.

51. All this variation, of course, is at the present time determined by the provisions of canon 1511, viz., that an action by the Apostolic See to recover its immovables, precious movables, or rights, and also to enforce its rights of action, personal or real, may be brought at any time within one hundred years after the cause of action has arisen, and that the aforesaid actions may be brought by other ecclesiastical moral persons (corporations) (not agencies of the Holy See) at any time within thirty years from the accrual of the action.

cited by place, type of case, name of judge and date as follows: *S.R.R. in causa Nullius seu Fulden., Iurisdictionis, coram Ansaldo,* tom. 4, dec. 439, n. 105; *Decisiones Sacrae Rotae Romanae coram R.P.D. Io. Maria Riminaldo* (8 vols., Romae, 1792), hereinafter cited by place, type of case, name of judge and date as follows: *S.R.R. in causa Auximana, seu Aesina, quarta funeralis, coram Riminaldo* (1765), tom. 2, dec. 197, n. 20; *S.R.R. in causa Caputaquen., Subventionis, super bono iure, coram De la Tremoille* (1702)—*Decisiones Nuperrimae,* tom. 7, dec. 358, n. 13; *Sacrae Romanae Rotae Decisiones seu Sententiae quae iuxta Legem Propriam et Constitutionem "Sapienti Consilio" Pii PP. X prodierunt, cura eiusdem S. Tribunalis editae* (23 vols. —, Romae, 1912—), hereinafter cited by place, type of case, name of judge and source as follows: *S.R.R. in causa Melevitana, Funerum,* 22 iul. 1911, *coram R.P.D. Ioanne Prior,* Dec. 34, n. 21—*Decisiones,* III (1911), 364; S. C. C., 16 febr. 1889—*ASS,* XXII (1889-1890), 20.

[88] S.C. Ep. et Reg., 28 apr. 1865—*ASS,* I (1865), 110.

CHAPTER III

GOOD FAITH

52. The need for good faith on the part of the one holding adversely has for centuries been a source of much dispute. It was in this that the Canon and Civil Laws were said to differ sharply.[1] In this connection it is of importance to recall that the Canonical and Civil *"praescriptio"* embraces three American institutes, viz., Adverse Possession and Prescription, which are modes of acquiring property or rights and of liberating one's self from an obligation,[2] and Limitation of Actions, which is intended to cut off a plaintiff's right of action in order to prevent suits being brought so long after the cause of action has arisen that the defendant has no longer a proper means of defense.[3] Considering, then, the possessor, one sees immediately that if he cannot conscientiously say that he is entitled to the property in question he is bound to restore it to the rightful owner. Considering, on the other hand, the plaintiff who has neglected to bring his suit within the appointed time, one sees that, regardless of the state of mind of the defendant regarding the property, the plaintiff is still not justified in disturbing the courts and the public in trying to recapture his property.[4]

53. It seems worthy of note that the requirement of the Canon Law, namely, that no *"praescriptio"* shall be good unless it rests on good faith not only at the beginning of the possession but likewise during the whole time required for *"praescriptio,"* [5] is placed in Book

[1] Cf. S. Raymundus, *Summa,* lib. II, tit. 5, q. 9, § *Bona fides*; Ricardus Anglicus, *Summa de Ordine Iudiciario* (in Quellen zur Geschichte des Roemisch-Kanonischen Processes im Mittelalter, herausgegeben von Dr. Ludwig Wahrmund, II Band, III Heft, Innsbruck, 1915), p. 101, hereinafter cited Ricardus, *De Ordine Iudiciario*; Hostiensis, *Summa Aurea,* ff. 164v-165, 167v-168.

[2] Canon 1508.

[3] Canons 1701 sqq.

[4] *"Mora sua cuilibet est nociva."*—Reg. 25, R.J. in VI°.

[5] Canon 1512.

Three of the Code of Canon Law, where there is question of one's acquisition of property or of one's liberation from an obligation, rather than in Book Four, where there is question of the Extinction of Actions (Limitation of Actions).[6] This seems to be in line with the distinction made above on the basis of whether it is the defendant's state of mind which is to be considered, or the plaintiff's failure, culpable, of course, to bring his suit within the statutory period.

Article 1. What Is "Good Faith"?

54. According to the decision of Innocent III [7] the extent of one's knowledge seems to be held relevant to the question of good faith. The *Glossa* [8] repeats this. Thus, one who knew that the thing belonged to another could not acquire it by adverse possession,[9] and knowledge, no matter how induced, was held sufficient to prevent adverse possession as to a mortgage.[10] Furthermore, the obligation to pay a debt could be outlawed in the external forum but remain recognized in the internal forum.[11]

55. This good faith was a judgment by which one prudently decided that the thing which he possessed was his own, or at least that it did not belong to anyone else. Bad faith was that by which one was said to possess if he knew or believed that the thing which he possessed belonged to another, or at least that it was not his own. Theological good faith was good conscience, i. e., one without sin; civil good faith was that which according to the law had no fault by which adverse possession would be prevented. The former without the latter was not sufficient for adverse possession. In this sense it was said that after joinder of issue one was a "possessor in bad faith,"

[6] Lib. III, tit. 27, in canon 1512 as against lib. IV, tit. 5, cap. 7, in canons 1701-1705.

[7] C. 17, X, *de praescriptionibus*, II, 26.

[8] In c. 10, C. XVI, q. 3, ad v. *Si Sacerdotes.*

[9] *Decisiones Sacrae Rotae Romanae coram R.P.D. Bartholomaeo Olivatio* (8 vols., Romae, 1784), hereinafter cited by place, type of case, name of judge and date as follows: *S.R.R. in causa Placentina, Canonum, coram Olivatio* (1763), tom. 4, dec. 387, n. 12.

[10] *S.R.R. in causa Romana, Salviani, coram Crescentio* (1731), tom. 1, dec. 127, n. 6.

[11] Schmalzgrueber, Part. III, tit. 26, n. 62.

scil. because the laws from that time on forbade adverse possession to continue,[12] whether or not one was subjectively certain of the right.

56. Good faith, under the American Law, is held to be an honest intention to abstain from taking any unconscientious advantage of another, even through the forms or technicalities of law, together with an absence of all information or belief of facts which would render the transaction unconscientious.[13] It means that honesty of intention and freedom from knowledge of circumstances which ought to put him on inquiry, which protects a purchaser, holder, or creditor from being implicated in an effort by one with whom he is dealing to defraud some party in interest.[14] Good faith, in a statute regulating chattel mortgages, and declaring unrecorded mortgages to be invalid as against purchasers and mortgagees in good faith, means the mental attitude of such persons as parted with something of value, or otherwise altered their position irretrievably, on the strength of the apparent ownership, and without notice. Good faith in this connection means actual reliance upon the ownership of the vendor or mortgagor, because one was without notice of the incumbrance.[15] These statements of the American Law, it seems, can well be considered by a court of Canon Law in determining what constitutes the good faith required for adverse possession or prescription.

57. As to the question whether one who from ignorance took a thing as his own would have the good faith requisite for adverse possession, it seemed certain to Schmalzgrueber that: 1—if his ignorance was such as could be readily overcome, or if it was "affected," he would not have the necessary good faith; 2—if the ignorance as to the facts could not be overcome it would not exclude good faith, e.g., if one received the goods from a thief not knowing they had

[12] Schmalzgrueber, Part. III, tit. 26, n. 55; Pirhing, lib. II, tit. 26, n. 45; Reiffenstuel, lib. II, tit. 26, n. 57; Wernz, tom. III, tit. II, n. 307; Wernz-Vidal, tom. IV, Vol. 2, p. 311.

[13] Wood v. Conrad, 2 S.D. 334, 50 N.W. 95; cf. also Winters v. Haines, 84 Ill. 588; Rawson v. Fox, 65 Ill. 200; Thornton v. Bledsoe, 46 Ala. 73; Bronner v. Loomis, 17 Hun (N.Y.) 442.

[14] Canal Bank v. Hudson, 111 U.S. 80, 4 Sup. Ct. 303, 28 L. Ed. 354.

[15] National Bank of the Metropolis v. Sprague, 21 N.J. Eq. 536.

been stolen, or from a prelate thinking that the chapter had given its consent; 3—if the law was doubtful and disputed, ignorance regarding it would not prevent adverse possession. The dispute, consequently, hinged on the question whether invincible ignorance of a clear and undisputed law would constitute one in bad faith. Schmalzgrueber adjudged it the more tenable opinion that it would prevent adverse possession in the ordinary periods of time unless the person was one in whom it was tolerated,[16] since this matter depended entirely on human law. It would prevent, he said, adverse possession of the object itself, not of the income from it,[17] in the ordinary periods of time, but not in the thirty- or forty-year periods which cut off all action by the plaintiff.[18]

Article 2. How Good or Bad Faith Arises

58. Good faith, under the Canon Law, could arise from a just reason for believing that one had a right to possess, e. g., from the assertion of a ruler or of a person of note.[19] St. Raymond of Peñafort (1175-1275),[20] in speaking of titles mentioned the formation of a "title in conscience" when one was in doubt or did not know his title, from the fact that one believed that the owner was satisfied since he saw what was going on and did not object, which of course meant that the holder was in good faith as to what he did.

59. If the deceased was not in bad faith the heirs could acquire by adverse possession through him.[21] The good faith of a predecessor in title also helped his successors, singular (e. g., a donee), or universal (e. g., an heir), because he transferred the thing to them

[16] E. g., a soldier, a minor, women, uneducated persons, etc., who did not have the assistance of experts.

[17] In such case there would be a mistake of fact.

[18] Part. III, tit. 26, n. 66; cf. also Pirhing, lib. II, tit. 26, nn. 55-58; Reiffenstuel, lib. II, tit. 26, nn. 71-78; Wernz, tom. III, tit. II, n. 308.

[19] *S.R.R. in causa Romana, Cottivii, coram Sacrato* (1606)—*Decisiones Recentiores,* Part. 3, dec. 120, n. 4. The "assertion of a ruler" is perhaps to be interpreted as a hint of the force of eminent domain. Cf. *infra,* n. 270.

[20] *Summa,* lib. II, tit. 5, q. 9.

[21] *S.R.R. in causa Romana, Divisionis, coram Bichio* (1640)—*Decisiones Recentiores,* Part. 8, dec. 238, n. 8.

with every right which he had. A *haeres extraneus* [22] then had the title *pro haerede* and acquired the thing in a shorter time than the *suus haeres*,[23] who had only such title as his ancestor had and was required to hold the object for the time the ancestor would have had to hold it, unless he renounced that condition of *suus* to hold by some other title, e. g., of agnation, cognation, succession by pretorian right, or as an emancipated child, in which case he acquired the object in his own name, not in that of the estate, by whatever of the aforesaid titles he adopted.[24]

60. Bad faith, according to the Canon Law, would be produced by demands, summonses, or other acts and interferences even extrajudicial,[25] and it could also appear from the injury done.[26] These demands, summonses, or other acts and interferences can be held to produce bad faith today if they actually cause the holder to come to the knowledge that he is not entitled to hold the property in question, or if they raise such a doubt about his right to hold it that he cannot in conscience continue to do so. This is said in regard to "theological bad faith"; in regard to "civil bad faith" one may hold that they produce it if the laws regard them as interrupting the adverse possession or prescription, as a barrier put across a walk interrupts the prescription of the easement of passage.

Article 3. Proof of Good or Bad Faith

61. On the question whether good faith must be proved by the one holding adversely it was said, under the Canon Law, that ordinarily it did not have to be proved but was presumed by the law, since it consisted in ignorance of the other's right, which was pre-

[22] One neither under the power of the testator at death, nor his slave.

[23] One under the testator's power at the time of his death.

[24] Schmalzgrueber, Part. III, tit. 26, n. 70.

[25] *S.R.R. in causa Romana, Salviani, coram De la Tremoille* (1701)—*Decisiones Nuperrimae,* tom. 7, dec. 188, nn. 5-8; *S.R.R. in causa Illerden., Iuris mulctandi super negocio principali, coram Muto* (1702)—*Decisiones Nuperrimae,* tom. 7, dec. 353, n. 3.

[26] *Decisiones Sacrae Rotae Romanae coram R.P.D. Iosepho Alphonso de Veri* (2 vols., Romae, 1787), hereinafter cited by place, type of case, name of judge and date as follows: *S.R.R. in causa Romana, Laesionis, coram de Veri* (1771), tom. 2, dec. 190, n. 19.

sumed in law whenever knowledge was not proved.[27] Furthermore, no one was presumed to be bad, hence it was held that the exception of fraud, deceit, falsehood, had to be conclusively proved,[28] and bad faith would be excluded by any reason whatsoever, even one that was colored,[29] though it would not be purged by recourse to an insufficient excuse.[30] Confronted with the problem that one cannot always prove good faith, the *Glossa* solved it by allowing the possessor in such a case to take an oath to the effect that he held the thing in good faith.[31]

62. The *Glossa* also taught that one who raised the objection of bad faith had to prove it.[32] Whether the one alleging bad faith on the part of the holder was bound to prove it was, however, a source of dispute for centuries, and even the later Rota decisions vary on this point, some requiring it, some not.[33]

63. It was suggested by Schmalzgrueber [34] that bad faith could

[27] Schmalzgrueber, Part. III, tit. 26, n. 80; cf. also Reiffenstuel, lib. II, tit. 26, n. 83; D (22.3) 21; *S.R.R. in causa Feltren. Praebendae, coram Coccino* (1605)—*Decisiones Recentiores,* Part. 1, dec. 91, n. 2.

[28] *Decisiones Sacrae Rotae Romanae coram R.P.D. Theodulpho Mertel* (Romae, 1853), hereinafter cited by place, type of case, name of judge and date as follows: *S.R.R. in causa Centumcellarum, Pecuniaria, coram Mertel* (1852), dec. 59, n. 3.

[29] Paulus Rubeus, *Annotationes* in *Decisiones Recentiores,* Part. 3, dec. 6, n. 132, hereinafter cited Rubeus, *Annotationes,* in *Decisiones Recentiores*; *S.R.R. in causa Romana, Vineae, coram Merlino* (1626)—*Decisiones Novissimae,* tom. 1, dec. 11, n. 10—*Decisiones Recentiores,* Part. 5, tom. 1; *S.R.R. in causa Romana, Divisionis, coram Bichio* (1640)—*Decisiones Recentiores,* Part. 8, dec. 238, n. 6.

[30] *S. Rotae Romanae Decisiones Recentissimae et Selectissimae D. Ioannis Gutierrez Operae Omnia* (2. ed. "*20 decisionibus aucta,*" *Coloniae Allobrogum,* 1735), hereinafter cited by place, type of case, name of judge, date and source as follows: *S.R.R. in causa Urbinaten., Legati, coram Millino* (1733)—*Decisiones Gutierrez,* dec. 102, n. 9.

[31] In c. 7, C. XVI, q. 3, ad v. *Offerre.*

[32] In c. 2, C. XVI, q. 4, ad v. *Inconcussam;* in c. 3, X, *de praescriptionibus,* II, 26, ad v. *Sincere*; in c. 20, *h. t.* ad v. *Bona Fide.*

[33] *S.R.R. in causa Mantuana, Bonorum, coram Ubaldo* (1614)—*Decisiones Recentiores,* Part 1, dec. 610, n. 2; *S.R.R. in causa Lucana, Unionis, coram Bichio* (1647)—*Decisiones Recentiores,* Part. 10, dec. 9, n. 25.

[34] Part. III, tit. 26, n. 80; cf. Reiffenstuel, lib. II, tit. 26, n. 83.

be discovered and proved from various conjectures: 1—if the possession was recent and without title; 2—if one bought the thing after hearing that it did not belong to the seller; 3—if one bought it without observing the formalities for the contract of sale; 4—if in the presence of others one said he knew the object belonged to another person; 5—if there was a rumor in the locality that the object belonged to some one other than the seller; 6—if this was proved by the depositions of witnesses; 7—if the one holding immediately after acquiring possession sought to acquire a title for his possession; 8—if one occupied the property of another during the owner's absence; 9—if one contracted with unusual precautions (indicative of fraud); 10—if one purchased from a spendthrift, a gambler, an unemancipated son, etc.; 11—if one purchased from an agent selling an object in the name of his principal and did not take care to have the proof of the agency shown to him at the time of the contract, for if afterward it was found that the authority to sell was invalid, or null, the buyer was presumed to be in bad faith; 12—if he, the possessor, had in his possession instruments, letters, and books which showed clearly that the property belonged to some one else, inasmuch as every man was presumed to know and understand the tenor of the instruments and writings which he had in his files, and especially of those which pertained to his own rights or to his office and administration; 13—if he could know from the common law, or from the municipal law, that the object belonged to another person.

64. While, under the American Law, the presumption of law that the holder is in good faith is sufficient in the absence of evidence, if the good faith of the party is put in issue by his adversary, he has a right to give affirmative evidence of it,[35] e. g., when the ownership of negotiable paper is put in issue, he may prove he became the owner in good faith.[36] A person to whom the want of good faith is imputed through a statement shown to have been made by him may be asked if he believed this statement to be correct.[37] After proof of circumstances relied on as showing want of good faith by putting a person on inquiry, he may explain them by showing the reasons in view of

[35] Macon County v. Shores, 97 U.S. 272, 24 L. Ed. 889.

[36] Ralls County v. Douglass, 105 U.S. 728, 26 L. Ed. 957.

[37] Rawls v. Ins. Co., 27 N.Y. 282, 84 Am. Dec. 280.

which he did not pursue the inquiry,[38] and after stating the explanation received upon inquiry he may testify that he was satisfied with it.[39] When the knowledge of a third person is in issue, proof of general reputation is sometimes competent as tending to show reasonable ground of belief or suspicion.[40] It is further held that good faith is not disproved by a forgotten conversation.[41] Good faith is always presumed in favor of the holder of a negotiable paper,[42] and such a holder takes the paper free from any infirmity in its origin except such as makes it void for illegality of consideration or want of capacity in the maker.[43] This is a presumption of law,[44] and it outweighs the presumption of payment.[45] One who has purchased for value and without notice, or also his transferee, is termed a holder in good faith,[46] and it is said that a holder of a negotiable instrument in due course must have taken it in good faith.[47]

The great difficulty in this matter of proof of good faith lies in the fact that it is a matter within the conscience of a man, which courts acting in the external forum cannot reach and judge unless there has been some act done, or unless there is a whole series of circumstances such as are incompatible with any assumption to the contrary. For the American Law, limiting itself to the external forum, the problem is left in this stage, namely, if bad faith cannot be shown good faith will be presumed. For the Canon Law, which must consider the state of a man's conscience as seeking to avoid anything that could seem to give approval to that which is sinful,

[38] Seybel v. Bank, 54 N.Y. 288, 13 Am. Rep. 583.

[39] Jennings v. Conboy, 73 N.Y. 236.

[40] Barrett v. Western, 66 Barb. (N.Y.) 205.

[41] Kenyon v. See, 29 Hun (N.Y.) 214.

[42] Dresser v. Construction Co., 93 U.S. 94, 23 L. Ed. 815; Collins v. Gilbert, 94 U.S. 754, 24 L. Ed. 170; Marfield v. Douglass, 3 N.Y. Super. Ct. 360.

[43] Bowditch v. Inc. Co., 141 Mass. 296, 4 N. E. 798, 55 Am. Rep. 474; Cromwell v. County of Sac, 96 U.S. 51, 24 L. Ed. 681.

[44] Jones v. Simpson, 116 U.S. 609, 6 Sup. Ct. 538, 29 L. Ed. 742.

[45] Louisville, N.A. & C. Ry. Co. v. Thompson, 107 Ind. 442, 8 N.E. 18, 9 N.E. 357, 57 Am. Rep. 120.

[46] McClure v. Oxford Tp., 94 U.S. 432, 24 L. Ed. 129.

[47] Neg. Instr. Act, § 52.

there is a greater problem, one which becomes almost insurmountable unless one keeps clearly in mind the distinction between Canon Law and Moral Theology, realizing that Canon Law as applied by an ecclesiastical court is bound to the limitations of what can be made to appear from the acts and proofs,[48] wherefore it must at times be content with a presumption of good faith when bad faith is not proved, whereas Moral Theology, treating of the state of a man's conscience and reaching that conscience in the internal forum of the tribunal of Penance, rightly is concerned with the actual state of that conscience, and can proceed to judge it when it is manifested.

Article 4. Necessity of Good Faith

65. The need of good faith is mentioned in various places in the *Glossa*,[49] although the *Glossa* in c. 1, C. XVI, q. 3, *in princ.* shows signs of correction, for it begins by saying that good faith is required only in the beginning, not in the intermediate period, and then reverses itself to say that according to the canons continuous good faith is required.[50]

66. The *Glossa* teaches that good faith is generally required because under the Canon Law good faith in the one acquiring by adverse possession is necessary whether in spiritual or in civil things. This good faith is understood to exist when one believes that the one delivering is the owner or had the right to alienate, although he errs as to the fact.[51] The doctrine of the *Glossa* on the need of good faith was of course based on several chapters of the Decretals.[52] Gratian had taught [53] that good faith was required only at the beginning of the adverse possession, in which he followed the Roman Law, hence the correction in the *Glossa* [54] in which is repeated the definition that, since anything which is not in accord with faith [55] is

[48] Canon 1869, § 2.

[49] In c. 1, C. XVI, q. 3, *in princ.* and ad v. *Dubitatio;* in c. 4, X, *de praescriptionibus,* II, 26, ad v. *Se posse tueri.*

[50] Cc. 5, 20, X, *de praescriptionibus,* II, 26.

[51] In c. 17, X, *de praescriptionibus,* II, 26 ad v. *Bona Fides.*

[52] Cc. 3, 5, 17, 19, 20, X, *de praescriptionibus,* II, 26.

[53] D. a. c. 16, C. XVI, q. 3, § 1.

[54] In c. 1, C. XVI, q. 3 *in princ.*

[55] *Glossa* in *h.c.*, ad v. *Ex fide,* says, "That is, conscience."

sinful, no adverse possession whether canonical or civil would be valid without good faith. The conclusion drawn was that one acquiring by adverse possession must not at any time be aware that the thing involved was the property of some one else. The foundation for this canon—c. 20, X, *de praescriptionibus,* II, 26—had been laid by the decision of Alexander III (1159-1181).[56] This doctrine was likewise summed up in Reg. 2, R.J. in VI°.[57]

67. The phrase "not at any time" raised a difficulty as to the condition of one who, after the adverse possession was complete, discovered that the property had belonged of right to some one else. The *Glossa* [58] said that in such a case one could not be said to hold in bad faith. St. Raymond of Peñafort [59] said that in this case the theologians held that one had to restore the property to the rightful owner, while the jurists held that it was not necessary to do so. He himself held that if one's conscience did not bother one on this point it was not necessary to restore the thing, but if it did bother one, he seemed to be in doubt as to the obligation of restitution.[60]

68. Gratian [61] had taught that adverse possession would be sustained, even if in bad faith, provided that it was continued for thirty years. The *Glossa,*[62] while recognizing with the law of the Decretals that good faith must exist at all times, regarded as an exception the case of a bishop holding territory which in the negligence of another bishop he had converted to the faith, saying that this was by virtue of the permission contained in the canon.[63] Again, the *Glossa* considered the possibility that one could acquire by adverse possession even though he was conscious that the property belonged to another in the case in which a judicial decree intervened.[64]

[56] C. 5, X, *de praescriptionibus,* II, 26.

[57] *"Possessor malae fidei ullo tempore non praescribit."*

[58] In c. 20, X, *de praescriptionibus,* II, 26, ad v. *Nulla temporis.*

[59] *Summa,* lib. II, tit. 5, q. 9; cf. *Glossa* in c. 5, X, *de praescriptionibus,* II, 26, ad v. *Noverit.*

[60] Cf. also Bernardus Papiensis, *Summa,* lib. II, tit. 18, n. 8.

[61] D.a.c. 16, C. XVI, q. 3, § 3.

[62] In c. 15, C. XVI, q. 3, ad v. *Pertineant.*

[63] C. 1, X, *de praescriptionibus,* II, 26.

[64] In c. 17, X, *de praescriptionibus,* II, 26, ad v. *Bona fides.*

69. Faced with the difficulty that the canons since 1215 [65] required good faith in adverse possession, both canonical and civil, the *Glossa* [66] explained, and this seems the better view, that the Pope seemingly intended to put an obstacle in the way of adverse possession by lay persons and in matters not subject to ecclesiastical cognizance and that some tried to say that the Pope had presumed to do this because of the sin involved, in which matter the Church is competent, with the result that the civil laws allowing adverse possession in bad faith if continued for thirty or forty years no longer held. Ioannes Teutonicus (+1245) may have understood the decree of the Council in this way, and he is thus quoted in this *Glossa,* but Bernard of Pavia (+1266) did not agree with him, feeling rather that by this constitution the Pope wanted to declare the divine law that a layman holding in bad faith committed a sin, and that the word "canonical" referred to spiritual things and the word "civil" referred to adverse possession under the Canon Law, so that the resulting interpretation required good faith in adverse possession of spiritual things and also in adverse possession of temporal goods under the Canon Law, but that nothing was said as to adverse possession under the Civil Law.

Another interpretation which Bernard offered was that which he attributed to Ioannes Teutonicus, namely, that the law considered the negligence of one who did not attempt to regain his property, while the canon considered the sin of the one who held in bad faith. This, of course, did not excuse the negligence of the true owner who failed to care for his property or to regain it. The result then was that no adverse possession was good whether canonical or civil which could not run without mortal sin. It was necessary, therefore, to observe the canon rather than the law, since the one holding was not excused from sin by reason of the law. The canon, consequently, intended to correct the law on this point because of the danger to souls, even though it was not observed in the secular courts.[67]

[65] C. 20, X, *de praescriptionibus,* II, 26.

[66] In *h.c.* ad v. *Quam civilis.*

[67] This observation of the *Glossa ordinaria* on the Canon Law, namely, that the secular courts did not observe the requirement of good faith, seems strange to one who reads the *Glossa ordinaria* on the Civil Law by Accursius

70. At any rate, in the ecclesiastical courts judgment was rendered in accordance with the law requiring good faith at all times,[68] even if laymen were defendants, since the Church could not contradict what it had already decreed and what it forbade in other cases.[69]

71. The later authors [70] also taught that good faith was necessary for adverse possession,[71] i. e., at Canon Law, though not under the

(1182-1260), C (7.33) 2, where it is stated that, in the case of adverse possession running for ten years provided that both parties are in the same jurisdiction, and for twenty years if they are not, good faith is required in the beginning and continuously for the whole time. In his *casus* wherewith he explained the Civil Law Accursius cited the Canon Law on this point. The same *Glossa,* C (7.39) 8, both in the *casus* and in the commentary on the text, taught that in the case of a thirty-year adverse possession good faith *"ab initio"* would be sufficient, even without title, to allow an action to recover against any but the true owner if the holder had been ejected, whereas if he had been in bad faith *"ab initio"* he had no action for recovery unless the third party had taken away the property (chattel) or ejected the holder (from realty), apparently with some degree of force, to judge from the connotation of the terms used to express the interference with his possession.

68 C. 20, X, *de praescriptionibus,* II, 26.

69 *Glossa* in c. 20, X, *de praescriptionibus,* II, 26, ad v. *Quam civilis.*

70 Schmalzgrueber, Part. III, tit. 26, n. 91; Pirhing, lib. II, tit. 26, n. 45; Reiffenstuel, lib. II, tit. 26, n. 58; Wernz, tom. III, tit. 11, n. 307; and modern authors generally.

71 Cf. *S.R.R. in causa Lucana, Bonorum, coram Lugdunen.* (1609)—*Decisiones Recentiores,* Part. 1, dec. 208, n. 6; *S.R.R. in causa Colonien., Occupationis bonorum, coram Panzirolo* (1637)—*Decisiones Recentiores,* Part. 7, dec. 191, n. 16; *S.R.R. in causa Cracovien., Decimarum, coram Taia* (1663)—*Decisiones Recentiores,* Part. 14, dec. 91, n. 9; *S.R.R. in causa Romana, Castri Orciani, coram Emerix* (1674), tom. 1, dec. 189, n. 17; *S.R.R. in causa Hostienen., Beneficii, coram Ansaldo* (1710), tom. 5, dec. 481, n. 22; *Decisiones Sacrae Rotae Romanae coram R.P.D. Alexandro Falconerio* (5 vols., Romae, 1730), hereinafter cited by place, type of case, name of judge and date as follows: *S.R.R. in causa Toletana, Decimarum, super bono iure, coram Falconerio* (1724), tom. 1, *De Decim.,* dec. 9, n. 17; *S.R.R. in causa Augustana, Decimarum, coram Lancetta* (1721), tom. 5, dec. 1257, n. 14; *S.R.R. coram Crescentio* (1762), tom. 4, dec. 156, nn. 2, 4; *S.R.R. in causa Cracovien., Decimarum, coram Riminaldo* (1772), tom. 4, dec. 410, n. 9; *S.R.R. in causa Vercellen., annexae praestationis, coram De la Tremoille* (1701)—*Decisiones Nuperrimae,* tom. 7, dec. 161, n. 10; *S.R.R. in causa Caputaquen., Subventionis super bono iure, coram De la Tremoille* (1702)—*Decisiones Nuperrimae,* tom. 7, dec. 358, nn. 23-24; *Decisiones Sacrae Rotae Romanae coram R.P.D.*

imperial laws, except on account of sin which made it necessary to have good faith even in the territory of the empire.[72] It was held in one case that any presumption of bad faith was excluded in the case of immemorial possession or even of a thirty- or forty-year possession,[73] but later it was held that good faith would be required even in immemorial possession.[74] Consequently Schmalzgrueber called it an undoubted opinion that good faith must exist not only in the beginning but even in the continuation right up to the completion of the adverse possession,[75] and this was the case with respect to both actions and obligations, as well as realty and personalty.[76]

72. Gratian[77] had taught that good faith was sufficient, even without title, if the adverse possession was continued for thirty years. This was qualified by a decision[78] to the effect that good faith suf-

Ioachim Ioanne Xaverio Isoard (3 vols., Romae, 1829), hereinafter cited by place, type of case, name of judge and date as follows: *S.R.R. in causa Romana, Haustus Aquae, coram Isoard* (1827), tom. 3, *de Servitut.* dec. 419, n. 2; *Sacrae Rotae Romanae Decisiones coram R.P.D. Io. Francisco Marco et Catalan* (3 vols., Romae, 1829), hereinafter cited by place, type of case, name of judge and date as follows: *S.R.R. in causa Perusina, manutentionis, super bono iure, coram Marco* (1828), tom. 2, dec. 400, n. 4; *S.R.R. in causa Anconitana, Hypothecae, coram Marco* (1826), tom. 2, dec. 288, n. 14; *Decisiones Sanctae Romanae Rotae coram Em. mo et Rev. mo D. no Cardinali Petro Marini* (3 vols., Romae, 1853), hereinafter cited by place, type of case, name of judge and date as follows: *S.R.R. in causa Perusina, Immissionis, coram Marini* (1832), tom. 1, dec. 76, n. 27; *S.R.R. in causa Romana, Restitutionis fructuum, coram Mertel* (1850), dec. 4, n. 4; *S.R.R. in causa Romana, Nullitatis contractus, coram Mertel* (1852), dec. 58, n. 9; Rubeus, *Annotationes,* in *Decisiones Recentiores,* Part. 3, dec. 6, n. 109.

[72] Rubeus, *Annotationes,* in *Decisiones Recentiores,* Part. 3, dec. 6, n. 104.

[73] *S.R.R. in causa Pampilonen., Decimarum, coram D. Card. Bononien.* (1610)—*Decisiones Recentiores,* Part. 2, dec. 285, n. 4.

[74] *S.R.R. in causa Cracovien., Iuris legendi, coram Ubaldo* (1629)—*Decisiones Novissimae,* tom. 1, dec. 265, n. 17—*Decisiones Recentiores,* Part. 5, tom. 1; *S.R.R. in causa Palentina, Decimarum, coram Cerro* (1657)—*Decisiones Recentiores,* Part. 12, dec. 283, n. 12; Rubeus, *Annotationes,* in *Decisiones Recentiores,* Part. 3, dec. 6, n. 108.

[75] Part. III, tit. 26, n. 57; cf. Pirhing, lib. II, tit. 26, n. 47; Reiffenstuel, lib. II, tit. 26, n. 58.

[76] Schmalzgrueber, Part. III, tit. 26, n. 61.

[77] D.a.c. 16, C. XVI, q. 3, § 1.

[78] C. 1, *de praescriptionibus,* II, 13, in VI°.

ficed when the common law or a presumption was not contrary to the holder, otherwise a title had to be alleged and proved, unless the period of adverse possession extended beyond the memory of living men.[79]

Article 5. Effect of Bad Faith

73. Bad faith prevented adverse possession at Canon Law,[80] and it was held to be an obstacle to adverse possession even though

[79] Cf. Schmalzgrueber, Part. III, tit. 26, n. 128; also *infra*, n. 126.

[80] *S.R.R. in causa Cavallicen., Legitima, coram Hervault* (1682)—*Decisiones Recentiores,* Part. 19, tom. 2, dec. 641, n. 8; *S.R.R. in causa Bituntina, Salviani, coram Emerix* (1669), tom. 1, dec. 2, n. 4; *Sacrae Rotae Romanae Decisiones coram R.P.D. Alexandro Caprara* (2 vols., Lucae, 1725), hereinafter cited by place, type of case, name of judge and date as follows: *S.R.R. in causa Romana, Domus, coram Caprara* (1694), tom. 1, dec. 228, n. 13; *S.R.R. in causa Recineten., Praedii, coram Falconerio* (1712), tom. 3, *de Societ.*, dec. 5, n. 3; *S.R.R. in causa Burgen., Iurisdictionis super remissoria, coram Falconerio* (1714), tom. 3, *de Prob.*, dec. 6, n. 11; *S.R.R. in causa Caven., Iurisdictionis super territorio separato, coram Falconerio* (1710), tom. 2, *de Offic. Ordin.*, dec. 3, n. 18; *S.R.R. in causa Vercellen., Reintegrationis, coram Falconerio* (1711), tom. 4, *de Miscell.*, dec. 89, n. 9; *Decisiones Sac. Rotae Romanae coram R.P.D. Thoma Ratto* (4 vols., Romae, 1754), hereinafter cited by place, type of case, name of judge and date as follows: *S.R.R. in causa Bononien., Statutorum, coram Ratto* (1727), tom. 2, dec. 148, n. 8; *S.R.R. in causa Bononien., Statutorum, coram Ratto* (1727), tom. 2, dec. 159, n. 16; *S.R.R. in causa Montis Falisci, Reintegrationis, coram Ratto* (1731), tom. 3, dec. 301, n. 8; *S.R.R. in causa Urbinaten., Legati, coram Millino* (1733)—*Decisiones Gutierrez,* dec. 102, n. 8; *Decisiones Sacrae Rotae Romanae coram R.P.D. Carolo Rezzonico (Clemente XIII)* (4 vols. in 3, Romae, 1762), hereinafter cited by place, type of case, name of judge and date as follows: *S.R.R. in causa Romana, Livelli, super Livellis decursis, coram Rezzonico* (1735), tom. 2, dec. 205, n. 21; *S.R.R. in causa Romana, Salviani, coram Crescentio* (1731), tom. 1, dec. 127, n. 4; *S.R.R. in causa Perusina, Pecuniaria, coram Crescentio* (1738), tom. 4, dec. 418, n. 3; *Decisiones Sacrae Rotae Romanae coram R.P.D. Clemente de Arostegui* (Romae, 1781), hereinafter cited by place, type of case, name of judge and date as follows: *S.R.R. in causa Civitatis Castelli, Salviani, coram Clemente* (1747), dec. 11, n. 4; *S.R.R. in causa Perusina, Immissionis, coram Clemente* (1747), dec. 14, n. 20; *S.R.R. in causa Cracovien., Decimarum super bono iure, coram Clemente* (1747), dec. 33, n. 15; *S.R.R. in causa Albanen., Dotis et fructuum, coram Olivatio* (1766), tom. 5, dec. 552, n. 5; *Decisiones Sacrae Rotae Romanae coram R.P.D. Francisco Herzan* (3 vols., Romae, 1789), hereinafter cited by place, type of case, name of judge and date

it lasted for only a very short time.[81] If the buyer knew that the seller did not have title to the whole thing sold he was in bad faith,[82] as was a despoiler,[83] but if the bad faith appeared after the adverse possession was complete then the holder could keep the thing with good conscience.[84] Nevertheless, the same protection, as against a

as follows: *S.R.R. in causa Camerinen., Immissionis, coram Herzan* (1773), tom. 1, dec. 49, n. 18; *S.R.R. in causa Urbevetana, Redintegrationis super reservatis, coram Riminaldo* (1770), tom. 4, dec. 337, n. 4; *S.R.R. in causa Monopolitana, Salviani, coram Manuel* (1693)—*Decisiones Nuperrimae,* tom. 4, dec. 179, n. 7, through very many decisions to *S.R.R. in causa Reatina, Immissionis, coram Scotto* (1705)—*Decisiones Nuperrimae,* tom. 9, dec. 100, n. 22; *Decisiones Sacrae Romanae Rotae coram R.P.D. Alexandro Malvasia* (3 vols., Romae, 1832), hereinafter cited by place, type of case, name of judge and date as follows: *S.R.R. in causa Romana, Manutentionis super bono iure, coram Malvasia* (1790), dec. 61, n. 11; *S.R.R. in causa Bononien., Salviani, coram Malvasia* (1786), dec. 195, n. 4; *Decisiones Sacrae Rotae Romanae coram R.P.D. Antonio Dominico Gamberini* (Romae, 1824), hereinafter cited by place, type of case, name of judge and date as follows: *S.R.R. in causa Veliterna, uti Praelato, coram Gamberini* (1820), dec. 22, n. 25; *S.R.R. in causa Romana, Locorum Montium, coram Isoard* (1819), tom. 2, *de Miscell.*, dec. 298, n. 10; *S.R.R. in causa Romana, Locorum Montium, coram Isoard* (1826), tom. 2, *de Miscell.*, dec. 300, n. 9. It was said in the case cited as *S.R.R. in causa Nolana, Parochialis, coram Rondinino* (1671)— *Decisiones Recentiores,* Part. 17, dec. 150, n. 12 that if there was not good faith the adverse possession could not be peaceful.

[81] *S.R.R. in causa Firmana, Salviani, coram Remboldo* (1624)—*Decisiones Recentiores,* Part. 4, tom. 3, dec. 513, n. 10; *S.R.R. in causa Romana, Executionis Laudi, coram Urgellen.* (1629)—*Decisiones Novissimae,* tom. 1, dec. 300, n. 13—*Decisiones Recentiores,* Part. 5, tom. 1; *S.R.R. in causa Messanen., seu Nullius, Feudi, coram Merlino* (1636)—*Decisiones Recentiores,* Part 7, dec. 94, nn. 33-34; *S.R.R. in causa Bituntina, Census, coram Corrado* (1645)—*Decisiones Recentiores,* Part. 9, tom. 2, dec. 373, n. 7 sqq.; *S.R.R. in causa Avenionen., Salviani, coram Bichio* (1648)— *Decisiones Recentiores,* Part. 10, dec. 204, n. 5; *S.R.R. in causa Toletana, coram Bevilaqua* (1660)—*Decisiones Recentiores,* Part. 13, dec. 221, n. 18; *S.R.R. in causa Farfen., Praedii, coram Emerix* (1673), tom. 1, dec. 152, n. 8.

[82] *S.R.R. in causa Recineten., Praedii, coram Falconerio* (1712), tom. 3, *de Societ.*, dec. 5, n. 4.

[83] *S.R.R. in causa Cornetana, Bonorum, coram Lancetta* (1722), tom. 6, dec. 1338, n. 4.

[84] *S.R.R. coram Crescentio,* tom. 4, *de Praescriptionibus,* dec. 156, n. 10.

third party, was afforded a holder in bad faith as was accorded to one who held by force, according to the *Glossa*.[85]

74. Bad faith passed from the deceased who had been in bad faith to his heirs,[86] even if they were in good faith; [87] and it extended to mediate as well as immediate heirs.[88]

75. The *Glossa,* however, said that bad faith on the part of the one delivering was not prejudicial to the one receiving, and that the contrary argument drawn from C (7.33) was to be understood in regard to the ten- and twenty-year periods, but not in regard to the thirty- and forty-year periods (which cut off all actions), in which case according to the laws it was not prejudicial.[89] The predecessor's bad faith did not prejudice a singular possessor inasmuch as the latter was held to have begun the possession in his own person in good faith, unless the object itself was affected by some real flaw, or was realty and the owner was unknown to the singular possessor.[90]

76. A universal immediate successor, even if he was in good faith, could not acquire by adverse possession in the ordinary period of time a thing which his predecessor had held in bad faith and had left to him as an inheritance. This was due to the fact that by the common law he was regarded as forming one person with the prede-

[85] In d.a.c. 16, C. XVI, q. 3, ad v. *Commodum.*

[86] *S.R.R. in causa Albanen., Dotis et fructuum, coram Olivatio* (1766), tom. 5, dec. 552, n. 7.

[87] *S.R.R. in causa Romana, Canonum, coram Ubaldo* (1622)—*Decisiones Recentiores,* Part. 4, tom. 2, dec. 372, n. 3; *S.R.R. in causa Ravennaten., Census, coram Dunozzetto* (1639)—*Decisiones Recentiores,* Part. 8, dec. 164, n. 7; *S.R.R. in causa Bituntina, Census, coram Corrado* (1645)—*Decisiones Recentiores,* Part. 9, tom. 2, dec. 373, nn. 12-13; *S.R.R. in causa Civitatis Plebis, Salviani, coram Bichio* (1647)—*Decisiones Recentiores,* Part. 10, dec. 118, n. 26.

[88] *S.R.R. in causa Romana, Canonum, coram Ubaldo* (1622)—*Decisiones Recentiores,* Part. 4, tom. 2, dec. 372, n. 5; *S.R.R. in causa Firmana, Salviani, coram Remboldo* (1624)—*Decisiones Recentiores,* Part. 4, tom. 3, dec. 513, n. 11; *S.R.R. in causa Ravennaten., Census, coram Dunozzetto* (1639)—*Decisiones Recentiores,* Part. 8, dec. 176, n. 3.

[89] In c. 17, X, *de praescriptionibus,* II, 26, ad v. *Bona Fides.*

[90] The thirty-year period was then required, which cut off all actions. Cf. Schmalzgrueber, Part. III, tit. 26, n. 71; Reiffenstuel, lib. II, tit. 26, n. 131 sq.; Pirhing, lib. II, tit. 26, n. 65 sq.

cessor, unless he held the thing by some other title besides that *pro haerede*, e. g., *pro donato, pro emptore*, or was a successor in dignity or in some ecclesiastical benefice,[91] and did not attempt to tack his possession to that of the predecessor. Particular statutes and municipal ordinances could provide otherwise regarding such transfer as involving also a transfer to the successor of the "bad faith" of his predecessor in title. If the possession was continued for thirty or forty years, the title was said to be not so much *pro haerede* as a presumed title.[92] The ancestor's bad faith did not, however, prejudice a mediate heir who had received the object from the immediate heir under the titles, *pro donato, pro emptore*, since this meant singular possession.[93]

77. On the question whether the bad faith of the predecessor in title of a province, city, collegiate person or other corporation would prejudice the successors so that they could not acquire by adverse possession the things or rights held by them even if they had good faith, it appeared to Schmalzgrueber [94] that, since the corporation was always the same person and did not change its possession or its title, the majority had to have good faith in the beginning, or else the adverse possession would never run.

78. On the question whether the bad faith of a prelate would be prejudicial to the adverse possession of his church it seemed to Schmalzgrueber [95] that, if it was notorious that the thing belonged to another, the church or monastery would have to give it back. If it was not notorious that the object belonged to another, and only the prelate knew it, then one had to see whether it could be proved to belong to the other party or not. If it could be so proved, the prelate would have to inform the chapter and give it back, otherwise it would be useless to give it back since the chapter could reclaim it in court. If the thing was held in common by the prelate and the chapter, then

[91] Then he did not have his possession from the predecessor, but from the one who conferred the benefice on him.

[92] Schmalzgrueber, Part. III, tit. 26, nn. 72-73.

[93] Schmalzgrueber, Part. III, tit. 26, n. 74.

[94] Part. III, tit. 26, nn. 76-77.

[95] Part. III, tit. 26, n. 78; cf. also Pirhing, lib. II, tit. 26, nn. 77-79; Reiffenstuel, lib. II, tit. 26, n. 79 sqq.

there could be no adverse possession since the prelate was not in good faith. If it was not held in common by them, then the party having the good faith could acquire by adverse possession. This reasoning seems to apply not only to the case of a prelate and chapter, but to any case of a corporation which has a board to govern it and some representative through whom its business is ordinarily transacted.

79. Bad faith as to one thing or one right did not prevent adverse possession of another held in good faith, e. g., as to one or the other portion of a piece of land. One knowing that the right of ownership belonged to another, but not knowing who was entitled to other rights in the object could acquire these other rights, and one doubting whether the seller had ownership could in good faith possess the thing under some title other than *pro emptore*. When, however, one held the land of A and thought it belonged to B, he could not acquire it by adverse possession.[96]

Article 6. Effect of Doubt

80. One who was in doubt could still be in good faith.[97] That doubt was not necessarily inconsistent with good faith was the teaching of the *Glossa*.[98] On the other hand, Schmalzgrueber taught[99] that doubt[100] would prevent adverse possession from beginning. If it came after the adverse possession had begun, then the common opinion, so he said, was that it was no bar unless it was a "practical" doubt, in which case one had to use moral diligence to find out the truth. A "practical" doubt interrupted even adverse possession which had been begun.

[96] Schmalzgrueber, Part. III, tit. 26, n. 79.

[97] D (41.3) (15.2); cf. also Schmalzgrueber, Part. III, tit. 26, nn. 64-65; Pirhing, lib. II, tit. 26, n. 55; Reiffenstuel, lib. II, tit. 26, n. 63.

[98] In c. 17, X, *de praescriptionibus,* II, 26, ad v. *Bona fides,* and in c. 20, *h. t.,* ad v. *Nulla temporis;* cf. Ioannes Teutonicus, *Glossa (Scholia) in Comp. IV,* lib. II, tit. 10, c. 3, ad v. *Quam civilis* in Antonii Augustini *Antiquae Collectiones Decretalium* (?); S. Raymundus, *Summa,* lib. II, tit. 5, q. 9, § *Si autem.*

[99] Part. III, tit. 26, nn. 64-65; cf. also Pirhing, lib. II, tit. 26, n. 55; Reiffenstuel, lib. II, tit. 26, n. 23.

[100] Obviously real, serious doubt.

Article 7. Fraud and Its Effect

81. In Equity, under the American Law, fraud by the defendant which prevented the plaintiff from knowing of his right to sue prevents the running of the statute of limitations,[101] even though there is a concurrent remedy at law.[102] This fraud requires that some trick or artifice shall have been used to prevent inquiry, or to elude investigation, or to hinder the party from obtaining information by the use of ordinary diligence; or it must appear that the facts were misrepresented to or concealed from the party by some positive act or declaration when inquiry was made.[103] Fraud would be, e. g., a wrongful entry of satisfaction of a judgment or mortgage whereby a subsequent assignee or purchaser suffers injury,[104] or a case wherein a tract of land was included in a deed by the active fraud of the grantee and without the knowledge of the grantor who continued in possession of the tract.[105]

82. Other examples of cases in which the rule is applied in equity are: 1—suits to reform written instruments on the ground of fraud; [106] 2—suits to have an absolute deed declared a mortgage; [107] 3—suits to rescind and cancel contracts, to set aside sales, deeds, and other transfers of property; [108] 4—suits to set aside a decree of sale and to charge the purchaser at the sale as trustee; [109] 5—suits for partition and to quiet title, where plaintiffs, in order to establish their title, are under the necessity of invalidating for fraud a certificate of final payment for school lands and a patent issued thereon; [110] 6—suits

[101] George Tucker Bispham, *The Doctrine of Equity* (7. Am. ed. by John Adams, Boston, 1881), § 203; Terry v. Fontaine's Adm'r, 83 Va. 451, 2 S.E. 743.

[102] U.S. Bank v. Biddle, 2 Pars. Eq. Cas. (Pa.) 31.

[103] Stone v. Brown, 116 Ind. 78, 18 N.E. 392; Felix v. Patrick, 145 U.S. 317, 12 Sup. Ct. 862, 36 L. Ed. 719.

[104] Day v. Dages, 17 Ind. A. 228, 46 N.E. 589.

[105] Davis v. Monroe, 187 Pa. 212, 41 Atl. 44, 67 Am. St. Rep. 581.

[106] Hammond v. Western Casualty, etc., Co., 100 Kan. 582, 165 Pac. 291.

[107] Brown v. Spradlin, 136 Ky. 703, 125 S.W. 150.

[108] U.S. v. Diamond Coal, etc., Co., 255 U.S. 323, 41 Sup. Ct. 335, 65 L. Ed. 660.

[109] Tuttle v. Tuttle, 146 N.C. 484, 59 S.E. 1008, 125 Am. St. Rep. 481.

[110] Murray v. Quigley, 119 Ia. 6, 92 N.W. 869, 97 Am. St. Rep. 276.

to cancel a state[111] or a United States[112] land patent; 7—suits to set aside releases and to vacate an order approving an administrator's final account based on such releases;[113] 8—suits to open or to set aside fraudulent accounts or settlements;[114] 9—suits to obtain an accounting,[115] unless the action is controlled by another statute of limitations which does not admit of exception in the case of fraud;[116] 10—suits to set aside a probated will on the ground that it is spurious and was imposed on the court by perjured testimony;[117] 11—suits for the purpose of securing a decree that a certain fund in defendant's possession be held for plaintiff's use and benefit;[118] 12—suits against officers of a manufacturing corporation under a statute requiring them to make an annual report of their paid-up capital stock and debts, and providing that the failure to make such reports, or the making of false reports, shall render them personally liable for all damages resulting from such failure while they are stockholders of the corporation.[119]

83. Constructive notice of fraud is sufficient to defeat the plaintiff's claim, e. g., if the means of discovery lie in public records,[120] provided that the plaintiff knew such facts as would put an ordinarily intelligent and prudent man on inquiry.[121] If the defrauded party discovers it within a reasonable time before the regular period of limitation expires he must sue within that regular period.[122] Notice to an attorney is notice to his client,[123] just as knowledge of an agent

111 People v. Blankenship, 52 Cal. 619.

112 U.S. v. Woolley, 262 Fed. 518; U.S. v. Albright, 234 Fed. 202; U.S. v. Wilson, 214 Fed. 630.

113 Pickens v. Campbell, 98 Kan. 518, 159 Pac. 21.

114 Kirby v. Lake Shore, etc., R. Co., 120 U.S. 130, 7 Sup. Ct. 430, 30 L. Ed. 569.

115 Johnson v. United R. Co., 243 Mo. 278, 147 S.W. 1077.

116 Steinberg v. Salzman, 139 Wis. 118, 125, 120 N.W. 1005.

117 *In re* Johnson, 182 N.C. 522, 109 S.E. 373.

118 Santa Marina Co. v. Canadian Bank of Commerce, 242 Fed. 142.

119 Brown v. Clow, 158 Ind. 403, 62 N.E. 1006.

120 Garfield Cty. v. Renshaw, 23 Okl. 56, 99 Pac. 638, 22 L.R.A. (N.S.) 207.

121 Houston v. Rosborough, 295 Fed. 137.

122 Johnson v. Johnson, 5 Ala. 90; Byrne v. Frere, 2 Molloy 157.

123 Deering v. Holcomb, 26 Wash. 588, 67 Pac. 240, 561.

within the scope of his employment is knowledge of his principal,[124] or knowledge of a partner is knowledge of the partnership.[125] If the ancestor had sufficient notice to put him on inquiry his heirs cannot claim against the running of the statute any fraud recently discovered.[126]

84. Examples of constructive notice are: 1 — a record of a deed [127] where the facts constituting the fraud appear on the face of the recorded deed, unless by construction of the statute in the particular jurisdiction actual notice is required; [128] 2—a record of a deed which would show the fraud which has been held on the one hand not such notice to a non-resident plaintiff, as to amount to a "constructive discovery" which will set the statute in motion,[129] but which, on the other hand, has also been held to constitute such notice, the theory being that it is notice to the world.[130] A record of a conveyance is notice only to those who are bound to search for it,[131] and in this behalf it is said that the recording of a deed is constructive notice only to those acquiring interests subsequent to the execution thereof.[132] A record of a deed which fraudulently included more land than was intended to be conveyed is not notice of the fraud to the grantor.[133] A record of a deed does not impart notice of matters wholly outside the deed, such as fraud not evident upon its face.[134]

85. The fact that there was an opportunity to discover the fraud earlier weighs against the plaintiff, but it is not conclusive evidence that he did discover it earlier.[135] In the case of a "continuing fraud"

[124] Boro v. Hidell, 122 Tenn. 80, 120 S.W. 961, 135 Am. St. Rep. 857.

[125] Morris v. Gwaltney, (Tex. Civ. A.), 215 S.W. 473.

[126] Clarke v. Johnston, 18 Wall. (U.S.) 493, 21 L. Ed. 904.

[127] Sanderlin v. Cross, 172 N.C. 234, 90 S.E. 213.

[128] Berkey v. Judd, 22 Minn. 287.

[129] Coulson v. Galtsman, 1 Neb. (Unoff.) 502, 96 N.W. 349.

[130] Teall v. Schroder, 158 U.S. 172, 15 Sup. Ct. 768, 39 L. Ed. 938 (construing the California statute).

[131] Davis v. Monroe, 187 Pa. 212, 41 Atl. 44, 67 Am. St. Rep. 581.

[132] Ackerson v. Elliott, 97 Wash. 31, 165 Pac. 899.

[133] Webb v. Logan, 48 Okl. 354, 150 Pac. 116.

[134] Donaldson v. Jacobitz, 67 Kan. 244, 246, 72 Pac. 846.

[135] Kilby Locomotive, etc., Works v. Lacy, 12 Ala. A. 464, 67 South. 754.

the statute will not run until the representations cease or their falsity is discovered.[136] If sources of information are exhausted without discovery of the fraud it is as though the plaintiff had never been put on inquiry.[137] The mere fact, however, that one has confidence in another is held no excuse for a lack of diligence in investigating,[138] e. g., when fiduciary relations have ceased.[139]

If the plaintiff plainly has no understanding of business affairs and has been lulled into a sense of security by the defendant perpetrating a fraud, he is not negligent in failing to make a diligent inquiry.[140] Mental weakness, however, or incapacity not amounting to absolute insanity is no excuse for failure to inquire where all material facts are known.[141] Inability to discover the whereabouts of the defendant and of the property is not inability to discover the fraud.[142] The necessity for using diligence and the question whether it was used depend upon the circumstances of the parties and of the case; there is no arbitrary rule.[143] Discovery of the fraud dates from the discovery of the acts, not from the discovery of the law making such acts "fraudulent."[144]

86. The courts of law consider that the limitation on actions to recover damages for fraud in the common acceptation of the term,[145] i. e., where there is no injury except for the fraud,[146] as a rule,[147] runs from the time when the fraud is successfully consummated, not from the discovery, even though the action purports to be in equity.[148]

87. Examples of the rule at law are: 1—if a purchase of prop-

[136] Martin v. Smith, 16 Fed. Cas. No. 9,164.

[137] Larson v. McMillan, 99 Wash. 626, 170 Pac. 324.

[138] Bass v. James, 83 Tex. 110, 18 S.W. 336.

[139] Curtis v. Connly, 257 U.S. 260, 42 Sup. Ct. 100, 66 L. Ed. 222.

[140] Carson v. Greeley, 107 Neb. 609, 619, 187 N.W. 47.

[141] Manby v. Bewicke, 3 Kay & J. 342, 69 Reprint 1140.

[142] Myers v. Center, 47 Kan. 324, 27 Pac. 978.

[143] Comfort v. Robinson, 155 Mich. 143, 118 N.W. 943.

[144] Noyes v. Parsons, 104 Wash. 696, 177 Pac. 651, 653.

[145] Bennett v. Jeeker, 61 Mont. 307, 202 Pac. 203.

[146] Penobscot R. Co. v. Mayo, 65 Me. 566.

[147] Ovid First Natl. Bank v. Steel, 146 Mich. 308, 109 N.W. 423.

[148] East River Natl. Bank v. Columbia Trust Co., 171 N.Y.S. 384.

erty is induced by fraud, the statute begins to run from the time when the sale is completed,[149] even though the action is brought in equity; [150] 2—if a purchase is induced by fraud the statute is held to run from the date of the sale, and not from the date when the purchaser is evicted; [151] 3—if the practice of fraud induces the plaintiff to enter into a contract of marriage, the cause of action accrues and the statute begins to run when the fraud is consummated by the making of the contract,[152] unless the deception is continued after the marriage; [153] 4—if the plaintiff suffers consequential damages only at a time subsequent to the making of the contract induced by the defendant's fraud, it is nevertheless considered that fraudulently inducing a man to enter into a contract works such a legal injury as will support an action.[154]

88. Examples of what is held no "fraud," with the result that the limitation runs, are: 1—an action for trespass on realty, although it is a secret trespass; [155] 2—an action merely to enforce a contract to recover damages for its breach,[156] unless the case is one wherein the violation of the contract is such as can properly be termed fraudulent; [157] 3—an action based on a violation of duty imposed by contractual relations; [158] 4—an action to recover money on the theory of an implied or quasi-contract when no fraud is chargeable to the defendant personally; [159] 5—an action in cases wherein the fraud is merely collateral to the cause of action; [160] 6—an action in which the cause of action is complete without fraud, not-

[149] Wilson v. Ivy, 32 Miss. 233.

[150] Dennin v. Powers, 96 Misc. 252, 160 N.Y. 636, though the rule may now be otherwise.

[151] Northrop v. Hill, 57 N. Y. 351, 15 Am. Rep. 501.

[152] Reilly v. Sabater, 43 N.Y.S. 383, 26 N.Y. Civ. Proc. 34; the Canon Law is regulated, however, by canon 1701 in this regard. Cf. *infra,* n. 162.

[153] Martin v. Smith, 16 Fed. Cas. No. 9,164.

[154] Wilson v. Ivy, 32 Miss. 233.

[155] Golden Eagle Min. Co. v. Imperator-Qulip Co., 93 Wash. 692, 161 Pac. 848.

[156] Hallidie v. Enginger, 175 Cal. 505, 166 Pac. 1.

[157] Gregory v. Spieker, 110 Cal. 150, 42 Pac. 576, 52 Am. St. Rep. 70.

[158] Miller v. Walser, 42 Nev. 497, 181 Pac. 437.

[159] Price v. Mulford, 107 N.Y. 303, 14 N.E. 298.

[160] Miles v. Berry, 19 S.C.L. 296.

withstanding unnecessary averments of fraud in the complaint; [161] 7—a breach of promise to do something in the future.[162]

89. Statutes providing a limitation on actions for relief on grounds of fraud do not bar the use of fraud as a plea against enforcement of a contract or transaction, under the American Law,[163] just as the exception of fraud is, along with other exceptions, perpetual at Canon Law.[164]

90. It seems that the rule in Equity is the one which is to be adopted in the courts of Canon Law in this country. Under this rule, until the fraud is discovered, the limitation will not run. Constructive notice is, however, to be considered, for were a plaintiff to disregard it he would be at fault and *"mora sua cuilibet est nociva."* The rule at law, i. e., that the limitation on the fraud runs from the time it occurs, seems too rigid for the Canon Law which has always adhered to the rule "fraus et dolus nemini patrocinari debet." [165] Fraud will, of course, as under the American Law, remain as a defense even if it is barred as a ground for a cause of action.

Article 8. Under the Present Code

91. The present Code of Canon Law provides that no *"praescriptio"* is valid unless it rests on good faith not only at the beginning of the possession, but during the whole time required for *"praescriptio."* [166] Thus, if one enters upon possession knowing that he is not entitled to such possession he is unable under the Code to claim title later by adverse possession or prescription. If he enters upon possession with a serious doubt in his mind whether he is entitled to do so, he must clear up such doubt or he cannot later claim title by adverse possession. If during the period of the adverse possession he comes to the knowledge that he is not entitled

[161] Glover v. Natl. Bank of Commerce, 156 App. Div. 247, 141 N.Y.S. 409.

[162] Mitchell Coal, etc., Co. v. Pennsylvania R. Co., 241 Pa. 536, 88 Atl. 743.

[163] Wilhite v. Hamrick, 92 Ind. 594; Caples v. Morgan, 81 Or. 692, 160 Pac. 1154, L.R.A. 1917 B, 760.

[164] Canon 1667.

[165] Herbert Broom, *Selection of Legal Maxims* (7. Am. ed., Philadelphia, 1868), Max. 97.

[166] Canon 1512.

to possession, the holder under the Code can no longer claim title by adverse possession. If a serious doubt as to his title arises during this period, then the holder must clear it up or he cannot claim title by adverse possession. The decision on the rights of the parties in these cases will depend on whether judgment is to be rendered in the external or in the internal forum, i. e., whether the court must base its decision on the evidence adduced in open court by the plaintiff or defendant, in which case it may have to presume good faith and absence of serious doubt on the part of the holder unless the contrary is proved clearly; or whether the tribunal bases its decision in the internal forum on a sincere admission of bad faith by the only person who can know the state of the holder's mind.

92. It is to be noted that the Code requires good faith for the entire time required for the *"praescriptio,"* saying nothing about good faith in the period after the required time has run. Hence it seems that the opinion of the medieval canonists is here adopted, viz., that when the period is ended and title has passed to the adverse holder, this holder is to be considered the owner. Knowledge subsequently induced that the property had in fact belonged to another will not destroy his title, passed to him by operation of law. The same may be said for a serious doubt arising after the period for adverse possession is complete; title having been transferred will not be destroyed by a subsequent serious doubt, and this, the writer thinks, can be held for the internal forum as well as for the external.

CHAPTER IV

TITLE

Article 1. What Is Meant by "Title"

93. Closely connected with the question of good faith is that of title, since the possessor can hardly be in good faith as to his right to possess unless he has received the property in such a way as to raise in his mind the idea that he is entitled to what he holds.

94. St. Raymond of Peñafort,[1] in speaking of titles, said that a title was any act by which ownership was customarily acquired, and thereupon mentioned the Roman Law titles: *pro soluto, pro emptore, pro transacto, pro haerede, pro donato, pro derelicto, pro legato, pro dote, pro socio, pro suo*. He spoke further of forming for one's self a title in conscience, when one was in doubt or did not know one's title, from the fact that one believed the owner was satisfied since he saw what was going on and did not object, in other words, when the adverse possession was open and notorious. He further allowed the present holder to presume that what he held from his ancestors was the result of their title, especially if they were upright men, because, as he said, it was sufficient if one had a title, whether this was true or presumed.

The later authors[2] considered title nothing else than a reason adequate in itself to transfer legal ownership, just as the *Glossa*[3] had taught that a title was a legal reason for the possession of that which was not already one's own. This could, it said, consist in the fact that a thing was handed over by one who was believed capable of conveying. Ignorance, however, of the law, it observed, was not of avail in adverse possession. This left the matter of ignorance of fact, e. g., if the person believed the property was conveyed with

[1] *Summa*, lib. II, tit. 5, q. 9.

[2] Schmalzgrueber, Part. III, tit. 26, nn. 81, 92-95; cf. also Pirhing, lib. II, tit. 26, n. 81; Reiffenstuel, lib. II, tit. 26, n. 128; Wernz, tom. III, tit. 11, n. 305.

[3] In c. 1, C. XVI, q. 3, ad v. *Quod autem praescriptione*.

the consent of the chapter, Schmalzgrueber[4] taught that in such a case invincible ignorance of fact did not destroy good faith. But he said nothing as to title, though adverse possession, in some cases, as he taught, could run without title. Thus the question, as far as he was concerned, was not one of pressing importance. Under the American Law title is the means whereby the owner of lands has the just possession of his property.[5] While this is true as to realty, as to personalty possession thereof is *prima facie* title thereto.[6]

95. The *Glossa*[7] remarked that a title must be alleged and proved whenever the common law or a presumption was contrary to the one asserting adverse possession. It, however, allowed[8] one who had proved adverse possession but could not prove his title to swear that he had the thing in his possession by a legal title.

96. This requirement of legal title meant that *pro conductore*,[9] the so-called "title" of a person who rents a thing; *pro commodatario*, the so-called "title" of one to whom a thing is lent for his own convenience; *pro depositario*, the so-called "title" of one with whom a thing is deposited, a bailee; *pro colono*, the so-called "title" of a tenant-farmer; and *pro inquilino*, the so-called "title" of one who rents an apartment or flat, were not sufficient for adverse possession.[10] It was likewise held that possession by a "title of household fellowship" was not sufficient for adverse possession.[11]

[4] Part. III, tit. 26, n. 66.

[5] Cf. Courcier v. Graham, 1 Ohio 349.

[6] Crawford v. Kimbrough, 76 Ga. 299.

[7] In c. 1, *de praescriptionibus*, II, 13, in VI°, ad v. *Episcopum*.

[8] In c. 7, C. XVI, q. 3, ad v. *Offerre*.

[9] *S.R.R. in causa Novarien., Decimarum, coram Pirovano* (1631)—*Decisiones Recentiores*, Part. 6, dec. 23, n. 6.

[10] Schmalzgrueber, Part. III, tit. 26, n. 84; Pirhing, lib. II, tit. 26, n. 81. It is to be noted that here the word "title" is used not in the true sense of a legal reason for ownership, but in a larger sense of a reason for having a thing in one's possession while not owning it.

[11] *S.R.R. in causa Veliterna, Bonorum, coram Marquemontio* (1607)—*Decisiones Recentiores*, Part. 3, dec. 144, n. 4. This "title" stems from a close personal association, but not that of members of the same family in the American sense of the term. It is derived from the broader sense of the Civil *familia*.

Article 2. Kind of Title Required

a. True Title

97. True title was not required for adverse possession and prescription at Canon Law; for true title would have given a right of ownership and there could then be no question of adverse possession, for the possessor would already be the true owner under such a title.[12] The title which was required instead, was such that of itself it was adequate to transfer ownership, though accidentally it did not transfer it.

b. Color of Title

98. Color of title (apparent title) was sufficient at Canon Law for adverse possession and prescription, but even this was said to be not necessarily required.[13] This, under the American Law, is an apparent title to land founded upon a written instrument, such as a deed, levy of execution, decree of a court, or the like,[14] so that a person taking lands under a judicial sale, though it is void, has color of title,[15] as has one whose deed is founded on a voidable decree in chancery,[16] or whose claim is founded on a will.[17] It is further said that color of title, for the purpose of adverse possession under the statute of limitations, is that which has the semblance or appearance of title, legal or equitable, but which in fact is no title,[18] so that a quit-claim deed,[19] a fraudulent deed accepted in good

[12] Cf. Ioannes Teutonicus, *Glossa (Scholia), in Comp. IV,* lib. II, tit. 10, c. 3; likewise *Glossa ordinaria* in c. 4, X, *de praescriptionibus,* II, 26, ad v. *Se posse tueri,* and in c. 17, *h. t.*, ad v. *Iustus titulus.*

[13] Schmalzgrueber, Part. III, tit. 26, n. 87; Pirhing, lib. II, tit. 26, n. 81; Reiffenstuel, lib. II, tit. 26, n. 126.

[14] 3 William Wait's *Actions and Defenses* (Albany, 1885),17; Brooks v. Bruyn, 35 Ill. 394; Torrey v. Forbes, 94 Ala. 135, 10 South. 320.

[15] Irey v. Mater, 134 Ind. 238, 33 N.E. 1018; Mullan's Adm'r v. Carper, 37 W. Va., 215, 16 S.E. 527.

[16] Whiteside v. Singleton, Meigs (Tenn.) 207.

[17] Doe v. Sherman, 27 N.C. 711.

[18] Sharp v. Furnace Co., 100 Va. 27, 40 S.E. 103.

[19] Parker v. Newberry, 83 Tex. 428, 18 S.W. 815.

faith,[20] a deed from an attorney who has no authority to convey,[21] a deed by an infant,[22] and a deed made by a husband and wife of the wife's interest in a former husband's estate,[23] will give color of title. Color of title is likewise said to be that which is a title in appearance, but not in reality,[24] an apparent right,[25] a title *prima facie* good.[26] It is said to exist whenever there is a reasonable doubt regarding the validity of an apparent title, whether such doubt arises from the circumstances under which the land is held, the identity of the land conveyed, or the construction of the instrument under which the party in possession claims title.[27]

99. Color of title has been described as a writing [28] upon its face professing to pass title, but which does not do so, either from a want of title in the person making it, or from the defective conveyance used; a title that is imperfect, but not so obviously that it would be apparent to one not skilled in the law.[29]

100. It has been held to be wholly immaterial how imperfect or defective the writing may be, considered as a deed; if it is in writing and defines the extent of the claim, it is a sign, semblance or

[20] Gregg v. Sayre, 8 Pet. (U.S.) 244, 8 L. Ed. 932.

[21] Hill's Heirs v. Wilton's Heirs, 6 N.E. 14; Munro v. Merchant, 28 N.Y. 9.

[22] 4 D. & B. 54; Weisinger v. Murphy, 2 Head (Tenn.) 674.

[23] Irey v. Markey, 132 Ind. 546, 32 N.E. 309.

[24] Wood v. Conrad, 2 S.D. 334, 50 N.W. 95; Cameron v. U.S., 148 U.S. 301, 13 Sup. Ct. 595, 37 L. Ed. 459.

[25] Newlin v. Rogers, 6 Kan. App. 910, 51 Pac. 315.

[26] Farley v. Smith, 39 Ala. 38; Converse v. R. Co., 195 Ill. 204, 62 N.E. 887.

[27] Cameron v. U.S., 148 U.S. 301, 13 Sup. Ct. 595, 37 L. Ed. 459.

[28] It has been said that taken strictly color of title cannot rest in parol, Armijo v. Armijo, 4 N.M. (Gild.) 57, 13 Pac. 92, though in some states a parol gift is held to give color of title if accompanied by actual entry and possession, since it manifests, equally with a sale, the intent of the donee to enter, and not as a tenant, and it equally proves an admission on the part of the donor that the possession is so taken, Clark v. Gilbert, 39 Conn. 98; Rannels v. Rannels, 52 Mo. 108; Magee v. Magee, 37 Miss. 138; Steel v. Johnson, 4 Allen (Mass.) 425; Outcalt v. Ludlow, 32 N.J.L. 239; *contra,* Roe v. Doe, 24 Ga. 494, 17 Am. Dec. 142.

[29] Williamson v. Tison, 99 Ga. 792, 26 S.E. 766; Head v. Phillips, 70 Ark. 432, 68 S.W. 878; Bloom v. Straus, 70 Ark. 483, 69 S.W. 549, 72 S.W. 563.

claim of title.[30] It has been said to be anything in writing, however defective, connected with the title, which serves to define the extent of the claim.[31]

It has been held that, to give color of title, a conveyance must describe the property,[32] and that it must designate a specified interest in the land.[33] It must be good in form, and profess to convey the title and be duly executed.[34] A state grant of land included in an older grant may be color of title.[35]

101. Possession in good faith under a void grant from the state gives color of title.[36] A writing signed by the heirs of an owner of lands allotting them to two of their number and relinquishing their own right thereto is also said to be color of title,[37] and so is a patent whether good against the sovereign or void,[38] and a record of proceedings in partition,[39] or a fraudulent deed accepted in good faith.[40] Likewise a tax deed, it has been held, though void for failure to comply with the statutes, affords color of title,[41] unless it be defective on its face.[42]

102. It is noted, however, under the American Law, that "color of title" and "claim of right" are not synonymous terms.[43] "Claim

[30] Street v. Collier, 118 Ga. 470, 45 S.E. 294; Mullan's Adm'r v. Carper, 37 W. Va. 215, 16 S.E. 527.

[31] McClellan v. Kellogg, 17 Ill. 498; Angell, *Limitations*, § 404.

[32] Packard v. Moss, 68 Cal. 123, 8 Pac. 818; Wood v. Conrad, 2 S.D. 334, 50 N.W. 95.

[33] Etowah, etc., Mining Co. v. Parker, 73 Ga. 53; Wilson v. Johnson, 145 Ind. 40, 38 N.E. 38, 43 N.E. 930.

[34] La Frambois v. Jackson, 8 Cow. (N.Y.) 589, 18 Am. Dec. 463; Latta v. Clifford, 47 Fed. 614; Irey v. Markey, 132 Ind. 546, 32 N.E. 309.

[35] Weaver v. Love, 146 N.C. 414, 59 S.E. 1041.

[36] Moody v. Fleming, 4 Ga. 115, 48 Am. Dec. 210.

[37] Henry v. Brown, 143 Ala. 446, 39 South. 325.

[38] Bogardus v. Trinity Church, 4 Sandf. Ch. (N.Y.) 633.

[39] Lindsay v. Beaman, 128 N.C. 189, 38 S.E. 811.

[40] Gregg v. Sayre, 8 Pet. (U.S.) 244, 8 L. Ed. 932.

[41] Lantry v. Parker, 37 Neb. 353, 55 N.W. 962; City of Chicago v. Middlebrooke, 143 Ill. 265, 32 N.E. 457; Van Gunden v. Iron Co., 52 Fed. 838, 3 C.C.A. 294.

[42] Bartlett v. Kauder, 97 Mo. 356, 11 S.W. 67; but cf. Wilson v. Atkinson, 77 Cal. 485, 20 Pac. 66, 11 Am. St. Rep. 299.

[43] Herbert v. Hanrick, 16 Ala. 581.

of title" does not necessarily include "color of title."[44] To constitute "color of title" there must usually be a paper title; but "claim of title" may rest wholly in parol.[45]

103. At Canon Law it was held that legal title could not arise from a contract which was simulated and illicit,[46] or from one which was illegal and void.[47]

104. Similarly, under the American Law certain defects prevent color of title from arising, e. g., if a will has but one subscribing witness and has never been proved, it does not give color of title.[48] Likewise a deed to a tenant in possession from one who has no title to the land is insufficient as a basis for adverse possession.[49] In the same way, a conveyance void on its face is not sufficient.[50] A sale by an administrator of the land of his solvent intestate, under a license of the probate court, does not give color of title, unless it be accompanied by a deed from the administrator.[51] Similarly, the sale of property by an intestate to his son, of which the possession is held by the wife, who is administratrix, while the son lives in the family, does not give color of title as against the intestate's creditors.[52]

105. The element of good faith, and the actual belief on the part of the claimant that he has title, give the claimant by color of title his advantage over the mere trespasser, who is restricted carefully to his actual occupation; and it may be said, generally, that

[44] Allen v. Mansfield, 108 Mo. 343, 18 S.W. 901.

[45] Hamilton v. Wright, 30 Ia. 480.

[46] *S.R.R. in causa Mediolanen., de Brioschis, coram Lugdunen.* (1606)—*Decisiones Recentiores,* Part. 2, dec. 164, n. 4.

[47] *Decisiones Sacrae Rotae Romanae coram R.P.D. Ioanne de Herrera* (Romae, 1731), hereinafter cited by place, type of case, name of judge and date, as follows: *S.R.R. in causa Casertana, Beneficii, coram Herrera* (1719), dec. 90, n. 14; *S.R.R. in causa Romana, Immissionis, coram Omanna* (1705)—*Decisiones Nuperrimae,* tom. 9, dec. 107, n. 8; *S.R.R. in causa Romana, Locorum Montium, coram Marco* (1827), tom. 2, dec. 358, n. 11.

[48] Doe v. Sherman, 27 N.C. 711.

[49] McRoberts v. Bergman, 132 N.Y. 73, 30 N.E. 261.

[50] Moore v. Brown, 11 How. (U.S.) 424, 13 L. Ed. 751; Marsh v. Weir, 21 Tex. 97.

[51] Livingston v. Pendergast, 34 N.H. 544.

[52] Snodgrass v. Andrews, 30 Miss. 472, 64 Am. Dec. 169.

whenever the facts and circumstances show that one in possession in good faith and in the belief that he has title holds for himself and to the exclusion of all others, his possession must be adverse, and according to his assumed title, whatever may be his relations in point of interest or priority to others.[53] Of course, the possession of the true owner must prevail over the claim by constructive possession on the part of one who holds under mere color of title.[54]

106. With all the liberality shown by the courts in giving color of title, it has been denied that a grant from a foreign government confers it, on the ground that the possession under such a title was rather a question between governments than individuals.[55] Thus, the courts of New York have been known to refuse to recognize claims under a grant of the French government in Canada, made prior to the treaty between Great Britain and France in 1763,[56] as conferring color of title. The soundness of the exception was, however, questioned in the same court,[57] and the grant of another state has been expressly held to give color of title in Pennsylvania, even as against one claiming under the grant of the latter state.[58]

For reasons of policy it has been held that a grant from the Indians gives no color of title,[59] nor does a grant by an Indian in contravention of a statute.[60]

c. Putative Title

107. Putative title (one believed to exist) was considered sufficient at Canon Law if the belief was reasonable.[61] It was held in

[53] Jackson v. Porter, 1 Paine 467, Fed. Cas. No. 7,143; Ewing v. Burnet, 11 Pet. (U.S.) 41, 9 L. Ed. 624.

[54] Anderson v. Jackson, 69 Tex. 346, 6 S.W. 575.

[55] Davidson's Lessee v. Beatty, 3 H. & McH. (Md.) 621.

[56] Jackson v. Ingraham, 4 Johns. (N.Y.) 163.

[57] La Frambois v. Jackson, 8 Cow. (N.Y.) 589, 18 Am. Dec. 463.

[58] Barney v. Sutton, 2 Watts (Pa.) 37.

[59] Johnson v. McIntosh, 8 Wheat. (U.S.) 571, 5 L. Ed. 681.

[60] Smythe v. Henry, 41 Fed. 705.

[61] Schmalzgrueber, Part. III, tit. 26, n. 87; Pirhing, lib. II, tit. 26, n. 81; Reiffenstuel, lib. II, tit. 26, n. 126. This was not, however, the case when the title was *pro emptore,* i.e., that of a purchaser, which required actual sale and delivery, not mere belief.

the Canon Law that a legally justified error which might cause such belief of a right to own the thing in question could be caused by a mixture of properties,[62] and if the error was legally justified the title would be good,[63] even if there was error of law, usually prejudicial to adverse possession, mixed in with it.[64] It was even said that the title might be doubtful and really non-existent,[65] and that it did not need to be clear.[66]

d. Presumptive Title

108. While presumptive title was not good at Canon Law in ten- and twenty-year adverse possessions, it was allowed in the thirty- and forty-year periods, which cut off all actions, and even more so in immemorial possession, that is to say, in immemorial possession it would be presumed that title had been acquired.[67] While some American courts speak of presumption of payment, it is unnecessary to speak of presumption of title, since it is transferred by operation of law on the lapse of the period of adverse pos-

[62] *S.R.R. in causa Romana, Vineae, coram Merlino* (1627)—*Decisiones Novissimae,* tom. 1, dec. 72, n. 5—*Decisiones Recentiores,* Part. 5, tom. 1.

[63] *S.R.R. in causa Constantin., Iurisdictionis, coram Attrebaten.* (1611)—*Decisiones Recentiores,* Part. 1, dec. 324, n. 8; *S.R.R. in causa Corduben., Redecimarum, coram Coccino* (1625)—*Decisiones Novissimae,* tom. 2, dec. 458, n. 73—*Decisiones Recentiores,* Part. 5, tom. 2; *S.R.R. in causa Detrusen., Vicariae, coram Carrillo* (1636)—*Decisiones Recentiores,* Part. 7, dec. 145, nn. 6-7; *S.R.R. in causa Barbastren., Decimarum, coram Taia* (1662)—*Decisiones Recentiores,* Part. 13, dec. 520, n. 17; *S.R.R. in causa Beneventana, Iurisdictionis, coram Taia* (1663)—*Decisiones Recentiores,* Part. 14, dec. 21, n. 12.

[64] *S.R.R. in causa Corduben., Redecimarum, coram Coccino* (1625)—*Decisiones Novissimae,* tom. 2, dec. 458, n. 78 sqq.—*Decisiones Recentiores,* Part 5, tom. 2; *S.R.R. in causa Romana, Divisionis, coram Bichio* (1640)—*Decisiones Recentiores,* Part. 8, dec. 238, nn. 4-5.

[65] *S.R.R. in causa Ravennaten. seu Ferrarien., Iurisdictionis super bono iure, coram Crescentio* (1735), tom. 3, dec. 326, n. 39.

[66] *S.R.R. in causa Mileten., Iurisdictionis, coram Falconerio* (1715), tom. 2, *de Offic. Ordin.,* dec. 9, n. 27.

[67] *Decisiones Sacrae Rotae Romanae coram R.P.D. Antonio Rusconi* (Romae, 1826), hereinafter cited by place, type of case, name of judge and year, as follows: *S.R.R. in causa Montis Alti, Decimarum, coram Rusconi* (1804), dec. 51, n. 6.

session as a rule, and is then true title, not merely presumed, much as the Canon Law presumed it when all actions were cut off as against the holder.

Article 3. Hostiensis' Doctrine on Titles

109. Hostiensis[68] includes in his work, for the benefit, as he says, of the Canonists, a lengthy discussion of the Roman Law on titles which may be summarized as follows:

110. *Pro soluto* (as satisfaction, in accord and satisfaction) was the title by which one held anything, whether so due or not, received in satisfaction of a debt.

111. *Pro emptore* (as purchaser) was the title by which one held: 1—things bought and paid for unconditionally and in good faith, and delivered actually; 2—land under constructive adverse possession in excess of what was actually purchased, provided that there was written evidence of the transaction when so required by law; 3—things received from one who had held them himself as purchaser; 4—things received from a husband who held them on a conveyance to him from his wife as donee; 5—things received as a "special" successor in title, i. e., not as an heir, with the result that one could raise a defense to a suit on grounds of fraud or deceit committed by the predecessor in title.

112. *Pro transacto* (as a transaction) was the title by which one held: 1—things given by one not really owning them but believing he did, as consideration for settling a suit out of court, i. e., what was given, not the object of the suit; 2—things given him as a supposed co-heir when he settled a suit for an estate out of court.

113. *Pro haerede* (as heir) was the title by which one held: 1—things which an ancestor had begun to acquire by adverse possession, i. e., tacking his holding, unless there was a flaw in the thing,[69] or a quasi-flaw,[70] or there was bad faith in the heir; 2—things delivered to a supposed co-heir as his supposed share of the estate, i. e., as to what was delivered, not as to what was thought to

[68] *Summa Aurea,* ff. 165 and 169v.

[69] This would be the case if the ancestor had obtained it *vi, clam, praecario.*

[70] E. g., if it was the property of the State, of the *fiscus,* or of a minor, or was in the hands of a magistrate.

be his share; 3—things which one held as an emancipated son who was made heir of his father whether the ancestor held the property himself as an heir or without any title, provided that the son believed the object was a part of the estate and provided there was no flaw in the thing; [71] 4—things which one held so as to make one liable to suit on an inheritance, whether he was such heir or not.[72] This did not afford a defense to a suit on grounds of fraud or deceit by the predecessor in title.

It did not avail: 1—as to what one took as universal successor, i. e., as true "heir"; 2—if one was not really an heir or did not with reason believe that he was; 3—if the ancestor was still alive; 4—if one was made universal successor by a person who held in bad faith and consequently could not transfer ownership.

114. *Pro donato* (as donee) was the title by which one held: [73] 1—a gift good in law and held in good faith, though it came from a non-owner; 2—a gift from husband to wife taken in good faith, unless he was liable (bailee) for the return of the object; [74] 3—a gift to a son from his father, provided that he was later disinherited and then ratified the gift or it was tacitly confirmed; 4—a gift if this was the real reason for transfer of title, even if there was apparently a sale. This entitled one to hold even though the donor tried to regain possession of the gift by a suit at law. It supposed an intent on the part of the donor to make the object the property of the donee when it was given.

115. *Pro derelicto* (as of a thing abandoned) was the title by which one held: 1—thinking, rightly or wrongly, that the previous owner had abandoned the object; 2—thinking the one who had abandoned it was the owner, otherwise it was not good. This required that one actually take possession. It was not good if the one abandoning was merely a joint owner of the property abandoned.

[71] Cf. *supra*, note 69.

[72] If there was no intent to tack one's possession one could acquire under the title *pro haerede* even though the ancestor could not have so acquired.

[73] Under a right to possess until the adverse possession was complete, since the gift did not transfer the right of ownership immediately, but gave one a right to possess until such time as it could not at law be revoked.

[74] Unless divorce intervened after her adverse possession was complete, in which case it remained hers.

116. *Pro legato* (as a bequest or devise) was the title by which one held: 1—the property of a third party which was really, though not legally, bequeathed or devised to him in good faith, even though ademption might have occurred; [75] i. e., the extinction or withholding of a legacy in consequence of some act of the testator which, though not directly a revocation of the bequest, is considered in law as equivalent thereto, or indicative of an intention to revoke; 2—property received by a legatee who thought the testator dead, though he was still alive. This required under the Civil Law that the holder should have legal capacity to be a legatee.

117. *Pro dote* (as dowry) was the title by which one held property of a third party given in good faith as a dowry. When such property was definitely determined at the time, this title did not arise,[76] but if it was not so determined this title arose after the marriage.

118. *Pro suo* (as one's own) was the title by which one held: a—strictly considered, one's own property known to be one's own; b—by analogy, when one believed justifiably he was the owner, either in common with another title he had, or in particular, supplying the defects of another title, provided there was probable error. This was good when a false reason was not prejudicial, e. g., when delivery had been made and one was in good faith, as to a child of a stolen slave, born during the adverse possession and held in good faith even if she, the slave, came to be known as stolen before the adverse possession was complete, provided the holder notified the owner, if possible. This covered, too, things occupied in the sea, on land, or in the air, or obtained by alluvion or out of things held by grant from another,[77] and income of a thing sold or granted to the holder. This was the title of a disinherited son not ratifying a gift from his father, made while he was still under the father's power. An undetermined dowry after a marriage binding in fact only, not in law and in fact, was held by this title. An undetermined dowry intended

[75] Provided he believed the will to be valid, or there was probable error as to the name, whether he was meant or another.

[76] *Pro suo* was the title in such a case.

[77] I. e., predecessor in title.

to pass before the marriage was also held by this title.[78] A determinate dowry intended to pass before the marriage was also held by this title. This was likewise the title used in the case of all legally justified reasons for possession by which ownership was customarily acquired when other specific titles were wanting, provided there was a legally justified reason, not the mere running of time.

Article 4. Importance of Title in Constructive Adverse Possession

119. Title was important at Canon Law since the adverse possession was not good beyond the extent of the title, in the case of constructive adverse possession,[79] and the possession was presumed to conform to the previous title.[80]

120. The American Law similarly holds that, when the claim rests upon color of title as well as possession, the possession will be regarded as co-extensive with the powers described in the title-deed,[81] unless the acts or declarations of the occupant restrict it. The constructive possession, however, of land arising from color of title cannot be extended to that part of it whereof there is no actual adverse possession [82] and extension of the inclosure within the time limited will not give title to the part included in the extension.[83] A trespasser who afterwards obtains color of title can claim constructively only from the time when the title was obtained.[84]

[78] Such title lasted until the marriage took place, when *pro dote* arose.

[79] *S.R.R. in causa Corduben., Redecimarum, coram Coccino* (1625)—*Decisiones Novissimae,* tom. 2, dec. 458, n. 70—*Decisiones Recentiores,* Part. 5, tom. 2; *S.R.R. in causa Ravennaten. seu Ferrarien., Iurisdictionis super bono iure, coram Crescentio* (1738), tom. 4, dec. 412, n. 49.

[80] *S.R.R. in causa Romana, Fideicommissi, coram Emerix* (1677), tom. 1, dec. 348, n. 7.

[81] Ewing v. Burnet, 11 Pet. (U.S.) 41, 9 L. Ed. 624; Bynum v. Thompson, 25 N.C. 578; Webb v. Sturtevant, 1 Scam. (Ill.) 181; Jackson v. Smith, 13 Johns. (N.Y.) 406; Proprietors of Kennebeck Purchase v. Springer, 4 Mass. 416, 3 Am. Dec. 227; Kile v. Tubbs, 23 Cal. 431.

[82] Beauplant v. McKeen, 28 Pa. 124, 70 Am. Dec. 115; Franklin Academy v. Hall, 16 B. Monr. (Ky.) 472.

[83] Hall v. Gitting's Lessee, 2 H. & J. (Md.) 391.

[84] Jackson v. Thomas, 16 Johns. (N.Y.) 293.

The American Law also holds that, when a man enters in good faith under a claim of title, his entry on a part is an entry on the whole; but if he claims no such title he has no seisin by his entry except by the ouster of him who was seised, which can only be by the actual and exclusive occupation of the land.[85] When a disseisor enters upon and cultivates part of a tract he does not thereby hold possession of the whole tract constructively unless this entry was by color of title by specific boundaries to the whole tract; color of title is valuable only in so far as it indicates the extent of the disseisor's claim.[86]

Article 5. Sufficiency of Title

121. In general, at Canon Law, "color of title" was sufficient for adverse possession.[87] Putative title was likewise held sufficient with no need that it be true and valid,[88] so long as it created in the holder justifiable error,[89] but it was not good if the title was false or erroneous.[90] Title would be supplied, it was held, by the mortgage contract for a mortgage,[91] or by the judgment for a judgment lien.[92]

[85] Proprietors of the Kennebeck Purchase v. Springer, 4 Mass. 416, 3 Am. Dec. 227.

[86] Ege v. Medlar, 82 Pa. 99; cf. also Allen v. Mansfield, 108 Mo. 343, 18 S.W. 901; Sholl v. Coal Co., 139 Ill. 21, 28 N.E. 748.

[87] *S.R.R. in causa Gerunden., Administrationis, coram Emerix* (1687), tom. 2, dec. 731, n. 13; *S.R.R. in causa Gerunden., Administrationis, coram Emerix* (1687), tom. 2, dec. 764, n. 14; *S.R.R. in causa Novarien., Parochialis, coram Ansaldo* (1707), tom. 4, dec. 425, n. 7; *S.R.R. in causa Nullius seu Fulden., Iurisdictionis, coram Ansaldo* (1708), tom. 4, dec. 439, n. 105; *S.R.R. in causa Ravennaten. seu Ferrarien., Iurisdictionis super bono iure, coram Crescentio* (1735), tom. 3, dec. 326, n. 36; *S.R.R. in causa Melevitana, Antianitatis, coram Priolo* (1694)—*Decisiones Nuperrimae*, tom. 4, dec. 252, n. 12.

[88] *S.R.R. in causa Tridentina, Decimarum, coram Scotto* (1705)—*Decisiones Nuperrimae*, tom. 9, dec. 15, n. 13.

[89] *S.R.R. in causa Tridentina, Decimarum, coram Scotto* (1705)—*Decisiones Nuperrimae*, tom. 9, dec. 15, n. 14.

[90] *S.R.R. in causa Perusina, Immissionis, coram Marini* (1832), dec. 76, n. 28; *S.R.R. in causa Perusina, Immissionis, coram Marini* (1832), dec. 90, n. 27.

[91] *S.R.R. in causa Veliterna, uti Praelato, coram Gamberini* (1820), dec. 22, n. 9.

[92] *S.R.R. in causa Veliterna, uti Praelato, coram Gamberini* (1820), dec. 22, n. 10.

122. Title alone was not sufficient for adverse possession to run if there were conditions to be fulfilled.[93] In matters of ecclesiastical jurisdiction title had to come from the Supreme Pontiff,[94] so that the right of the Metropolitan was not sufficient to give color of title,[95] nor did a concession by a secular prince give color of title.[96] It was also held that mere color of title was not sufficient against an Apostolic Constitution which contained a decree nullifying the possession in question,[97] or that if such color of title was alleged it rather gave rise to bad faith.[98]

123. If the title had flaws in it, it would not avail him if it was offered by the one claiming adverse possession, though it would not hurt him if it was held forth by some one else.[99] It was said to be better to have no title than to have a faulty one,[100] because a faulty title prejudiced even a centenary possession.[101]

[93] *S.R.R. in causa Romana, Salviani, coram Merlino* (1630)—*Decisiones Novissimae,* tom. 1, dec. 407, n. 13—*Decisiones Recentiores,* Part. 5, tom. 1.

[94] *S.R.R. in causa Ravennaten. seu Ferrarien., Iurisdictionis super bono iure, coram Crescentio* (1735), tom. 3, dec. 326, n. 40.

[95] *S.R.R. in causa Ravennaten. seu Ferrarien., Iurisdictionis super bono iure, coram Crescentio* (1735), tom. 3, dec. 326, nn. 41-42.

[96] *S.R.R. in causa Ravennaten. seu Ferrarien., Iurisdictionis super bono iure, coram Crescentio* (1735), tom. 3, dec. 326, n. 38; *S.R.R. in causa Ravennaten. seu Ferrarien., Iurisdictionis, super bono iure, coram Crescentio* (1738), tom. 4, dec. 412, n. 48.

[97] *S.R.R. in causa Vratislavien., Iuris approbandi Confessarios, coram Lancetta* (1722), tom. 6, dec. 1319, n. 17.

[98] *S.R.R. in causa Vratislavien., Iuris approbandi Confessarios, coram Lancetta* (1722), tom. 6, dec. 1319, n. 15.

[99] *S.R.R. in causa Romana seu Portuen., Tenutarum, coram Emerix* (1694), tom. 3, dec. 1188, nn. 2-3.

[100] *S.R.R. in causa Bononien., Dismembrationis, coram Verospio* (1658)—*Decisiones Recentiores,* Part. 12, dec. 320, n. 20 sqq.; *S.R.R. in causa Herbipolen., Monasterii, coram Lancetta* (1713), tom. 3, dec. 782, n. 22; *Decisiones Sacrae Romanae Rotae coram R.P.D. Hercule Consalvi* (Romae, 1822), hereinafter cited by place, type of case, name of judge and date, as follows: *S.R.R. in causa Romana, seu Parmen., Salviani, coram Consalvi* (1795), dec. 34, n. 9; *Coram Lega habitae Sacrae Romanae Rotae Decisiones sive Sententiae annis 1909-1914* (2. ed., Romae, 1926), dec. 7, n. 12, hereinafter cited as follows, *S.R.R. in causa Ripana, Iurium, coram Lega.*

[101] Schmalzgrueber, Part. III, tit. 26, n. 85.

124. The title could not be changed during the adverse possession,[102] because each such change meant a new possession,[103] and one could not have several titles at the same time to the same thing,[104] despite what Hostiensis had said about the title *pro suo*.[105] It is to be noted, however, that some of the states in the United States seem to allow a change of possession, so that it is under different titles at different times, provided the claim is always adverse.[106]

Article 6. Necessity of Title

125. Gratian had already remarked[107] that possession without title was usurpation and that consequently adverse possession would not run. He further noted that a just (legal) title was necessary[108] and proceeded to illustrate this by the rule that a layman could not acquire spiritual things since he could not have a just (legal) title thereto. Rufinus (+ca. 1190)[109] taught the same. Bernard of Pavia (+1266)[110] mentioned the need for a title in adverse possession running ten or twenty years, for after thirty years, or forty in the case of churches, every action was cut off and title was presumed. One can say, therefore, that title was required for adverse possession.[111] Indeed, it was in this requirement of title that adverse

[102] *S.R.R. in causa Mediolanen., Curae animarum,* 23 mart. 1909, *coram R.P.D. Michaele Lega,* Dec. I, n. 11—*S.R.R. Decisiones,* I (1909), 101; *AAS,* I (1909), 314-325.

[103] *S.R.R. in causa Lucana, Bonorum, coram Lugdunen.* (1611)—*Decisiones Recentiores,* Part. I, dec. 304, n. 7.

[104] *S.R.R. in causa Romana seu Parmen., Salviani, coram Consalvi* (1795), Dec. 34, n. 13.

[105] Cf. *supra,* n. 118.

[106] Cf. Fanning v. Wilcox, 3 Day (Conn.) 258; Shannon v. Kinney, 1 A. D. Marsh (Ky.) 4, 10 Am. Dec. 705.

[107] D.a.c. 8, C. XVI, q. 3.

[108] D.a.c. 16, C. XVI, q. 3.

[109] *Summa,* p. 359.

[110] *Summa,* lib. II, tit. 18, § 3.

[111] Schmalzgrueber, Part. III, tit. 26, n. 128; *S.R.R. in causa Cathacen., Praetensae Obedientiae, coram Bichio* (1650)—*Decisiones Recentiores,* Part. 11, dec. 30, n. 12; *S.R.R. in causa Beneventana, Iurisdictionis, coram Taia* (1663)—*Decisiones Recentiores,* Part. 14, dec. 21, n. 18; *S.R.R. in causa Cracovien.,*

possession differed from custom, which was so often treated together with adverse possession by writers in the period before the Code.[112]

Title was also nècessary, for when preference was given to one of two claimants of possession it was given to the one having title, at Canon Law.[113] Under the American Law in cases of mixed possession, or of a possession at the same time by two or more persons, each under a separate colorable title, the seisin is in him who has the better or prior title,[114] for it is said that, though there may be a concurrent possession, there cannot be a concurrent seisin; and, one only being seised, the possession must be adjudged to be in him, because he has the better right.[115] Of course, in such a case, if one has color of title, and the other is a mere trespasser or intruder, the possession is in him who has color of title.[116]

126. Title was not required, at Canon Law, in the case of a servitude which was real and continual,[117] but if it was non-continual then a title was necessary for the ordinary periods of possession, if not for immemorial.[118] Title was likewise not required in forty-year

Bonorum, coram Emerix (1695), tom. 3, dec. 1264, n. 10; *S.R.R. in causa Toletana, Decimarum super bono iure, coram Falconerio* (1724), tom. 4, *de Decim.*, dec. 9, n. 17; *S.R.R. in causa Melevitana, Antianitatis, coram Priolo* (1694)—*Decisiones Nuperrimae*, tom. 4, dec. 252, n. 10; *S.R.R. in causa Perusina, Manutentionis, coram Marco* (1828), dec. 400, n. 4; *S.R.R. in causa Perusina, Immissionis, coram Marini* (1832), dec. 76, n. 29; *S.R.R. in causa Perusina, Immissionis, coram Marini* (1832), dec. 90, n. 21; *S.R.R. in causa Melevitana, Funerum*, 22 iul. 1911, *coram R.P.D. Ioanne Prior*, Dec. XXXIV, n. 21—*S.R.R. Decisiones*, III (1911), 364; *AAS*, III (1911), 611-628; S.C.C., 16 febr. 1889—*ASS*, XXII (1889-1890), 20.

112 *S.R.R. in causa Barchinonen., Mulctae, coram Falconerio* (1721), tom. 2, *de Offic. Ordin.*, dec. 22, n. 3.

113 *S.R.R. in causa Hispalen., Primitiarum, coram Novarro* (1622)—*Decisiones Recentiores*, Part. 4, tom. 2, dec. 391, n. 36.

114 White v. Burnley, 20 How. (U.S.) 235, 15 L. Ed. 886; Doe v. Butler, 3 Wend. (N.Y.) 149.

115 Mather v. Ministers of Trinity Church, 3 S. & R. (Pa.) 509, 8 Am. Dec. 663.

116 Hall v. Gittings' Lessee, 2 Harr. & J. (Md.) 112; Hall v. Powel, 4 S. & R. (Pa.) 465, 8 Am. Dec. 722.

117 Schmalzgrueber, Part. III, tit. 26, n. 91.

118 Schmalzgrueber, *ibid.*

possession when the law was not opposed to the holding,[119] though it was certainly required for possession which was contrary to the law,[120] so that it was remarked that reprobated acts would not afford a legal reason for possession.[121]

Since title was sometimes, i. e., in the case of "presumed" title, not required at Canon Law, and since the American Law does not always require even color of title, and since when all actions are cut off title is in the holder,[122] it seems that Canon Law will not always require title even now. It suffices to consider what St. Raymond said about forming for oneself a title in conscience,[123] and what was said concerning putative title [124] and presumptive title [125] when all actions were cut off to see that title is not always required even at Canon Law.

119 *S.R.R. in causa Gerunden., Administrationis, coram Emerix* (1687), tom. 2, dec. 731, n. 11; *S.R.R. in causa Gerunden., Administrationis, coram Emerix* (1687), tom. 2, dec. 764, n. 9; *S.R.R. in causa Leodien., Beghinagii, coram Emerix* (1695), tom. 3, dec. 1257, n. 23.

120 *S.R.R. in causa Feltren., Praebendae, coram Coccino* (1605)—*Decisiones Recentiores,* Part. 1, dec. 91, n. 1; *S.R.R. in causa Pampilonen., Decimarum, coram Emerix* (1681), tom. 1, dec. 473, n. 3; *S.R.R. in causa Gerunden., Administrationis, coram Emerix* (1687), tom. 2, dec. 764, n. 8; *S.R.R. in causa Colonien., Decanatus, coram Falconerio* (1711), tom. 1, *de Elect.,* dec. 4, n. 5; *S.R.R. in causa Marsicen., Decimarum, coram Muto* (1697)—*Decisiones Nuperrimae,* tom. 5, dec. 308, n. 34; *S.R.R. in causa Caputaquen., Subventionis, coram De la Tremoille* (1702)—*Decisiones Nuperrimae,* tom. 7, dec. 358, n. 23; cf. canons 12; 27, § 2; 147, § 1; 150.

121 *S.R.R. in causa Caputaquen., Subventionis, coram De la Tremoille* (1702) —*Decisiones Nuperrimae,* tom. 7, dec. 358, n. 24.

122 James Barr Ames, *Lectures on Legal History* (Cambridge, 1913), § 197.

123 Cf. *supra,* n. 94.

124 Cf. *supra,* n. 107.

125 Cf. *supra,* n. 108.

CHAPTER V

MANNER OF HOLDING

ARTICLE 1. ACTUAL POSSESSION

127. At Canon Law, actual civil possession was required, so that one who did not actually hold in this manner could not claim adverse possession, especially against one who had so held.[1] Civil possession was, however, not good so long as another, not one's agent or tenant, still had the natural possession,[2] even if the possession was granted by judicial decree.[3] This was especially true if a long time had elapsed after the issuance of the decree and the one actually holding had not been cited and had no knowledge of it.[4]

128. Adverse possession, it was said, had to be a natural acquisition of a possession which was open to be taken,[5] but natural possession was not sufficient if civil possession (title) was still in an-

[1] *S.R.R. in causa Reatina, Immissionis, coram Scotto* (1706)—*Decisiones Nuperrimae,* tom. 9, dec. 253, n. 16.

[2] *S.R.R. in causa Veliterna, Bonorum, coram Marquemontio* (1607)—*Decisiones Recentiores,* Part. 3, dec. 144, n. 4; *S.R.R. in causa Romana, Salviani, coram Roias* (1643)—*Decisiones Recentiores,* Part. 9, tom. 1, dec. 212, n. 2; *S.R.R. in causa Romana seu Portuen., Tenutarum, coram Emerix* (1694), tom. 3, dec. 1189, n. 3; *S.R.R. in causa Romana, Castri Orciani, coram Emerix* (1674), tom. 1, dec. 189, n. 17; *S.R.R. in causa Nullius seu Fulden., Iurisdictionis, coram Ansaldo* (1708), tom. 4, dec. 439, n. 138; *S.R.R. in causa Melevitana, Antianitatis, coram Priolo* (1694)—*Decisiones Nuperrimae,* tom. 4, dec. 252, n. 10; *S.R.R. in causa Romana seu Farfen., Reintegrationis, coram Priolo* (1699)—*Decisiones Nuperrimae,* tom. 6, dec. 96, n. 5; *S.R.R. in causa Bononien., Salviani, coram Malvasia* (1786), dec. 195, n. 6; *S.R.R. in causa Montis alti, Decimarum, coram Rusconi* (1804), dec. 51, n. 7.

[3] *S.R.R. in causa Romana seu Portuen., Tenutarum, coram Emerix* (1694), tom. 3, dec. 1189, n. 4.

[4] *S.R.R. in causa Romana seu Portuen., Tenutarum, coram Emerix* (1694), tom. 3, dec. 1189, n. 5.

[5] *S.R.R. in causa Veliterna, Bonorum, coram Marquemontio* (1607)—*Decisiones Recentiores,* Part. 3, dec. 144, n. 4.

other person,[6] so that the holder clearly had no right whatsoever to own the property. This, then, is stricter than the American rule. Possession could be acquired through a window, when one was prevented from taking actual seisin.[7] Though civil possession usually meant taking hold of the thing with the idea of being owner, a real, actual seisin was not necessary. It was sufficient if by fiction of law it was acquired by some act equivalent to a seizing,[8] but one had to hold for himself and in his own name.[9]

129. Since there had to be actual possession, what was good for one thing was not good for another,[10] even if there was greater reason to say the possession covered that other thing.[11] Certainly it was not extended where the possession was prejudicial.[12] Hence it did not cover things later acquired,[13] i. e., the time had to run on these things from the date of their acquisition. It was also necessary that the one holding have intent to acquire by such possession.[14]

130. The American Law likewise requires that there be an actual occupation with intent to claim against the true owner. In Pennsylvania this rule has been announced with special distinct-

[6] Schmalzgrueber, Part. III, tit. 26, nn. 44, 128; *S.R.R. in causa Lucana, Bonorum, coram Lugdunen.* (1609)—*Decisiones Recentiores,* Part. 1, dec. 208, n. 5.

[7] *S.R.R. in causa Gnesnen., Parochialis, coram Emerix* (1682), tom. 2, dec. 551, n. 2.

[8] Consequently the deeds recognized by the American Law are good in this sense. Cf. also canon 1499, § 1.

[9] Schmalzgrueber, Part. III, tit. 26, nn. 42-44.

[10] *S.R.R. in causa Barchinonen., Iurium Parochialium, coram Rezzonico* (1735), tom. 2, dec. 239, n. 20; *S.R.R. in causa Barchinonen., Iurium Parochialium, coram Rezzonico* (1735), tom. 2, dec. 241, n. 12; *S.R.R. in causa Derthusen., Iurisdictionis, coram Pio* (1697)—*Decisiones Nuperrimae,* tom. 5, dec. 217, nn. 24-25.

[11] *S.R.R. in causa Barchinonen., Iurium Parochialium, coram Rezzonico* (1735), tom. 2, dec. 241, n. 13.

[12] *S.R.R. in causa Gerunden., Anniversariorum, coram Paulutio* (1685)—*Decisiones Nuperrimae,* tom. 1, dec. 175, n. 7.

[13] *S.R.R. in causa Hispalen., Decimarum, coram Bichio* (1649)—*Decisiones Recentiores,* Part. 10, dec. 333, n. 31.

[14] *S.R.R. in causa Beneventana, Iurisdictionis, coram Taia* (1664)—*Decisiones Recentiores,* Part. 14, dec. 189, n. 7.

ness. "The owner of land," says the Supreme Court,[15] "can only be barred by such possession as has been actual. . . ."[16] Adverse and exclusive occupation for the statutory period of a railroad's right of way does not, however, prevail against the railroad since it is for a public purpose and the statute does not run against it.[17]

131. When the claim is by possession, without any color or pretense of title (Canon Law usually requires colored or putative title because good faith would not otherwise be possible), it cannot, under the American Law, extend beyond the actual limits of the inclosure,[18] and constructive possession of land arising from color of title can not be extended to that part of it whereof there is no actual adverse possession,[19] nor will a subsequent conflicting possession, whether under color of title or not, be extended by construction beyond the limits of the actual adverse possession for the purpose of defeating a prior constructive possession.[20] Similarly, there cannot be any constructive adverse possession against the owner when there has been no actual possession which he could treat as a trespass and bring suit for.[21]

Article 2. Hostile to True Owner

132. At Canon Law the possession had to be hostile, as is apparent from what has been said regarding persons who because of their juridical relationship to the true owner cannot acquire by adverse possession against such owner.[22]

[15] Mercer v. Watson, 1 Watts (Pa.) 341.

[16] Cf. Paldi v. Paldi, 95 Mich. 410, 54 N.W. 903; Murray v. Hoyle, 97 Ala. 588, 12 South. 797; Sharon v. Tucker, 144 U.S. 533, 12 Sup. Ct. 720, 36 L. Ed. 532; Evans v. Templeton, 69 Tex. 375, 6 S.W. 843, 5 Am. St. Rep. 71; Gildehaus v. Whiting, 39 Kan. 706, 18 Pac. 916; Haffendorfer v. Gault, 84 Ky. 124; Colvin v. Land Ass'n, 23 Neb. 75, 36 N.W. 361, 8 Am. St. Rep. 114.

[17] Southern Pac. Co. v. Hyatt, 132 Cal. 240, 64 Pac. 272, 54 L. R. A. 522.

[18] Watrous v. Southworth, 5 Conn. 305; Hatch v. R. Co., 28 Vt. 142; Bell v. Longworth, 6 Ind. 273.

[19] Beauplant v. McKeen, 28 Pa. 124, 70 Am. Dec. 115; Franklin Academy v. Hall, 16 B. Monr. (Ky.) 372.

[20] Jackson v. Vermilyea, 6 Cow. (N.Y.) 677; Ralph v. Bayley, 11 Vt. 521.

[21] Steedman v. Hilliard, 3 Rich. (S.C.) 101.

[22] Cf. *supra*, nn. 13-20.

133. Under the American Law the same is true, as the Supreme Court of Pennsylvania in the decision cited above,[23] said, "The owner of land can only be barred by such possession as has been . . . hostile or adverse." [24] The possession must be in such manner and under such circumstances as to amount to an invasion of the owner's rights, thereby giving him a cause of action.[25] The possession must be adverse. If it is permissive,[26] or by mistake,[27] or unintentional,[28] or confessedly in subordination to another's right,[29] it does not avail to bar the owner's right.

134. If the occupation is such and by such a person that it may be for the true owner, it will be presumed to be for the latter, unless it be shown that the adverse claimant gave notice that he held adversely and not in subordination.[30] Such notice must further be clear and unequivocal.[31]

135. If the act of the tenant or adverse claimant may be a trespass as well as a disseisin, the true owner may elect which he will consider it, regardless of the wishes of the trespasser, who cannot be allowed to qualify his own wrong.[32] Thus, if the adverse claimant sets up his trespasses as amounting to adverse possession, the owner may reply that they are no disseisin, but trespasses only; while, on the other hand, the true owner may elect, if he please, for the sake of his remedy, to treat them as a disseisin.[33] This is called a disseisin by election, in distinction to a disseisin by fact—a distinc-

[23] Cf. *supra, h. c.*, note 15.

[24] Cf. also *supra, h. c.*, note 16.

[25] Abell v. Harris, 11 Gill & J. (Md.) 371; Jackson v. Huntington, 5 Pet. (U.S.) 438, 8 L. Ed. 170; Somerville v. Hamilton, 4 Wheat. (U.S.) 230, 4 L. Ed. 558.

[26] 2 Jac. & W. 1.

[27] Comegys v. Carley, 3 Watts (Pa.) 280, 27 Am. Dec. 356.

[28] Burrell v. Burrell, 11 Mass. 296.

[29] 5 B. & Ald. 223; Kirk v. Smith, 9 Wheat. (U.S.) 241, 6 L. Ed. 81; Jackson v. Denison, 4 Wend. (N.Y.) 558; Dikeman v. Parrish, 6 Pa. 210, 47 Am. Dec. 455.

[30] 1 Barr. Ch. 373; 5 Burr. 2604.

[31] 1 Burr. 60.

[32] 1 Burr. 60; Proprietors of Tp. No. 6 v. McFarland, 12 Mass. 325; Prescott v. Nevers, 4 Mas. 329, Fed. Cas. No. 11,390.

[33] Bryant v. Tucker, 19 Me. 383.

tion which was taken for the benefit of the owner of the land. Whenever the act done of itself necessarily works an actual disseisin, it is a disseisin in fact, as when a tenant for years or at will conveys in fee. On the other hand, those acts which are susceptible of being made a disseisin by election are no disseisin till the election of the owner makes them so.[34]

Article 3. Distinct and Exclusive

136. The Canon Law held that the possession had to be exclusive of others.[35] Hence two persons could not hold adversely in common,[35a] but one could acquire a right of ownership, the other a life-tenancy; or one could acquire the ownership, the other a leasehold; one could acquire one part, the other another; or they could acquire concurrent jurisdiction in the same place,[36] so that a particular possession, e. g., of donee, could arise in one, and the universal possession, e. g., of heir, in another,[37] unless the possession of the part was through a universal title, i. e., of an heir, existing in another.[38]

137. Under the American Law, to quote again the Supreme Court of Pennsylvania,[39] it is held that "the owner of land can only be barred by such possession as has been . . . distinct. . . ."[40] A possession not actual, but constructive, not exclusive, but in participation with the owner or others, falls short of that kind of adverse possession which deprives the true owner of his title.[41]

[34] Jackson v. Rogers, 1 Johns. (N.Y.) 36.

[35] *S.R.R. in causa Ripana, Iurium,* 2 apr. 1910, *coram R.P.D. Michaele Lega,* Dec. XIV, n. 16—*S.R.R. Decisiones,* II (1910), 129; *AAS,* II (1910), 418-431.

[35a] But cf. *supra,* n. 78, note 95.

[36] Schmalzgrueber, Part. III, tit. 26, n. 46; cf. *supra,* n. 125, notes 114-115.

[37] *S.R.R. in causa Urgellen., Plebaniae, coram Emerix* (1686), tom. 2, dec. 698, n. 7.

[38] Cf. preceding note.

[39] Cf. *supra, h. c.,* note 15.

[40] Cf. *supra, h. c.,* note 16.

[41] Ward v. Cochran, 150 U.S. 597, 14 Sup. Ct. 230, 37 L. Ed. 1195.

ARTICLE 4. PEACEFUL

138. That the possession must not be violent in its inception was mentioned by Gratian.[42] The *Glossa* likewise taught that one who took [43] or detained a thing by violence did not acquire by adverse possession.[44] This idea went back to the Roman Law.[45] On the other hand, the *Glossa* mentioned that unless the recaption was made on fresh pursuit the law did not permit it to be done in a riotous or forceful manner.[46] The Roman interdict *"unde vi"* lay to recover land from which the plaintiff had been forcibly ejected, so self-help was not considered necessary.

139. The *Glossa,* after explaining that things affected by some flaw cannot be acquired by adverse possession stated that such things were those mentioned in the Roman Law,[47] viz., freemen, sacred or religious things, a fugitive slave,[48] which can never be acquired as property through adverse possession.

140. If the taking or holding was violent the Canon Law, following the Roman, held that there was a flaw in the object held,[49] so that it was what was known as *res vitiosa,* which faulty condition passed with the possession to the holder's heirs.[50] The same was true if the possession was not open and notorious, or if the object was stolen, or if the relationship between the parties prevented adverse possession.

141. According to the Decretals [51] adverse possession had to be "peaceful," which the *Glossa* [52] interpreted to mean "without any

[42] D.a.c. 16, C. XVI, q. 3, § 3.

[43] Schmalzgrueber, Part. III, tit. 26, n. 71; Pirhing, lib. II, tit. 26, n. 13.

[44] In c. 1, C. XVI, q. 3, ad v. *Maxime*; in c. 2, X, *de praescriptionibus,* II, 26, ad v. *Futuris.*

[45] I (2.6) 8.

[46] In d.a.c. 16, C. XVI, q. 3, ad v. *Commodum*; cf. the similar statute, 5 Rich. II.

[47] I (2.6) (1.2).

[48] In c. 1, C. XVI, q. 3.

[49] Schmalzgrueber, Part. III, tit. 26, n. 71; Pirhing, lib. II, tit. 26, n. 13.

[50] *S.R.R. in causa Romana, locorum montium, coram Marco* (1827), tom. 2, dec. 358, n. 12.

[51] C. 3, X, *de praescriptionibus,* II, 26.

[52] In c. 3, X, *de praescriptionibus,* II, 26, ad v. *Quiete.*

interruption and without disturbance," in other words that there had to be quiet enjoyment. Disturbance even by a third party interrupted adverse possession if it caused the holder to lose possession. This was called *"interruptio naturalis,"* running for all, not merely for the one interrupting.[53]

The decisions held simply that adverse possession had to be peaceful,[54] so that, in the case of advowson, presentations made by the true patron would be opposed to an adverse claim of a right to present,[55] and if there was bad faith and a suit was pending the possession was held not to be peaceful.[56]

142. The interruption could occur in various ways, other than the one mentioned above, called *"interruptio naturalis,"* which could arise from the intervention of a third party or from natural causes. A change in one's claim acted,[57] according to the *Corpus Iuris Canonici*,[58] as a renunciation of one's previous holding.

Article 5. Continuous

143. The adverse possession, at Canon Law, had to be continued.[59] This was established by proof of the beginning, middle and end of the possession, for more than that it was impossible to prove; and if it was proved that one had held the thing previously, one was

[53] Cf. D (41.3) 5.

[54] *S.R.R. in causa Romana, Statutorum, coram Taia* (1665)—*Decisiones Recentiores,* Part. 14, dec. 307, n. 4; *S.R.R. in causa Comen., Decimarum, coram Caprara* (1705), Part. 2, dec. 741, n. 7; *S.R.R. in causa Herbipolen., Monasterii, coram Ansaldo* (1712), tom. 5, dec. 589, n. 22; *S.R.R. in causa Ravennaten. seu Ferrarien., Iurisdictionis, coram Crescentio* (1735), tom. 3, dec. 326, n. 29; *S.R.R. in causa Viterbien., Servitutis, coram De Veri* (1770), tom. 2, dec. 146, n. 13; *S.R.R. in causa Mediolanen., Iurium Parochialium, coram Caccia* (1688) —*Decisiones Nuperrimae,* tom. 2, dec. 150, n. 10.

[55] *S.R.R. in causa Lauden., Canonicatus, coram Emerix* (1696), tom. 3, dec. 1320, n. 14.

[56] *S.R.R. in causa Nolana, Parochialis, coram Rondinino* (1671)—*Decisiones Recentiores,* Part. 17, dec. 150, n. 12.

[57] Cf. *supra,* n. 124.

[58] C. 19, X, *de praescriptionibus,* II, 26.

[59] *S.R.R. in causa Romana, Divisionis, coram Bichio* (1640)—*Decisiones Recentiores,* Part. 8, dec. 238, n. 12; *S.R.R. in causa Perusina, Immissionis, coram Marini* (1832), tom. 1, dec. 76, n. 27.

not supposed to have changed one's mind and was presumed to possess at the present time. If it was proved that one had held previously and still did so at the present time, it was presumed that one also held for the intervening time, if one had to prove ten-year possession. If one had to prove more than ten-year possession it was sufficient to prove the beginning of each ten-year period.[60] This seems to afford a rule which courts of Canon Law may follow even today in similar cases.

144. Under the American Law, to quote again the Supreme Court of Pennsylvania,[61] it is held that "the owner of land can only be barred by such possession as has been . . . continued. . . ."[62] It must be continuous for the whole period. If one trespasser enters and leaves, and then another trespasser, a stranger to the former and without purchase from or respect to him, enters, the possession is not continuous.[63] A slight connection, however, of the latter with the former trespasser, as by a purchase by parol contract, will be sufficient to give the possession continuity,[64] and so will a purchase at a sale or execution.[65]

145. To give continuity to the possession by successive occupants there must be privity of estate,[66] and such a privity that each possession may be referred to one and the same entry, as that of a tenant to his landlord, or of the heir of a disseisor to his ancestor.[67] It is not essential that one and the same person shall have been all the time the adverse holder, if the latter succeeds to the asserted

[60] Schmalzgrueber, Part. III, tit. 26, n. 47; *S.R.R. in causa Beneventana, Iurisdictionis, coram Taia* (1663)—*Decisiones Recentiores,* Part. 14, dec. 21, n. 18.

[61] Cf. *supra, h. c.,* note 15.

[62] Cf. *supra, h. c.,* note 16.

[63] Schrack v. Zubler, 34 Pa. 38; Christy v. Alford, 17 How. (U.S.) 601, 15 L. Ed. 256; Stout v. Taul, 71 Tex. 438, 9 S.W. 329.

[64] Cunningham v. Patton, 6 Pa. 355; 1 Term. 448.

[65] Scheetz v. Fitzwater, 5 Pa. 126; Cleveland Ins. Co. v. Reed, 24 How. (U.S.) 284, 16 L. Ed. 686.

[66] Melvin v. Proprietors of Locks and Canals, 5 Metc. (Mass.) 15, 38 Am. Dec. 384; Angell, *Limitations,* § 414.

[67] King v. Smith, 1 Rice (S.C.) 10.

rights of the preceding holders or occupants as grantee or transferee.[68] An administrator's possession may be connected with that of his intestate,[69] and that of a tenant holding under the ancestor, with that of the heir.[70]

Article 6. Open and Notorious

a. In General

146. That the possession at Canon Law had to be open and notorious is indicated in the *Glossa*,[71] which stated that if the chapter knew of the alienation the alienee was immediately safe. This was likewise the later law.[72] In the case of servitudes, too, the pre-

[68] Black v. Coke Co., 85 Ala. 504, 5 South. 89; cf. *supra*, nn. 93 sqq.

[69] Moffitt v. McDonald, 11 Humphr. (Tenn.) 457.

[70] Williams v. McAliley, Cheves (S.C.) 200.

[71] In c. 10, C. XVI, q. 3, ad v. *Si Sacerdotes.*

[72] *S.R.R. in causa Romana, Supplementi legitimae, coram Sacrato* (1613)—*Decisiones Recentiores*, Part. 3, dec. 538, n. 4, through many decisions to *S.R.R. in causa Forosempronien., Salviani, coram Albergato* (1678)—*Decisiones Recentiores*, Part. 19, tom. 1, dec. 231, n. 7; *S.R.R. in causa Ravennaten., Decimarum, coram Emerix* (1672), tom. 1, dec. 87, n. 10; *S.R.R. in causa Ravennaten., Decimarum, coram Emerix* (1672), tom. 1, dec. 117, n. 8; *S.R.R. in causa Romana seu Portuen., Tenutarum, coram Emerix* (1694), tom. 3, dec. 1189, n. 6; *S.R.R. in causa Lauden., Canonicatus, coram Emerix* (1696), tom. 3, dec. 1320, n. 13; *S.R.R. in causa Cracovien., Cantoriae, coram Caprara* (1701), Part. 2, dec. 536, n. 10; *S.R.R. in causa Aquinaten., Fideicommissi, coram Ansaldo* (1699), tom. 1, dec. 92, n. 52; *S.R.R. in causa Toletana, Decimarum, coram Falconerio* (1724), tom. 1, *de Decim.*, dec. 9, n. 16; *S.R.R. in causa Baren., Legitimae, coram Crescentio* (1727), tom. 1, dec. 1, n. 28; *S.R.R. in causa Aesina, Pecuniaria super reservatis, coram Riminaldo* (1763), tom. 1, dec. 122, n. 27; *S.R.R. in causa Urbevetana, Redintegrationis, coram Riminaldo* (1770), tom. 4, dec. 337, n. 5; *S.R.R. in causa Fanen., Dotis, coram Ursino* (1685)—*Decisiones Nuperrimae*, tom. 1, dec. 207, n. 14; *S.R.R. in causa Albanen, Domus, coram Rondinino* (1688)—*Decisiones Nuperrimae*, tom. 2, dec. 183, n. 3; *S.R.R. in causa Forosempronien., Immissionis, coram Manuel* (1693)—*Decisiones Nuperrimae*, tom. 4, dec. 103, n. 3; *S.R.R. in causa Illerden., Iuris mulctandi, coram Muto* (1702)—*Decisiones Nuperrimae*, tom. 7, dec. 229, n. 13; *S.R.R. in causa Carpentoraten., Immissionis, coram Priolo* (1705)—*Decisiones Nuperrimae*, tom. 9, dec. 90, n. 17; *S.R.R. in causa Reatina, Immissionis, coram Muto* (1702)—*Decisiones Nuperrimae*, tom. 9, dec. 171, n. 12; *S.R.R. in causa Civi-*

scription had to be open and notorious.[73] The quasi-possession of a right had to be certain, unequivocal and public.[74]

147. The American Law requires that the adverse possession be open, so open that the true owner ought to know it and must be presumed to know it.[75] The Supreme Court of Pennsylvania, so often quoted on this matter, said: [76] "The owner of land can only be barred by such possession as has been . . . visible, notorious. . . ." [77]

b. Owner's Knowledge

148. Adverse possession, at Canon Law, did not run against an owner who did not know of it,[78] though he would presumably know of it if both parties were present in the same place,[79] or if he had made a demand, the holder had refused, and the owner had acquiesced in this refusal.[80] It did, in fact, run against anyone who ac-

tatis Castelli, Canonicatus Poenitentiarii, coram Mattheio (1685)—*Decisiones Nuperrimae,* tom. 1, dec. 180, n. 7; *Decisiones Sacrae Rotae Romanae coram R.P.D. Karolo ex Ducibus Odescalchi* (3 vols., Romae, 1827), hereinafter cited by place, type of case, name of judge and date, as follows: *S.R.R. in causa Romana, Liberationis a molestiis, coram Odescalchi* (1817), tom. 1, dec. 41, n. 9; *Decisiones S. Rotae Romanae coram R.P.D. Cosma De Cursiis* (5 vols., Romae, 1855), hereinafter cited by place, type of case, name of judge and date, as follows: *S.R.R. in causa Romana, Crediti, coram De Cursiis* (1841), tom. 5, dec. 679, n. 1; *S.R.R. in causa Romana, Nullitatis contractus, coram Marini* (1845), tom. 3, dec. 622, n. 11; *S.R.R. in causa Romana, Nullitatis contractus, coram Marini* (1844), tom. 3, dec. 594, n. 11.

[73] *S.R.R. in causa Romana, haustus aquae, coram Isoard* (1827), tom. 3, *de Servitut.,* dec. 419, n. 10.

[74] *S.R.R. in causa Ripana, Iurium,* 2 apr. 1910, *coram R.P.D. Michaele Lega,* Dec. XIV, n. 16—*S.R.R. Decisiones,* II (1910), 129; *AAS,* II (1910), 418-431.

[75] Jackson v. Huntington, 5 Pet. (U.S.) 402, 8 L. Ed. 170; Tourtelotte v. Pearce, 27 Neb. 57, 42 N.W. 915.

[76] Cf. *supra, h. c.,* note 15.

[77] Cf. *supra, h. c.,* note 16.

[78] Rubeus, *Annotationes,* in *Decisiones Recentiores,* Part. 3, dec. 3, n. 47.

[79] Rubeus, *Annotationes,* in *Decisiones Recentiores,* Part. 3, dec. 20, n. 20.

[80] *S.R.R. in causa Romana seu Ferentina, Iuris Privativi Molendinorum, coram Marini* (1831), tom. 1, dec. 71, n. 8; *S.R.R. in causa Ferentina, Molendini, coram Marini* (1834), tom. 1, dec. 181, n. 6.

quiesced in the matter.[81] It was called an accepted doctrine in the courts that adverse possession never ran against those who had no knowledge of it.[82] There had been a great dispute among the authors whether adverse possession ran against those having no knowledge of it,[83] and some even contradicted themselves,[84] but it was held that if it did run it did so only as to the common and ordinary law, not as to the extraordinary remedy of restoration of the *status quo (restitutio in integrum)*.[85]

The ignorance of which there is question here is ignorance of the facts. This statement is not weakened by the fact that the Rota considered the Statute of the City of Rome as an excuse, for it held this in regard to strangers for whom of course the question, What is the law of Rome?, was one of fact, not one of law, since it concerned the law of a jurisdiction not their own. When the American Law requires that the adverse possession shall be open and notorious, or visible and notorious, it prevents adverse possession by one whose actions were such that the true owner could not know the true state of the facts, i. e., such that the true owner labored under ignorance of fact. Both the Canon Law and the American Law assume that a reasonably prudent man will not be ignorant of the law as it

[81] *S.R.R. in causa Forosempronien., Immissionis, coram Manuel* (1693)—*Decisiones Nuperrimae,* tom. 4, dec. 103, n. 3; *S.R.R. in causa Bononien., Remotionis arborum, coram De Cursiis* (1828), tom. 3, dec. 331, n. 10.

[82] *S.R.R. in causa Romana, Census, coram Lancetta* (1703), tom. 1, dec. 262, n. 15; *S.R.R. in causa Imolen., Salviani, coram Lancetta* (1703), tom. 1, dec. 263, n. 3; *S.R.R. in causa Neapolitana seu Tricaricen., Iuris Redimendi, coram Lancetta* (1703), tom. 1, dec. 271, n. 8; *S.R.R. in causa Romana, Expurgationis Aquaeductus, coram Olivatio* (1759), tom. 1, dec. 125, n. 5 (as to the ten- and twenty-year periods); *S.R.R. in causa Sancti Severini, Servitutis, coram Malvasia* (1791), dec. 212, n. 9.

[83] Rubeus, *Annotationes,* in *Decisiones Recentiores,* Part. 3, dec. 3, nn. 2-3.

[84] Rubeus, *Annotationes,* in *Decisiones Recentiores,* Part. 3, dec. 3, n. 4.

[85] Rubeus, *Annotationes,* in *Decisiones Recentiores,* Part 3, dec. 3, n. 27; *S.R.R. in causa Ravennaten., Salviani, coram Sacrato* (1614)—*Decisiones Recentiores,* Part. 3, dec. 573, n. 1; *S.R.R. in causa Romana, Census, coram Albergato* (1672)—*Decisiones Recentiores,* Part. 17, dec. 330, n. 21; *S.R.R. in causa Romana, executionis laudi, coram Rondinino* (1675)—*Decisiones Recentiores,* Part. 18, tom. 2, dec. 443, n. 3 sqq.

affects him and his rights, hence both rule out ignorance of law in this matter.

149. It was on occasion held that the creditor's knowledge had to be fully proved,[86] and strangers were granted restoration of the *status quo* against statutory adverse possession, especially in the case of probable ignorance of the Statute of the City of Rome.[87] An heir, under the same circumstances, was granted restoration of the *status quo* because of probable ignorance of the Statute.[88] Furthermore, the Statute of the City of Rome, like ordinary adverse possession, did not run against successors in title who had no knowledge,[89] or against a woman as the heir of a creditor,[90] for her husband's knowledge did not always affect her right to reclaim what she had brought as a dowry.[91] In the case of a mortgage, the action of

[86] *S.R.R. in causa Romana, Salviani, coram De la Tremoille* (1701)—*Decisiones Nuperrimae,* tom. 7, dec. 188, n. 13.

[87] *S.R.R. in causa Fulginaten., Pecuniaria, coram Caccia* (1689)—*Decisiones Nuperrimae,* tom. 2, dec. 287, n. 4; *S.R.R. in causa Fulginaten., Pecuniaria, coram Manuel* (1691)—*Decisiones Nuperrimae,* tom. 3, dec. 150, n. 8; *S.R.R. in causa Romana seu Crotonen., super fructibus, coram Scotto* (1703)—*Decisiones Nuperrimae,* tom. 8, dec. 171, n. 7.

[88] *S.R.R. in causa Narnien., Legati, coram Calataio* (1676)—*Decisiones Recentiores,* Part. 16, dec. 417, n. 11; *S.R.R. in causa Romana, Immissionis, coram Caprara* (1697), Part. 1, dec. 336, n. 12, *Sacrae Rotae Romanae Decisiones coram R.P.D. Francisco Carolo Kaunitz* (2 vols., Romae, 1734), hereinafter cited by place, type of case, name of judge and date, as follows: *S.R.R. in causa Montis Pelusii, Pignoris conventionalis, coram Kaunitz* (1704), Part. 1, dec. 66, n. 11; *S.R.R. in causa Fulginaten., Pecuniaria, coram Caccia* (1689)—*Decisiones Nuperrimae,* tom. 2, dec. 287, n. 5, through many decisions to *S.R.R. in causa Reatina, Immissionis, coram Muto* (1705)—*Decisiones Nuperrimae,* tom. 9, dec. 171, n. 22.

[89] *S.R.R. in causa Albanen., Dotis et fructuum, coram Olivatio* (1766), tom. 5, dec. 552, n. 10; *S.R.R. in causa Perusina, Dotis, coram De la Tremoille* (1702) —*Decisiones Nuperrimae,* tom. 7, dec. 247, n. 24 (restoration of the *status quo* was allowed to them—*ibid.,* n. 25).

[90] *S.R.R. in causa Romana, Dotis, coram Rondinino* (1687)—*Decisiones Nuperrimae,* tom. 2, dec. 34, n. 2; *S.R.R. in causa Perusina, Dotis, coram De la Tremoille* (1702)—*Decisiones Nuperrimae,* tom. 7, dec. 247, n. 6.

[91] *S.R.R. in causa Spoletana, Salviani, coram Hervault* (1693)—*Decisiones Nuperrimae,* tom. 4, dec. 138, n. 16.

a creditor who did not know of the alienation was not barred,[92] and ignorance was presumed in an heir regarding the Statute.[93]

150. Adverse possession likewise did not run against one who did not know his own rights,[94] e. g., if a woman did not know that her dowry, which had been substituted for her legitimate portion of her ancestor's estate, was subject to the limitation in the Statute of the City of Rome, or, if the Statute was held to run she was to be granted a rescission.[95] Likewise a creditor under the Statute of the City of Rome who did not know the rights of his credit was excused,[96] as was an heir who was under age.[97] This was due to the fact that the Statute changed and shortened the period which had been required for adverse possession under the Civil Law. Thus, it was not always possible to hold that the shorter period was understood and observed by the plaintiff in question. If the plaintiff was acquainted with the shorter statutory period he was bound by the

[92] *S.R.R. in causa Romana, Salviani, coram Ansaldo* (1698), tom. 1, dec. 50, n. 24; *S.R.R. in causa Perusina, Immissionis, coram Lancetta* (1717), tom. 4, dec. 1017, n. 6; *Decisiones Sacrae Rotae Romanae coram R.P.D. Alexandro Tanario* (2 vols., Romae, 1748), hereinafter cited by place, type of case, name of judge and date, as follows: *S.R.R. in causa Viterbien., Salviani, coram Tanario* (1738), tom. 1, dec. 96, n. 8; *S.R.R. in causa Eugubina, Salviani, coram Mattheio* (1685)—*Decisiones Nuperrimae,* tom. 1, dec. 173, n. 18; *S.R.R. in causa Romana, Dotis, coram Rondinino* (1687)—*Decisiones Nuperrimae,* tom. 2, dec. 34, n. 2; *S.R.R. in causa Romana, Salviani, coram Caccia* (1688)—*Decisiones Nuperrimae,* tom. 2, dec. 94, n. 10; *S.R.R. in causa Spoletana, Salviani, coram Hervault* (1693)—*Decisiones Nuperrimae,* tom. 4, dec. 138, n. 15.

[93] *S.R.R. in causa Romana seu Terracinen., Immissionis, coram Falconerio* (1723), tom. 1, *de Fidei com.,* dec. 73, n. 8.

[94] *S.R.R. in causa Romana seu Florentina, Commendae, coram Emerix* (1680), tom. 1, dec. 457, n. 4; *S.R.R. in causa Terracinen. seu Corana, Donationis, coram Falconerio* (1722), tom. 1, *de Donat.,* dec. 5, n. 18.

[95] *S.R.R. in causa Aesina, Pecuniaria, super reservatis, coram Riminaldo* (1763), tom. 1, dec. 89, n. 13.

[96] *S.R.R. in causa Romana, Pecuniaria, coram Priolo* (1694)—*Decisiones Nuperrimae,* tom. 4, dec. 239, n. 12.

[97] *S.R.R. in causa Romana seu Montis Falisci, Bonorum, coram Ansaldo* (1700), tom. 2, dec. 148, n. 20; *S.R.R. in causa Hostunen., Beneficii, coram Ansaldo* (1710), tom. 5, dec. 481, n. 3; *S.R.R. in causa Romana, Census, coram Lancetta* (1710), tom. 3, dec. 643, n. 7; *S.R.R. in causa Romana, Domorum, coram Scotto* (1695)—*Decisiones Nuperrimae,* tom. 4, dec. 361, n. 17.

limitation. Since the periods established in the various states by the American Law are the customary periods at the present time, it seems that the liberality shown in the past by the Rota in its decisions concerning the shorter statutory period no longer needs to be observed, but one may consider these present customary periods of the American Law just as the Rota was wont to consider the established periods of the Civil Law, i. e., without such liberality.

c. *Discovery by the Possessor*

151. It was held in the Canon Law that the one acquiring by adverse possession did not need to prove that the other party had knowledge, provided that he, the holder, had title [98] either express, or tacit, resulting from a one-hundred-year possession.[99] Other cases, however, held that the holder had to prove the owner's knowledge of the adverse possession.[100] Such knowledge had to be certain and undoubted, it was held, not just likely and presumed,[101] especially in prejudicial matters,[102] but presumed knowledge was held sufficient in the case of a debtor who had a credit to set off against his creditor.[103]

[98] Obviously color of title, cf. *supra,* n. 97 sq.

[99] *S.R.R. in causa Marsicen., seu Nullius, Iurisdictionis, coram Muto* (1700) —*Decisiones Nuperrimae,* tom. 6, dec. 340, n. 70.

[100] *S.R.R. in causa Gerunden., Administrationis, coram Verospio* (1629)—*Decisiones Novissimae,* tom. 1, dec. 252, n. 11—*Decisiones Recentiores,* Part. 5, tom. 1; *S.R.R. in causa Civitatis Castelli, Salviani, coram Roias* (1641)—*Decisiones Recentiores,* Part. 9, tom. 1, dec. 4, n. 9; *S.R.R. in causa Avenionen., Bonorum, coram Mattheio* (1674)—*Decisiones Recentiores,* Part. 18, tom. 1, dec. 231, n. 20; *S.R.R. in causa Viterbien., seu Civitatis Vetulae, Associationis, coram Rezzonico* (1731), tom. 1, dec. 17, n. 13; *S.R.R. in causa Eugubina, Salviani, coram Mattheio* (1685)—*Decisiones Nuperrimae,* tom. 1, dec. 173, n. 19.

[101] *S.R.R. in causa Perusina, Immissionis, coram Lancetta* (1717), tom. 4, dec. 1017, n. 7; *S.R.R. in causa Perusina, Cambii, coram Ratto* (1730), tom. 3, dec. 275, n. 20; *S.R.R. in causa Viterbien., seu Civitatis Vetulae, Associationis, coram Rezzonico* (1731), tom. 1, dec. 17, n. 14.

[102] *S.R.R. in causa Reatina, Immissionis, coram Muto* (1705)—*Decisiones Nuperrimae,* tom. 9, dec. 171, n. 18.

[103] *S.R.R. in causa Romana, Pecuniaria, coram Lancetta* (1712), tom. 3, dec. 716, n. 19.

By way of conclusion it seems correct to say that the one holding property may find himself in the condition of being: a—convinced that he is the rightful owner thereof, in which case he will not think of any necessity of notifying another that he holds against him, for his holding will be done openly against all the world; b—in doubt as to his right to the property, in which case good faith requires that he clear up this cloud on his title, not only for the sake of his own conscience, with which good faith is concerned, but also for the sake of his successors in title, whose claim may be defeated if some one else is able to prove a better right to the property; c—convinced that he is not the rightful owner thereof, in which case he must restore the property [104] or notify the rightful owner, if known, or the public in general, that the rightful owner may come forward, and meanwhile hold the property as bailee, for failure to do otherwise would be unconscionable, and if positive efforts to conceal the true state of affairs were involved, fraud could be charged.[105]

Article 7. Proof of Possession

152. According to the Canon Law there has to be placed some act which shows possession.[106] The extent of the possession determined the extent of what was eventually acquired.[107]

[104] Cf. canon 1512.

[105] Cf. *supra*, n. 81 sqq.

[106] *S.R.R. in causa Romana, Salviani, coram Merlino* (1630)—*Decisiones Novissimae*, tom. 1, dec. 407, n. 13—*Decisiones Recentiores*, Part. 5, tom. 1; *S.R.R. in causa Ariminen., Census, coram Albergato* (1659)—*Decisiones Recentiores*, Part. 13, dec. 47, n. 3; *S.R.R. in causa Ianuens., Abbatiae, coram Manuel* (1689)—*Decisiones Nuperrimae*, tom. 2, dec. 341, n. 7.

[107] Schmalzgrueber, Part. III, tit. 26, n. 43; *S.R.R. in causa Legionen., Decimarum, coram Pirovano* (1613)—*Decisiones Recentiores*, Part. 3, dec. 484, n. 3; *S.R.R. in causa Conchen., Decimarum, coram Manzanedo* (1617)—*Decisiones Recentiores*, Part. 4, tom. 1, dec. 502, n. 6; *S.R.R. in causa Cracovien., Iuris Legendi, coram Ubaldo* (1629)—*Decisiones Novissimae*, tom. 1, dec. 265, n. 34—*Decisiones Recentiores*, Part. 5, tom. 1; *S.R.R. in causa Nullius seu Fulden., Iurisdictionis, coram Ansaldo* (1708), tom. 4, dec. 439, n. 138; *S.R.R. in causa Senogallien., seu Fanen., Bonorum, coram Crescentio* (1738), tom. 4, dec. 449, nn. 3, 8; *S.R.R. in causa Caliguritana, Decimarum, coram Paulutio* (1685)—*Decisiones Nuperrimae*, tom. 1, dec. 151, n. 7; *S.R.R. in causa Barchinonen., Cantus, coram Caccia* (1689)—*Decisiones Nuperrimae*, tom. 2,

153. As to proof of possession, aside from the provision made in the present Code of Canon Law,[108] one may consider from the pre-Code law various decisions. It was, for instance, said that a private and arbitrary declaration in a record book was not sufficient to give proof of ownership,[109] though a record was deserving of more faith than a private expert or a weak witness.[110] If the record book was old it afforded no proof for what could have happened later,[111] especially if, when the record was made, a suit was in progress as to the limits of the property,[112] and in such a case the limits of the land were recognized to be what a transaction subsequent to the record showed.[113] The record showed only the manner of possession at the time when it was made, which could have been modified and increased; [114] but if the record was very carefully kept, and the survey was made by experts, and public authority confirmed the record, it was held deserving of the greatest faith.[115] Mere words did not destroy one's possession.[116]

Further evidence of possession were prohibitions imposed and penalties inflicted for their transgression,[117] and such evidence was also

dec. 223, n. 11; *S.R.R. in causa Derthusen., Iurisdictionis, coràm Pio* (1697), tom. 5, dec. 217, n. 24; *S.R.R. in causa Bonenien., Remotionis arborum, coram De Cursiis* (1828), tom. 3, dec. 331, n. 9.

[108] Lib. IV, tit. 10, canons 1747-1836.

[109] *S.R.R. in causa Tyburtina, Spolii, coram Consalvi* (1796), dec. 46, n. 13; *S.R.R. in causa Tyburtina, Spolii, coram Consalvi* (1798), dec. 72, n. 18.

[110] *S.R.R. in causa Urbevetana, Retractus, coram Consalvi* (1794), dec. 20, n. 17.

[111] *S.R.R. in causa Bonònien., seu Ferrarien., Reintegrationis, coram Consalvi* (1793), dec. 3, n. 13.

[112] *S.R.R. in causa Bononien., seu Ferrarien., Reintegrationis, coram Consalvi* (1794), dec. 13, nn. 9, 11.

[113] *S.R.R. in causa Bononien., seu Ferrarien., Reintegrationis, coram Consalvi* (1794), dec. 13, n. 12.

[114] *S.R.R. in causa Firmana, Manutentionis, coram Consalvi* (1794), dec. 12, n. 2.

[115] *S.R.R. in causa Firmana, Immissionis, coram Consalvi* (1797), dec. 63, n. 3; *S.R.R. in causa Firmana, Immissionis, coram Consalvi* (1797), dec. 64, n. 1.

[116] *S.R.R. in causa Tyburtina, Spolii, coram Consalvi* (1797), dec. 70, n. 15.

[117] *S.R.R. in causa Romana, Liberationis a molestiis, coram Odescalchi* (1817), tom. 1, dec. 41, n. 4.

derivable from the effected collection of fruits or income.[118] It was also held that two acts were sufficient for one to acquire by adverse possession or prescription if the thing in question was such as rarely occurred,[119] but in general one or another event was held insufficient evidence.[120] For a chapter to acquire, by adverse possession or prescription, the right to inflict punishment in the bishop's stead it had to show frequent and multiple acts,[121] and in the case of advowson it was necessary to show continued presentations.[122]

154. Under the American Law many acts of occupation are considered unequivocal evidence of possession with adverse intent, such as fencing the land or erecting a house on it,[123] actual improvement and cultivation of the soil,[124] building on land and putting a fence around it,[125] digging stones and cutting timber from time to time,[126] driving piles into the soil covered by a mill-pond and thereon erecting a building,[127] cutting roads into a swamp, and cutting trees and making shingles therefrom,[128] and setting fish-traps in a non-navigable stream, building dams across it, and using it every year during the entire fishing season for the purpose of catching fish.[129] Filling up flats and building a wharf there, and using the same, if the use is

[118] *S.R.R. in causa Bononien., seu Ferrarien., Reintegrationis, coram Consalvi* (1794), dec. 13, n. 3; *S.R.R. in causa Romana, Liberationis a molestiis, coram Odescalchi* (1817), tom. 1, dec. 41, n. 3.

[119] *S.R.R. in causa Majoricen., Quartae Funeralis, coram Olivatio* (1758), tom. 1, dec. 86, n. 12.

[120] *S.R.R. in causa Romana, Electionis, coram Riminaldo* (1768), tom. 3, dec. 275, n. 16.

[121] *S.R.R. in causa Illerden., Iuris mulctandi, coram Muto* (1702)—*Decisiones Nuperrimae*, tom. 7, dec. 229, n. 11.

[122] *S.R.R. in causa Novarien., Praepositurae, coram Emerix* (1690), tom. 2, dec. 1000, n. 1.

[123] Jackson v. Huntington, 5 Pet. (U.S.) 402, 8 L. Ed. 170; Tourtelotte v. Pearce, 27 Neb. 57, 42 N.W. 915.

[124] Brandt v. Ogden, 1 Johns. (N.Y.) 156.

[125] Poignard v. Smith, 6 Pick. (Mass.) 172.

[126] 14 East. 332; Boaz v. Heister, 6 S. & R. (Pa.) 21.

[127] Boston Mill Corp. v. Bulfinch, 6 Mass. 229, 4 Am. Dec. 120.

[128] Tredwell v. Reddick, 23 N.C. 56.

[129] Williams v. Buchanan, 23 N.C. 535, 35 Am. Dec. 760.

exclusive, is evidence of adverse possession.[130] The nature of the acts necessary to constitute adverse possession varies. If the ground is uncultivated and the region sparsely populated, much less unequivocal acts are necessary on the part of the adverse holder.

155. On the other hand, under the American Law, other acts do not show intent to possess adversely. Entering upon uninclosed flats, when covered by the tide, and sailing over them with a boat or vessel for the ordinary purposes of navigation, is not an adverse possession.[131] Likewise entering upon a lot and marking its boundaries by splitting the trees does not establish adverse possession,[132] nor does the getting of rails and other timber for a few weeks each year from timberland,[133] nor the overflowing of land by the stoppage of a stream,[134] nor the survey, allotment, and conveyance of a piece of land, and the recording of the deed; unless there is open occupation.[135]

156. Evidence of adverse possession, under the American Law, must be strictly construed, for every presumption is in favor of the true owner.[136] The claim by adverse possession must have some definite boundaries,[137] since there must be something to indicate to what extent the adverse possessor claims. A sufficient inclosure will establish the limits, without actual continued residence on the land,[138] but it must be an actual, visible, and substantial inclosure.[139] An inclosure on three sides, by a trespasser as against the real owner, is not enough,[140] nor is an unsubstantial brush fence,[141] nor one

130 Wheeler v. Stone, 1 Cush. (Mass.) 313; McFarlane v. Kerr, 10 Bosw. (N.Y.) 249.

131 Drake v. Curtis, 1 Cush. (Mass.) 395.

132 Woods v. Banks, 14 N.H. 101.

133 Bartlett v. Simmons, 49 N.C. 295.

134 Green v. Harman, 15 N.C. 158.

135 Thayer v. McLellan, 23 Me. 417.

136 Fairfield v. Barrette, 73 Wis. 463, 41 N.W. 624.

137 Munshower v. Patton, 10 S. & R. (Pa.) 334, 13 Am. Dec. 678; Hapgood v. Burt, 4 Vt. 155.

138 Johnston v. Irvin, 3 S. & R. (Pa.) 291; Brown v. Porter, 10 Mass. 93.

139 Smith v. Hosmer, 7 N.H. 436, 28 Am. Dec. 354.

140 Dennett v. Crocker, 8 Greenl. (Me.) 239; Armstrong v. Risteau's Lessee, 5 Md. 256, 59 Am. Dec. 115.

141 Hale v. Glidden, 10 N.H. 397.

formed by the lapping of fallen trees.[142] Natural barriers may be a sufficient inclosure.[143] The enclosure must be fixed, not roving from part to part.[144] Possession and occupancy of land not enclosed by a fence may, however, be adverse.[145] If one has by mistake enclosed land of another, and claimed it as his own to certain fixed monuments or boundaries, his actual and uninterrupted possession as owner for the statutory period will work a disseisin, and his title will be perfect.[146] The Canon Law, too, considers adverse possession odious and therefore to be treated as a thing of strict law.[147] It is to be restricted as much as possible by strict interpretation within the bounds of what is expressed,[148] so the American decisions cited above afford a good guide for courts of Canon Law in this country.

157. It is said, under the American Law, that when the claim rests upon color of title as well as possession, the possession will be regarded as coextensive with the powers described in the title-deed.[149] This doctrine of constructive possession, however, applies only to land taken possession of for the ordinary purpose of cultivation and use, and not to a case in which a few acres are taken possession of in an uncultivated township for the mere purpose of thereby gaining title to the entire township.[150]

[142] Coburn v. Hollis, 3 Metc. (Mass.) 125; Jackson v. Schoonmaker, 2 Johns. (N.Y.) 230.

[143] Goodwin v. McCabe, 75 Cal. 584, 17 Pac. 705.

[144] Ewing v. Burnett, 11 Pet. (U.S.) 53, 9 L. Ed. 624.

[145] Beecher v. Galvin, 71 Mich. 391, 39 N.W. 469.

[146] Levy v. Yerga, 25 Neb. 764, 41 N.W. 773; 13 Am. St. Rep. 525; White v. Spreckels, 75 Cal. 610, 17 Pac. 715; Erch v. Church, 87 Tenn. 575, 11 S.W. 794, 4 L.R.A. 641.

[147] *S.R.R. in causa Toletana, Decimarum, coram Millino* (1729)—*Decisiones Gutierrez*, dec. 98, n. 9.

[148] Rubeus, *Annotationes*, in *Decisiones Recentiores*, Part. 9, tom. 1, dec. 20, nn. 12, 19; *S.R.R. in causa Civitatis Castelli, Salviani, coram Roias* (1641) —*Decisiones Recentiores*, Part. 9, tom. 1, dec. 4, nn. 10-11.

[149] Ewing v. Burnet, 11 Pet. (U.S.) 41, 9 L. Ed. 624; Bynum v. Thompson, 25 N.C. 578; Webb v. Sturtevant, 1 Scam. (Ill.) 181; Jackson v. Smith, 13 Johns. (N.Y.) 406; Proprietors of Kennebeck Purchase v. Springer, 4 Mass. 416; 3 Am. Dec. 227; Kile v. Tubbs, 23 Cal. 431.

[150] Chandler v. Spear, 22 Vt. 388; Jackson v. Woodruff, 1 Cow. (N.Y.) 286, 13 Am. Dec. 525.

It may be said, in conclusion, that with a little liberalization of the rule in the case of wild, remote, and uncultivated lands, the sort of possession necessary to acquire title is adverse, open, public, and notorious, and not clandestine and secret. It is possession, exclusive, uninterrupted, definite as to boundaries, and fixed as to its locality. This is an expression of the doctrine under the American Law.[151] As has been seen, it can serve as well to express the doctrine of the Canon Law as it was before the Code. Hence the Code in adopting the American Law in this point is not changing materially its traditional background except in so far as there is question of modern applications of the law, applications which were not brought to the attention of courts of Canon Law in the past.

[151] 2 Bouvier 2017.

CHAPTER VI

THE CANON LAW OF LIMITATION OF ACTIONS

158. As has been noted above,[1] *"praescriptio"* may mean a mode of acquiring property and rights, as also of freeing oneself from an obligation,[2] which is known to the American Law as Adverse Possession or Prescription. It may also mean a defense to a suit on the ground that the said suit is now brought at a time when the law says it may no longer be brought,[3] which is known to the American Law as Limitation of Actions. It is true that when suit is brought against him the defendant may plead his possession of the property in question for a long period of time, but this means usually that he asserts title in himself contrary to the plaintiff's assertion of title in himself, so that the issue before the court is one of fact: Who is entitled to the property in question? When, however, limitation of the action is pleaded, the defendant is not really putting the question of title in issue, but is raising a question of law: Whether the plaintiff is entitled to maintain his action in the present case.

159. Adverse Possession and Prescription will not always appear as defenses to an action, for it is conceivable that without any action being brought against him the holder may become aware of a flaw in his title and apply to a proper court to have it removed on the showing of a possession sufficiently long to cut off all actions by whosoever may be concerned. Limitation of Actions, however, will appear as a defense, and must, indeed, be pleaded; else it will be considered to be waived.[4]

160. Adverse Possession and Prescription imply that a title or right has been acquired by the defendant raising this plea traversing

[1] N. 4.

[2] Canon 1508.

[3] Canons 1701 sqq.

[4] Burnet v. Desmornes y Alvarez, 226 U.S. 145, 33 Sup. Ct. 63, 57 L. Ed. 159; Vyse v. Richards, 208 Mich. 383, 175 N.W. 392; and very many other cases in all jurisdictions.

the declaration of the plaintiff, whereas Limitation of Actions does not directly assert a title in the defendant demurring, but merely objects that the action is now outlawed, i. e., barred by the Statute, so that it cannot be brought before this court.

161. Since Adverse Possession and Prescription imply that a title or right has been acquired, more is required for them as regards good faith. This good faith must be "positive," i. e., based upon some reason for believing one is entitled to hold the property or to exercise the right in question. Limitation of Actions, on the contrary, implies some fault on the part of the plaintiff. As a result, less is required of the defendant as regards good faith. His good faith needs only to be "negative," i. e., an absence of any unconscionable action producing plaintiff's condition, so that whatever harm plaintiff suffers is to be attributed solely to his own fault.

One may now proceed to consider this matter of Limitation of Actions more at length.

Article 1. General Rules

162. The Code of Canon Law establishes that contentious actions,[5] both real and personal, are extinguished by *"praescriptio"* according to the rules stated in canons 1508-1512, i. e., according to the civil laws of the respective nation, except for the particular provisions of Canon Law as explained above,[6] while actions as to the status of persons, e. g., religious, clergy, married persons, are never extinguished.[7]

163. A criminal action, at Canon Law,[8] is extinguished in three ways: 1—by death of the accused; 2—by condonation of the legitimate authority; 3—by lapse of the time limited for presenting the criminal action.[9] Aside from the particular provisions[10] regarding

[5] Actions in which the object of the judgment are the rights of persons, physical or moral (corporations), to be obtained or vindicated, or the juridical deeds of the same persons, to be declared.—Canon 1552, § 2, 1°.

[6] Chap. II, art. 2, and Chap. III.

[7] Canon 1701.

[8] An action in which the object of the judgment is a crime with regard to the inflicting of a penalty or the declaring of it as incurred.—Canon 1551, § 2, 2°.

[9] Canon 1702.

[10] Canon 1555, § 1.

crimes concerning which judgment is reserved to the Sacred Congregation of the Holy Office, which follows its own practice and customs, the time limited for presenting a criminal action is three years.[11] It is to be noted, however, that when one speaks of "crimes" one must be careful to remember that in Canon Law there is no verbal distinction between Crime and Tort such as exists in the American Law, though there is a corresponding actual distinction. Hence, though the object of the action may seem to be the same, i. e., as to the facts involved, still one must distinguish whether the action is brought by the public authority in prosecution of the crime, in which case the action is a criminal action and is limited as provided in the canons relating to limitation of criminal actions, or whether it is brought by a private individual seeking compensation for the wrong done to him, in which case the action is a contentious action, however much the facts may appear to be criminal, and is limited in accord with the provisions made by specific canons excepted from the general rule, or with the provisions of the American Law for these cases.

Article 2. Exceptions

164. Certain exceptions as to the limit on *criminal* actions are mentioned in canon 1703: 1—an action for libel [12] is limited to one year; [13] 2—an action on qualified delicts against the sixth [14] and seventh commandments [15] is limited to five years; [16] 3—an action against simony [17] or murder [18] is limited to ten years.[19]

165. Exceptions to the general rule as to *contentious* actions as specified by Canon Law are: 1—an action, namely, by one who is being disturbed in his possession, for an injunction against the

[11] Canon 1703.
[12] Canon 2355.
[13] Canon 1703, 1°.
[14] Canons 2357, 2359.
[15] Canon 2354.
[16] Canon 1703, 2°.
[17] Canons 727-730, 2392.
[18] Canon 2354.
[19] Canon 1703, 3°.

author of the disturbance in order to cause him to desist is limited to one year from the date of the disturbance; [20] 2—an action against a despoiler is limited to one year from the date the one despoiled had notice; [21] 3—an action to rescind a contract because of damage greater than half the value, caused through error on the part of the one suffering the damage, is limited to two years; [22] 4—an action for restoration of the *status quo* is limited to four years, to be counted from the day one attains his majority when there is question of a minor who was injured, or from the day the injury was done, and ceased, when there is question of one who was in his majority at the time, or of moral persons (corporations); [23] 5—an action because of the nullity of a sentence is limited to thirty years from the day of the publication of the sentence.[24]

Article 3. Computation of Time

166. At Canon Law [25] in contentious cases the time runs from the moment that the action could first be presented legally; in criminal cases from the day the delict was committed. When the Canon Law establishes that in contentious cases the time begins to run from the moment that the action could first be presented legally, it takes into consideration the questions of plaintiff and defendant in being, disabilities, fulfillment of conditions precedent, as well as that of accrual of the cause of action. It is the writer's opinion that once the time has begun to run it is continuous (*tempus continuum*) except in those cases in which the law allows a suspension of the running of the limitation.[26] This is supported not only by the rule adopted [27] from the American Law which is that once the limitation has begun to run the courts will not recognize exemptions,[28] but

[20] Canon 1695, § 2.
[21] Canon 1698, § 2.
[22] Canon 1684, § 2; cf. *infra*, n. 189.
[23] Canon 1688, § 1.
[24] Canon 1893.
[25] Canon 1705, § 1.
[26] Cf. *infra*, n. 185.
[27] Canon 1701.
[28] Cf. *infra*, n. 186.

by the fact that the time established is sufficiently long to enable an ordinarily prudent man to act to protect his rights, together with the fact that to consider the time as "useful" (*tempus utile*) would be to prolong the period of limitation unduly, make it practically impossible of computation, and thus destroy the benefits of this institute.

When the Canon Law establishes that the time runs in criminal cases from the day the delict was committed, it does this with the understanding that the authorities are to be vigilant in noting and punishing such delicts.[29]

Since, as was seen, canon 1701 provides that contentious actions, whether real or personal, are extinguished by limitation of actions according to canons 1508-1512, which canonize the civil law of the territory in this regard, it will be useful to consider what the American Law establishes with regard to the computation of time in the matter of limitation of actions, comparing it with the Canon Law of previous times.

167. At Canon Law the day of the beginning had to be certain.[30] Examples of the Canon Law rule for the time of the beginning of an action are: 1—when the right was acquired the time would run, not before; [31] 2—when the action had accrued the time would run; [32] 3—when there was no due date the time could not begin to run; [33] 4—when there was a due date the time would run from it; [34] 5—

[29] Cf. canons 336; 1939.

[30] *S.R.R. in causa Anconitana, Mannae, coram Corrado* (1644)—*Decisiones Recentiores,* Part. 9, tom. 1, dec. 284, n. 42.

[31] *S.R.R. in causa Bononien., Emphyteusis, coram Varesio* (1667)—*Decisiones Recentiores,* Part. 15, dec. 143, n. 14.

[32] *S.R.R. in causa Romana, Pecuniaria, coram Pio* (1692)—*Decisiones Nuperrimae,* tom. 3, dec. 165, n. 16; *S.R.R. in causa Urbevetana, Pecuniaria, coram Ursino* (1692)—*Decisiones Nuperrimae,* tom. 3, dec. 228, n. 16; *S.R.R. in causa Mechoacan., Crediti,* 1 iun. 1911, *coram R.P.D. Guglielmo Sebastianelli,* Dec. XX, n. 17—*S.R.R. Decisiones,* III (1911), 212; *AAS,* III (1911), 428-438.

[33] *S.R.R. in causa Anconitana, Mannae, coram Corrado* (1644)—*Decisiones Recentiores,* Part. 9, tom. 1, dec. 284, n. 39 sqq.

[34] *S.R.R. in causa Romana, Immissionis, coram Caprara* (1697), tom. 1, dec. 336, n. 10.

when the accounts were closed it ran from that day; [35] 6—when a right was confirmed, i. e., it ran from the day of the confirmation, not from the day of the concession; [36] 7—when one was despoiled it ran from the day of the spoliation; [37] 8—when the debtor ceased payment and the creditor, though he knew that the goods subject to the mortgage had been taken away, ceased to demand them, the limitation ran from that day; [38] 9—when a prohibition and demand was made, in the case of negative servitudes, it ran from that day; [39] 10—when a demand had been made, refused, and the one demanding acquiesced, it ran from the day of acquiescence; [40] 11—when a servant left the master's employ the limitation ran from that day as to his salary; [41] 12—when the husband became bankrupt, the limitation as to the wife's dowry ran from the day of his bankruptcy; [42] 13—when the harmful effects of wrongs or the wrongs themselves continued the limitation

[35] *S.R.R. in causa Romana, Pecuniaria, coram Pio* (1692)—*Decisiones Nuperrimae,* tom. 3, dec. 224, n. 5.

[36] *S.R.R. in causa Lucana, Bonorum, coram Lugdunen.* (1611)—*Decisiones Recentiores,* Part. 1, dec. 304, n. 3.

[37] *S.R.R. in causa Tiburtina, Spolii, coram Coccino* (1634)—*Decisiones Novissimae,* tom. 2, dec. 563, n. 2—*Decisiones Recentiores,* Part. 5, tom. 2.

[38] *S.R.R. in causa Romana, Salviani, coram Merlino* (1630)—*Decisiones Novissimae,* tom. 1, dec. 407, n. 18—*Decisiones Recentiores,* Part. 5, tom. 1; *S.R.R. in causa Romana, Salviani, coram Albergato* (1665)—*Decisiones Recentiores,* Part. 14, dec. 365, n. 6; *S.R.R. in causa Perusina, Immissionis, coram Lancetta* (1717), tom. 4, dec. 1017, n. 6; *S.R.R. in causa Romana, Salviani, coram Pio* (1695)—*Decisiones Nuperrimae,* tom. 4, dec. 455, n. 5 (in which it was said that it was not to be counted from the day on which a third party had taken possession).

[39] *S.R.R. in causa Farfen., Molendini, coram Hervault* (1687)—*Decisiones Nuperrimae,* tom. 2, dec. 21, n. 5.

[40] *S.R.R. in causa Romana, Concordiae, coram Cavalerio* (1610)—*Decisiones Recentiores,* Part. 1, dec. 221, n. 8; *S.R.R. in causa Carthaginen., Iuris deputandi custodem, coram Verospio* (1616)—*Decisiones Recentiores,* Part. 4, tom. 1, dec. 213, n. 4; *S.R.R. in causa Ravennaten., Decimarum, coram Emerix* (1672)—*Decisiones Recentiores,* Part. 17, dec. 232, n. 12.

[41] *S.R.R. in causa Pisauren., Haereditatis, coram Muto* (1698)—*Decisiones Nuperrimae,* tom. 5, dec. 580, n. 30.

[42] *S.R.R. in causa Romana, Salviani, coram Roias* (1643)—*Decisiones Recentiores,* Part. 9, tom. 1, dec. 212, n. 1.

would not begin to run;[43] 14—when the crimes were successive or permanent the limitation would not begin to run; [44] 15—when the crimes were wholly occult the limitation ran from the day the accuser or inquisitor first had knowledge thereof.[45]

168. Under the American Law it is held that the statute of limitations begins to run from the time when a complete cause of action accrues, i. e., from the time when there is a right to apply to the court for relief, e. g., on breach of the contract.[46]

Examples of the rule under the American Law are: 1—when a note is payable on demand, the statute begins to run from its date; [47] 2—when the note is payable immediately, or when requested, or when called for, the time commences to run immediately; [48] 3—when a note is payable in certain days after demand, sight, or notice, the statute begins to run from the demand, sight, or notice; [49] 4—when a note is payable on demand, demand must be made within the time limited for bringing the action on the note; else a note limited to six years might be kept open indefinitely by a failure to make a demand; [50] 5—when a bill is payable "after sight" or "after notice," demand must be made within a reasonable time on the ex-

[43] *S.R.R. in causa Rossanen., Monitorii et Exercitiorum Spiritualium,* 13 iul. 1909, *coram R.P.D. Michaele Lega,* Dec. VI, n. 13—*S.R.R. Decisiones,* I (1909), 121; *AAS,* I (1909), 630; cf. also canon 1705, §§ 2, 3.

[44] Schmalzgrueber (Part. III, tit. 26, n. 122) said the limitation ran only from the last one. Cf. also S.C. EE. et RR., 22 mart. 1898—*ASS,* XXX (1897-1898), 689, and canon 1705, §§ 2, 3.

[45] S.C. EE. et RR.—*loc. cit.*; cf. also canon 1705, § 3.

[46] Aachen, etc., F. Ins. Co. v. Morton, 156 Fed. 654, 84 C. C. A. 366, 15 L.R.A. (N.S.) 156, 13 Ann. Cas. 692; Clinton v. Clinton, 148 Mich. 496, 111 N.W. 1087.

[47] 2 M. & W. 467; Little v. Blunt, 9 Pick. (Mass.) 488; Caldwell v. Rodman, 50 N.C. 139; Young v. Weston, 39 Me. 492; Hill v. Henry, 17 Ohio 9; Laidley v. Smith, 32 W. Va. 387, 9 S.E. 209; 25 Am. St. Rep. 825; Mills v. Davis, 113 N.Y. 243, 21 N.E. 68, 3 L.R.A. 394; Darby v. Darby, 120 La. 848, 45 South. 747, 14 L.R.A. (N.S.) 1208, 14 Ann. Cas. 805.

[48] Sandford v. Lancaster, 81 Me. 434, 17 Atl. 402.

[49] Wenman v. Ins. Co., 18 Wend. (N.Y.) 267, 28 Am. Dec. 464; 8 Dowl. & Ry. 374; Palmer v. Palmer, 36 Mich. 487, 24 Am. Rep. 605.

[50] Codman v. Rogers, 10 Pick. (Mass.) 120.

piration of which the statute begins to run; [51] 6—when a note is on interest, this does not become barred by the statute till the principal, or some distinct portion of it, becomes barred; [52] 7—when a note or due bill is payable on demand, demand is not a condition precedent to a right of action; [53] 8—when the note is entitled to grace, the statute runs from the last day of grace; [54] 9—when a promissory note past due is indorsed for a valuable consideration, making it a new contract, the statute begins to run in favor of the indorser only from the date of the indorsement; [55] 10—when a reasonable time for the presentment of a check has lapsed the time begins to run in favor of the drawer; [56] 11—when money is deposited with a person for safe custody, a right of action does not accrue until demand is made therefor; [57] 12—when money is payable in instalments the statute runs as to each instalment from the time of the failure to pay it; [58] but if the contract provides that on failure to pay one instalment the whole amount shall fall due, the statute runs as to the whole from such failure; [59] 13—when securities are deposited as collateral to demand notes they do not prevent the running of the statute from the date of maturity of such notes; [60] 14—when a premium note is payable in such portions and at such times as may be necessary to cover losses, the statute runs only from the time of loss, and the assessment thereof; [61] 15—when money is paid by mistake, the statute begins to run from the time of payment,[62] or from the time the mistake should, in the exercise of reasonable diligence,

[51] Wallace v. Agry, 4 Mas. 336, Fed. Cas. No. 17,096; 9 M. & W. 506.

[52] Ferry v. Ferry, 2 Cush. (Mass.) 92.

[53] Appeal of Andress, 11 W.N.C. (Pa.) 294.

[54] Pickard v. Valentine, 13 Me. 412; Kinball v. Fuller, 13 La. Ann. 602.

[55] Graham v. Roberson, 79 Ga. 72, 3 S.E. 611.

[56] Scroggin v. McClelland, 37 Neb. 644, 56 N.W. 208, 22 L.R.A. 110, 40 Am. St. Rep. 520.

[57] (1893) 3 Ch. 154.

[58] Burnham v. Brown, 23 Me. 400; Bush v. Stowell, 71 Pa. 208, 10 Am. Rep. 694.

[59] 3 G. & D. 402.

[60] Hartranft's Estate, 153 Pa. 530, 26 Atl. 104, 34 Am. St. Rep. 717.

[61] Howland v. Cuykendall, 40 Barb. (N.Y.) 320.

[62] Clarke v. Dutcher, 9 Cow. (N.Y.) 674.

have been found out; [63] also in the case of usury, though a shorter time is frequently limited by statute; [64] and when money is paid for another as surety; [65] 16—when money is paid by a bank on a forged check, the right of action to recover the same accrues immediately upon such payment; [66] 17—when overpayments were made on a contract to deliver logs it was held that the time began to run when the amount delivered was ascertained, rather than at the date of payment; [67] 18—when the contract takes effect upon some condition or contingency, or the happening of some event, the statute runs from the performance of the condition,[68] or the happening of the contingency or event,[69] and not from the date of the contract; 19—when there has been an agreement to devise, the statute runs from the death of the promissor; [70] 20—when money is paid and there is afterwards a failure of consideration, the statute runs from the failure.[71]

169. Under the American Law in the case of torts *quasi ex contractu* the rule is that in cases of negligence, unskillfulness, and the like, the statute runs from the time when these happen respectively, and not from the time when damages accrue therefrom.[72] Thus if an attorney negligently invests money in a poor security, the statute runs from the investment,[73] and if a party neglects to remove goods from a warehouse, whereby the plaintiff is obliged to pay damages, the statute runs from the neglect, not from the payment of damages.[74]

[63] West v. Fry, 134 Ia. 675, 112 N.W. 184, 11 L.R.A. (N.S.) 1191; Snyder v. Miller, 71 Kan. 410, 80 Pac. 970, 69 L.R.A. 250, 114 Am. St. Rep. 489.

[64] Davis v. Converse, 35 Vt. 503; Pritchard v. Meekins, 98 N.C. 244, 3 S.E. 484.

[65] Bennett v. Cook, 45 N.Y. 268.

[66] Leather Mfrs.' Bank v. Bank, 128 U.S. 26, 9 Sup. Ct. 3, 32 L. Ed. 342.

[67] Busch v. Jones, 94 Mich. 223, 53 N.W. 1051.

[68] Gardner v. Webber, 17 Pick. (Mass.) 407; Angell, *Limitations*, § 113.

[69] Morgan v. Plumb, 9 Wend. (N.Y.) 287; Louisiana v. U.S., 22 Ct. Cl. 284.

[70] Bash v. Bash, 9 Pa. 260.

[71] Eames v. Savage, 14 Mass. 425; 9 Bing. 748.

[72] Wilcox v. Plummer, 4 Pet. (U.S.) 172, 7 L. Ed. 821; Thruston v. Blackiston, 36 Md. 501; Northrop v. Hill, 61 Barb. (N.Y.) 136; Pennsylvania Co. v. Ry. Co., 44 Ill. 132.

[73] 2 Brod. & B. 73.

[74] McKerras v. Gardner, 3 Johns. (N.Y.) 137.

In a case in which the defendant agreed to go into another state and collect some money, and on his return to pay off a certain judgment, the statute was held to run from the return and demand upon him.[75] A cause of action for an act which is in itself lawful, as to the person who bases thereon an action for injury subsequently accruing from and consequent upon the act, does not accrue until the injury is sustained.[76]

170. The breach of a contract is the gist of the action, not the damages resulting therefrom.[77] As a result, it was held when the defendant had contracted to sell the plaintiff a quantity of salt, but was unable, by reason of the destruction of the salt, to deliver on demand, and prolonged negotiations for settlement till the statutory limitation had expired, and then refused, the statute ran from the demand, the non-delivery being a breach of the contract.[78] It is also held, under the American Law, that when a notary public neglects to give seasonable notice of non-payment of a note, and the bank employing him was held responsible for the failure, upon suit brought by the bank against the notary to recover the damages it had been obliged to pay, the action is held to be barred, if it is not within the time limited running from the notary's default, though within the time limited running from the time when the bank was required to pay damages.[79] If an attorney makes a mistake in a writ, whereupon, after prolonged litigation, non-suit follows, but not till an action against the indorser on the note originally sued has become barred, the mistake is held to set the statute in motion.[80] If an attorney collects money for a client and uses no fraud or falsehood in regard to its receipt, the statute runs from the time of its collection.[81] If the attorney dies before the legal proceedings are terminated, the statute runs from his death.[82] If directors of a bank

[75] Baines v. Williams, 25 N.C. 481.

[76] Houston Water Works v. Kennedy, 70 Tex. 233, 8 S.W. 36.

[77] 5 B. & C. 259; Argall v. Bryant, 1 Sandf. (N.Y.) 98; 3 B. & Ald. 288.

[78] 1 E. L. & Eq. 44.

[79] President, etc., of Bank of Utica v. Childs, 6 Cow. (N.Y.) 238.

[80] Wilcox v. Plummer, 4 Pet. (U.S.) 172, 7 L. Ed. 821; Mardis' Adm'rs v. Shackleford, 4 Ala. 495.

[81] Douglas v. Corry, 46 Ohio St. 349, 21 N.E. 440, 15 Am. St. Rep. 604.

[82] Johnston v. McCain, 145 Pa. 531, 22 Atl. 979.

are made liable by statute for mismanagement, they are discharged after the time limited has run from the day the insolvency of the bank is made known.[83]

171. In some states a distinction is made in cases in which a public officer has neglected duties imposed on him by law, and the statute is in such cases said to run from the time when the injury is developed.[84] Thus it has been held that if a sheriff makes an insufficient return, and there is in consequence a reversal of judgment, the statute runs from the return, and not from the reversal of judgment.[85] Further, if a sheriff collects money and makes due return but fails to pay over, the statute runs from the return,[86] or from the demand by the creditor.[87] If the sheriff suffers an escape, the time runs from the escape.[88] If the sheriff takes insufficient bail, the time runs from the return of *non est inventus* upon execution against the principal debtor,[89] and if he receives money on a *scire facias,* it runs from its reception.[90] If the sheriff neglects to attach sufficient property, the time runs on the return of the writ and not from the time when the insufficiency of the property is ascertained.[91] The statute also runs on a cause of action for wrongful attachment from the time thereof.[92] An action, furthermore, by a sheriff upon the bond of his deputy for a default accrues when the sheriff has paid the debt occasioned by the default.[93] When the American Law

[83] Hinsdale v. Larned, 16 Mass. 68.

[84] Bank of Hartford County v. Waterman, 26 Conn. 324; but cf. Betts v. Norris, 21 Me. 314, 38 Am. Dec. 264; Owen v. Western Sav. Fund, 97 Pa. 47, 39 Am. Rep. 794.

[85] Miller v. Adams, 16 Mass. 456.

[86] Governor v. Stonum, 11 Ala. 679, the one entitled knows from the time of the return that the money is being held by the sheriff, and presumably could act, so this is good at Canon Law, too.

[87] Weston v. Ames, 10 Metc. (Mass.) 244.

[88] 2 Mod. 212.

[89] Mather v. Green, 17 Mass. 60; Harriman v. Wilkins, 20 Me. 93.

[90] Thompson v. Bank, 9 Ga. 413.

[91] Garlin v. Strickland, 27 Me. 443.

[92] McCusker v. Walker, 77 Cal. 208, 19 Pac. 382; Garrett v. Bicklin, 78 Ia. 115, 42 N.W. 621.

[93] Adkins v. Fry, 38 W. Va. 549, 18 S.E. 737; Adkins v. Stephens, 38 W. Va. 557, 18 S.E. 740.

mentions a sheriff in the previous cases, the law expressed there can be applied to the "*cursor*" mentioned in Canon Law.

An action against a recorder of deeds for damages caused by a false certificate of search against incumbrances on real property must be brought within the time limit computed from the date of the search, and not from the date of the discovery of the lien overlooked, or of the loss suffered by the plaintiff.[94]

172. A covenant against incumbrances is not broken until eviction or the actual suffering of damage, and no right of action accrues until such time, and not until then does the statute begin to run.[95] This is likewise the law as regards breach of a warranty in a warranty deed.[96]

173. The statute begins to run against a surety claiming contribution only when his own liability is ascertained.[97]

174. In cases of nuisance, the statute begins to run from the injury to the right, without reference to the question of the amount of the damage, the law holding the violation of the right as some damage.[98] The same is true if a party having a right to use land for a specific purpose puts it to other uses, or wrongfully disposes of property rightfully in possession, i. e., the statute begins to run from the perversion.[99]

175. In trover the statute runs from the conversion,[100] in replevin it runs from the unlawful taking or detention. The limitations in the statute of James, of actions for slander to two years next after the words spoken, applies only to cases wherein the words are actionable in themselves, and not when they become actionable by

[94] Owen v. Saving Fund, 97 Pa. 47, 39 Am. Rep. 794; Russell & Co., v. Abstract Co., 87 Ia. 233, 54 N.W. 212, 43 Am. St. Rep. 381.

[95] *In re* Hanlin's Estate, 133 Wis. 140, 113 N.W. 411, 17 L.R.A. (N.S.) 1189, 126 Am. St. Rep. 938; Seibert v. Bergman, 91 Tex. 411, 44 S.W. 63.

[96] Brooks v. Mohl, 104 Minn. 404, 116 N.W. 931, 17 L.R.A. (N.S.) 1195, 124 Am. St. Rep. 629.

[97] (1893) 2 Ch. 514.

[98] 8 East. 4; Bolivar Mfg. Co. v. Mfg. Co., 16 Pick. (Mass.) 241; Pastorius v. Fisher, 1 Rawle (Pa.) 27; Lyles v. Ry. Co., 73 Tex. 95, 11 S.W. 782; cf. canon 1695, § 2.

[99] Rogers v. Stoever, 24 Pa. 186.

[100] Melville v. Brown, 15 Mass. 82; 5 B. & C. 149.

reason of special damage arising from the speaking thereof.[101] The limitation extends neither to slander of title,[102] nor to libel.[103] In the case of trespass, criminal conversation, etc., the statute runs from the time the injury was committed.[104]

176. The Code of Canon Law provides quite simply [105] for the determination of the opening day of the period: 1—if it is not assigned explicitly or implicitly the time is computed from moment to moment; and if it is continuous the months and years are taken as they appear in the calendar; [106] 2—if the beginning of the period coincides with the beginning of the day, i. e., midnight, the first day is to be counted and the period ends with the beginning of the last day marking the same date; 3—if the beginning of the period [107] does not coincide with the beginning of the day, i. e., midnight, the first day is not counted and the period ends with the end of the last day marking the same date.

177. Under the American Law the courts have discussed much the day when the statute begins to run, whether it is to be included or excluded, but without any satisfactory result. Consequently courts of Canon Law will prefer simply to follow the provisions of the Code on this point despite canon 1508, and thus avoid difficulties.

178. The Canon Law held that adverse possession did not run against those who could not appear in court, or act, or protect their rights, or administer their goods, because it was said in such a case

[101] 1 Salk. 206; Pearl v. Koch, 32 Wkly. Law Bul. 52.

[102] Cro. Car. 140.

[103] John Frederick Archbold's *Practice* (ed. John Jervis, New York, 1846), 29. In this connection it will be necessary to recall what was said above, n. 163, regarding the distinction, under the American Law, between torts and crimes.

[104] Sanborn v. Neilson, 5 N.H. 314.

[105] Canon 34, §§ 2; 3, 2°, 3°.

[106] Cf. also Rubeus, *Annotationes* in *Decisiones Recentiores,* Part. 3, dec. 3, n. 1; *S.R.R. in causa Mediolanen., Pecuniaria, coram Motmanno* (1629)—*Decisiones Novissimae,* tom. 1, dec. 234, n. 10—*Decisiones Recentiores,* Part. 5, tom. 1.

[107] This will be the more common case.

the holder lacked either good faith or title, or was prevented from acquiring for other reasons.[108] Under the American Law, it is held that if, when the right of action would otherwise accrue and the statute begin to run, there is no person who can exercise the right, the statute does not begin to run until there is such a person,[109] for this would be contrary to the intent of the various statutes. Thus, if a note matures after the decease of the promisee, and prior to the issue of letters of administration, the statute runs from the date of the letters of administration unless otherwise specified in the statute,[110] and there must be a person in being to be sued, otherwise the statute will not begin to run.[111]

179. The Canon Law recognized certain disabilities to the effect that, if the plaintiff labored under them when the adverse possession began, the time prescribed in the limitation of actions would be lengthened. These were: 1—vacancy of the church, i. e., when the corporation had no one to represent it, whether this was due to death, transfer, or malice of the representative; [112] 2—time of schism, in the case of the Roman Church; [113] 3—time of hostilities; [114] 4—

[108] Schmalzgrueber, Part. III, tit. 26, n. 19; Pirhing, lib. II, tit. 26, n. 10.

[109] Richards v. Ins. Co., 8 Cra. (U.S.) 84, 3 L. Ed. 496.

[110] 5 B. & Ald. 204; Wenman v. Ins. Co., 13 Wend. (N.Y.) 267, 28 Am. Dec. 464; Levering v. Rittenhouse, 4 Whart. (Pa.) 130; Hobart v. Turnpike Co., 15 Conn. 145; cf. also *S.R.R. in causa Leodien., Beneficii, coram Peutingero* (1648)—*Decisiones Recentiores,* Part. 10, dec. 149, n. 14.

[111] Montgomery v. Hernandez, 12 Wheat. (U.S.) 129, 6 L. Ed. 575.

[112] Cc. 1, 4, 15, X, *de praescriptionibus,* II, 26, and *Glossa* in c. 16, C. XVI, q. 3, ad v. *Interrupta,* and in the *casus* contained in the *Glossa* in c. 1, X, *de praescriptionibus,* II, 26, and *Glossa* in c. 2, X, *de praescriptionibus,* II, 26, ad v. *Futuris.* Cf. also Rufinus, *Summa,* p. 363, and *Glossa* in c. 4, X, *de praescriptionibus,* II, 26, ad v. *Caruisset.*

[113] C. 14, X, *de praescriptionibus,* II, 26.

[114] C. 10, X, *de praescriptionibus,* II, 26; *S.R.R. in causa Ferrarien. seu Bononien., Nullitatis adiudicationis et reintegrationis, coram Gamberini* (1823), dec. 128, n. 5. That hostilities had really created a disability was considered to be proved by the fact that the person acted as soon thereafter as he could, *S.R.R. in causa Barchinonen, Haereditatis, coram Rondinino* (1688)—*Decisiones Nuperrimae,* tom. 2, dec. 101, n. 15, while the contrary was regarded as manifest by the fact that he had brought other suits during that time, *S.R.R., loc. cit.*

minority;[115] 5—insanity;[116] 6—coverture, as long as it lasted, with regard to the property the wife brought with her as dowry.[117] The Canon Law also considered a special case, on the pattern of the Roman Law, of one who could not act within four years of his return, e. g., from captivity, and was therefore given an extension of time corresponding to the number of days in which he had been unable to act.[118]

Other disabilities under the Canon Law were those of a spendthrift who was not allowed to handle his property,[119] as well as all others who were forbidden by law to alienate their property, since "*praescriptio*" involved alienation. Likewise, if the courts were not functioning during the time of a pestilence the limitation did not

[115] D.a.c. 16, C. XVI, q. 3, § 5; *Glossa* in c. 13, C. XVI, q. 3, ad v. *Postliminio*; *Glossa* in d.a.c. 16, C. XVI, q. 3, ad v. *Interrupta*; *Glossa* in c. 17, C. XVI, q. 3, ad v. *Usucapione*, where it is mentioned that the Church may claim restitution according to the law for minors (cf. canon 1687, § 1, together with canon 100, § 3); Schmalzgrueber, Part. III, tit. 26, nn. 19, 33, 38, 131; *S.R.R. in causa Conchen., Nullitatis ordin., coram Penia* (1606)—*Decisiones Recentiores*, Part. 3, dec. 105, n. 17 sqq.; *S.R.R. in causa Romana, locorum montium, coram Marco* (1827), dec. 358, n. 10. A son who was not emancipated was under disability because he was not free to act—Schmalzgrueber, Part. III, tit. 26, nn. 19, 131; *S.R.R. in causa Fulginaten., Pecuniaria, coram Caccia* (1688)—*Decisiones Nuperrimae*, tom. 2, dec. 205, n. 3; *S.R.R. in causa Fulginaten., Pecuniaria, coram Manuel* (1691)—*Decisiones Nuperrimae*, tom. 3, dec. 150, n. 5. This was the case, for instance, when a statute gave the father a life-estate (curtesy)—*S.R.R. in causa Romana, Domus, coram Caprara* (1694), tom. 1, dec. 228, n. 12; *S.R.R. in causa Perusina, Dotis, coram De la Tremoille* (1702)—*Decisiones Nuperrimae*, tom. 7, dec. 247, nn. 19, 20; Gratian (d.a.c. 16, C. XVI, q. 3, § 5) supposed in this case that such minors were without guardians who could, and were bound to, care for their rights.

[116] D.a.c. 16, C. XVI, q. 3, § 5; Schmalzgrueber, Part. III, tit. 26, n. 19; Pirhing, lib. II, tit. 26, n. 10; *S.R.R. in causa Romana, locorum montium, coram Isoard* (1819), tom 2, *de Miscell.*, dec. 298, n. 10; *S.R.R. in causa Romana, locorum montium, coram Isoard* (1826), tom. 2, *de Miscell.*, dec. 300, n. 9; *S.R.R. in causa Romana, locorum montium, coram Marco* (1827), dec. 358, n. 10.

[117] *Glossa* in c. 13, C. XVI, q. 3, ad v. *Postliminio*; in c. 12, X, *de praescriptionibus*, II, 26, ad v. *Non obstante*; cf. C. (5.12) 30.

[118] *Glossa* in c. 13, C. XVI, q. 3, ad v. *Postliminio*.

[119] Schmalzgrueber, Part. III, tit. 26, n. 19.

run.[120] A person who was under a notorious general impediment which he could not remove was also considered at Canon Law to be under a disability, but it was said that if the impediment was not notorious the adverse possession would be allowed, and only on proof of the impediment was restoration of the *status quo* to be granted.[121] A trustee who could not act until a condition was fulfilled was under an impediment,[122] unless he could have removed the impediment.[123]

Absence was a disability at Canon Law,[124] but it was also held that absence of the creditor did not interrupt the running of the limitation because he could send a proxy.[125] The disability was held, however, to exist if one was absent because he had been banished.[126]

180. Under the American Law, the statute provides that infants, married women, persons *non compos mentis,* those imprisoned, and those beyond seas, out of the realm, or out of the country, are to be regarded as affected by the incapacity to sue, or, in other words, as being under disability, and are to have, therefore, the right of action secured to them until the expiration of the time limited, after the removal of the disability,[127] e. g., the statute of

[120] Schmalzgrueber, Part. III, tit. 26, n. 131.

[121] Schmalzgrueber, Part. III, tit. 26, n. 131.

[122] *S.R.R. in causa Romana, locorum montium, coram Ansaldo* (1700), tom. 2, dec. 129, nn. 9, 12, 15.

[123] *S.R.R. in causa Romana, Cambii, coram Ansaldo* (1698), tom. 1, dec. 26, nn. 29, 30.

[124] *S.R.R. in causa Romana, Pecuniaria, coram Emerix* (1694), tom. 3, dec. 1152, n. 10 (as to the sixteen-year statutory adverse possession and limitation); *S.R.R. in causa Romana, Cambii, coram Ansaldo* (1698), tom. 1, dec. 26, n. 25; *S.R.R. in causa Albanen., Dotis, coram Olivatio* (1766), tom. 5, dec. 552, n. 10; *S.R.R. in causa Romana seu Crotonen., super Fructibus, coram Scotto* (1703)—*Decisiones Nuperrimae,* tom. 8, dec. 171, n. 8.

[125] Rubeus, *Annotationes* in *Decisiones Recentiores,* Part. 3, dec. 6, n. 24; but cf. *S.R.R. in causa Romana, Pecuniaria, coram Rondinino* (1672)—*Decisiones Recentiores,* Part. 18, tom. 1, dec. 392, n. 17, where it was held that, if it would not be allowed against the absent creditor, it would not run for an absent debtor who could not be served with process.

[126] *S.R.R. in causa Firmana, Bonorum, coram Mattheio* (1674)—*Decisiones Recentiores,* Part. 18, tom. 1, dec. 281, n. 8.

[127] 2 Bouvier 2004.

limitations cannot be pleaded in bar to an action by a wife against a husband to recover present and future maintenance.[128]

181. These personal exceptions have been strictly construed under the American Law, and the party alleging the disability has been very uniformly held to be obliged to bring himself exactly within the express words of the statute to entitle himself to use the benefit of the exception. To bring himself within the spirit or supposed reason of the exception is not enough.[129] The privilege under the American Law is accorded, however, although the person laboring under the statute disability could in fact bring suit. Thus, an infant may sue before he arrives at his majority, but he is not obliged to, and his right is saved if he does not.[130] It is also held that the time during which a Negro was held as a slave should not be counted in determining whether an action by him is barred by the statute.[131]

The disability must be continuous and identical. One disability cannot be superadded to another so as to prolong the time,[132] and if the statute once begins to run, whether before a disability exists or after it has been removed, no intervention of another and subsequent disability can stop it.[133] When, however, there are two or more coexisting disabilities at the time when the right of action accrues, suit need not be brought until all are removed.[134]

182. The foregoing statements [135] show that the courts of Canon Law will find no novelty in the application of the American Law as

[128] Carr v. Carr, 6 Ind. App. 277, 33 N.E. 805.

[129] Sacia v. De Graaf, 1 Cow. (N.Y.) 356; Beardsley v. Southmayd, 15 N.J.L. 171; 17 Ves. Ch. 87.

[130] 2 Saund. 117.

[131] Berry v. Berry's Adm'r, (Ky.), 22 S.W. 654.

[132] East Tennessee Iron & Coal Co. v. Wiggin, 37 U.S. App. 129, 68 Fed. 446, 15 C.C.A. 510.

[133] Workman v. Guthrie, 29 Pa. 495, 72 Am. Dec. 654; Fritz v. Joiner, 54 Ill. 101; Turnipseed v. Freeman, 2 McCord (S.C.) 269; Hardy v. Riddle, 24 Neb. 670, 39 N.W. 841; Alvis v. Oglesby, 87 Tenn. 172, 10 S.W. 313; Royse v. Turnbaugh, 117 Ind. 539, 20 S.W. 485; Bauserman v. Blunt, 147 U.S. 647, 13 Sup. Ct. 466, 37 L. Ed. 316.

[134] Plowd. 375; Keeton's Heirs v. Keeton's Adm'r, 20 Mo. 530; Demarest v. Wynkoop, 3 Johns. Ch. (N. Y.) 129, 8 Am. Dec. 467.

[135] Nn. 180, 181.

to disabilities. There is, however, to be noted the fact that in this connection the American Law treats also of the absence of the debtor on whom process cannot be served, and considers this as a disability. The Canon Law was not accustomed to mention the absence of the debtor among the disabilities, for it considered these as affecting the plaintiff directly rather than indirectly, as when he is unable to sue because of something depending upon the other party. It is possible, too, that the problem of absence of the debtor was not so often presented to the courts, since "*praescriptio*" so often meant adverse possession or prescription, in which case the holder was present in the place where the property was situated and where suit was brought.

Under the American Law the time during which a debtor is absent, residing out of the state of his own free will and accord, is to be deducted in estimating the time in which an action must be brought against him,[136] notwithstanding that he continues to have a usual place of residence in the state where service of the summons could be made on him.[137] In this sense it also holds that a foreign corporation is a person out of the state.[138]

183. When the phrase "beyond seas" occurs in the statute of limitations, it means, generally, outside the jurisdiction of the state or government in which the question arises.[139] It has also been held to mean "out of the United States." [140] Other cases hold that it means "out of the state." [141] In the various statutes of limitation

[136] Hoffman v. Pope's Estate, 74 Mich. 235, 41 N.W. 907; Ament v. Lowenthall, 52 Kan. 706, 35 Pac. 804.

[137] Bauserman v. Blunt, 147 U.S. 647, 13 Sup. Ct. 466, 37 L. Ed. 316.

[138] Larsen v. Aultman & Taylor Co., 86 Wis. 285, 56 N.W. 915, 39 Am. St. Rep. 893.

[139] 32 E. L. & Eq. 84; Forbes' Adm'r v. Foot's Adm'r, 2 McCord (S.C.) 331, 13 Am. Dec. 732; Galusha v. Cobleigh, 13 N.H. 79; Hatch v. Spofford, 24 Conn. 432.

[140] Thurston v. Fisher, 9 S. & R. (Pa.) 288; Earle v. McDowell 12 N.C. 16; Davie v. Briggs, 97 U.S. 638, 24 L. Ed. 1086; Keeton's Heirs v. Keeton's Adm'r, 20 Mo. 530; Darling v. Meechum, 2 G. Greene (Ia.) 602.

[141] Byrne v. Crowninshield, 1 Pick. (Mass.) 263; Pancoast's Lessee v. Addison, 1 Harr. & J. (Md.) 350, 2 Am. Dec. 520; Forbes' Adm'r v. Foot's Adm'r, 2 McCord (S.C.) 331, 13 Am. Dec. 732; Mansell's Adm'r v. Israel, 3 Bibb (Ky.)

the phrase "out of the state" is now generally used, and the United States courts adopt and follow the decisions of the respective states upon the interpretation of their respective laws.[142] What constitutes absence out of the state within the meaning of the statute is wholly undeterminable by any rule to be drawn from the decisions, but it seems to be agreed that temporary absence is not enough; though what is a temporary absence is by no means generally agreed.

The absence of one of several joint-plaintiffs does not prevent the running of the statute,[143] but the absence of one of several joint-defendants does.[144] This, at least, seems to be the settled law of England; but the cases in the several states are conflicting on these points.[145] If a claimant beyond seas when the claim accrued returned to this country, the statute began to run and was not suspended by his departure to foreign parts.[146]

184. The word "return," as applied to an absent debtor, applies as well to foreigners, or residents out of the state coming to the state, as to citizens of the state who have gone abroad and have returned.[147] In order to set the statute in motion the return must be open, public, and accompanied with such circumstances as will give a party

510; Houston v. Moore, 3 Wheat. (U.S.) 433, 4 L. Ed. 428; Galusha v. Cobleigh, 13 N.H. 86; Stephenson v. Doe, 8 Blackf. (Ind.) 515, 46 Am. Dec. 489; Richardson's Adm'rs v. Richardson's Adm'rs, 6 Ohio 126, 25 Am. Dec. 745; Thomason v. Odum, 23 Ala. 486; Wakefield v. Smart, 8 Ark. 489. Cf. also Sleght v. Kane, 1 Johns. Cas. (N.Y.) 76, and to this effect is the very uniform current of authorities, 1 Bouvier 340-341.

142 Shelby v. Guy, 11 Wheat. (U.S.) 361, 6 L. Ed. 495. This seems to afford a norm for courts of Canon Law in deciding cases presented to them, i. e., they should consider absence as it is considered in the courts of the state in which they sit. Cf. canon 1508.

143 4 Term 516.

144 29 E. L. & Eq. 271.

145 Cf. Bruce v. Flagg, 25 N.J.L. 219; Denny v. Smith, 18 N.Y. 567; Harlan's Heirs v. Seaton's Heirs, 18 B. Monr. (Ky.) 312; Seay v. Bacon, 4 Sneed (Tenn.) 99, 67 Am. Dec. 601.

146 Savage v. U.S., 23 Ct. Cl. 255.

147 Ruggles v. Keeler, 3 Johns. (N. Y.) 267, 3 Am. Dec. 482; Bulger v. Roche, 11 Pick. (Mass.) 36, 22 Am. Dec. 359; Crocker v. Arey, 3 R.I. 178.

who exercises ordinary diligence an opportunity to bring his action.[148] The creditor, however, must at least take some steps from time to time to ascertain whether he can reach the debtor.[149] Though the return is temporary it will be sufficient if the creditor knows of it,[150] but a stay even of several weeks without the creditor's knowledge will not be sufficient,[151] nor will a secret visit.[152] It has also been held that there must be a return with an intention to reside.[153]

185. It was mentioned above [154] that the Canon Law considered that the plaintiff was under a disability during the time of hostilities. One may also say that during that time the running of the limitation is suspended, saving the disability concept for the period prior to the running of the statute. In this sense it was also said that, if the adverse possession had been begun against the deceased, it would be interrupted while the latter's child was under fourteen if a boy, twelve if a girl.[155] The Canon Law terminology usually reserves "interruption" for the idea of some subsequent act which stops the continuity of adverse possession, whether this be something which stops it as to all the world,[156] or something which stops it as to the one interrupting, e. g., the one bringing suit against the holder.[157]

[148] Byrne v. Crowninshield, 1 Pick. (Mass.) 263; Berrien v. Wright, 26 Barb. (N.Y.) 208; 24 Ont. App. Rep. 718; Steen v. Swadley, 126 Ala. 616, 28 South. 620.

[149] Dukes v. Collins, 7 Houst. (Del.) 3, 30 Atl. 639.

[150] Faw v. Roberdeau, 3 Cra. (U.S.) 174, 2 L. Ed. 402; *contra* Wilson v. Daggett, 88 Tex. 375, 31 S.W. 618, 53 Am. St. Rep. 766.

[151] Mazozon v. Foot, 1 Aik. (Vt.) 282, 15 Am. Dec. 679.

[152] Steward v. Stewart, 152 Cal. 162, 92 Pac. 87, 14 Ann. Cas. 940.

[153] Lee v. McKoy, 118 N.C. 518, 24 S.E. 210.

[154] N. 179.

[155] Schmalzgrueber, Part. III, tit. 26, n. 33; *S.R.R. in causa Faventina, Dotis, coram Caprara* (1696), tom. 1, dec. 271, n. 5; *S.R.R. in causa Aesina, Manutentionis, coram Ursino* (1687)—*Decisiones Nuperrimae*, tom. 2, dec. 38, n. 14. Cf. *supra*, n. 179, note 115; *contra infra*, n. 186, note 159.

[156] *Interruptio naturalis.*

[157] *Interruptio civilis*, cf. canon 1725, 4°.

186. Under the American Law the courts will not recognize exemptions where the statute has once begun to run.[158] When the statute begins to run before the death of the testator or intestate, it is not interrupted by his death.[159] nor by the death of the administrator,[160] nor by his removal from the state.[161] This is presumably based on the assumption that there is someone who can and should act for the heirs of the deceased. If there should be no one in that position, it seems that the Canon Law rule allowing suspension of the running of the limitation is preferable.[162] Under the American Law, too, subsequent mental incapacity of a party will likewise not interrupt the running of the limitation.[163] It is likewise said under the American Law that an insolvent's discharge as effectually removes him from pursuit by his creditor as absence from the state; but it is not an exception within the statute, and cannot avail as a suspension.[164]

The American Law has always held that a statutory impediment to the assertion of title will not help the party so impeded,[165] nor do the courts feel that they can create an exception to the operation of the statute not made by the statute itself, when the party designedly eludes the service of process.[166]

There are many authorities, however, to show that, if by the interposition of courts, by the necessity of the case, or by the provisions of a statute, a person cannot be sued for a limited time, the running of the statute is suspended during that period. In other

[158] Douglas v. Irvine, 126 Pa. 643; 17 Atl. 802; Northrop v. Marquam, 16 Or. 173, 18 Pac. 449.

[159] 4 M. & W. 43; Frost v. Frost, 4 Edw. Ch. (N.Y.) 733; Handy v. Smith, 30 W. Va. 195, 3 S.E. 604; Hardy v. Riddle, 24 Neb. 670, 39 N.W. 841.

[160] Pipkin v. Hewlett, 17 Ala. 291.

[161] Lowe's Adm'r v. Jones, 15 Ala. 545.

[162] Cf. *supra,* n. 185.

[163] De Arnaud v. U.S., 151 U.S. 483, 14 Sup. Ct. 374, 38 L. Ed. 244. Here again, if there is no one to act for him, the Canòn Law spirit would prompt the court to allow a suspension.

[164] Sletor v. Oram, 1 Whart. (Pa.) 106; Sacia v. De Graaf, 1 Cow. (N.Y.) 356; Collester v. Hailey, 6 Gray (Mass.) 517.

[165] McIver v. Ragan, 2 Wheat. (U.S.) 25, 4 L. Ed. 175.

[166] Amy v. Watertown, 130 U.S. 320, 9 Sup. Ct. 537, 32 L. Ed. 953.

words, if the law interposes to prevent suit, it will see to it that he who has a right of action shall not be prejudiced thereby.[167] Thus an injunction will suspend the statute,[168] but it is also held that an injunction against the commencement of an action does not prevent the running of the statute of limitations unless it so provides.[169] The courts of Canon Law will, therefore, consider that, if their action prevents the plaintiff from bringing his suit within the time limited, said action not being caused by his fault, they will allow a suspension of the limitation for the time that they have impeded his suit, and in the decree impeding his suit they will take cognizance of such suspension of the limitation. When title cannot be asserted because of some prohibition of the canons, the courts will not feel bound to allow such assertion or to suspend the running of the statute on that account.

Under the American Law, too, the running of the statute is suspended when a state of war exists between the governments of the debtor and creditor,[170] and it revives in full force on the restoration of peace.[171] The rule is thus slightly different from that of the Canon Law mentioned above,[172] which had its origin in a period of the world's history when armed conflict was perhaps more frequent and not always between organized governments.

[167] Tarver v. Cowart, 5 Ga. 66; Montgomery v. Hernandez, 12 Wheat. (U.S.) 129, 6 L. Ed. 575.

[168] Hutsonpiller's Adm'r v. Stover's Adm'r, 12 Gratt. (Va.) 579; Sands v. Campbell, 31 N.Y. 345.

[169] Hunter v. Ins. Co., 73 Ohio St. 110, 76 N.E. 563, 3 L.R.A. (N.S.) 1187, 112 Am. St. Rep. 699, 4 Ann. Cas. 146.

[170] Ross v. Jones, 22 Wall. (U.S.) 576, 22 L. Ed. 730; Bell v. Hanks, 55 Ga. 274; McMerty v. Morrison, 62 Mo. 140.

[171] Cf. Chancy v. Powell, 103 N.C. 159, 9 S.E. 298.

[172] Cf. *supra*, n. 179.

CHAPTER VII

LIMITATION ON VARIOUS CLASSES OF ACTIONS [1]

ARTICLE 1. IN GENERAL

187. It is to be noted first of all that the length of time prescribed for the bringing of an action, the lapse of which affords the occasion for the use on the part of the defendant of the plea *(exceptio)* of limitation of the action, varies not only from state to state but also from time to time within the same state. It will, therefore, be necessary for the courts of Canon Law to consult someone versed in the law of the state in which they sit whenever a case involving limitation of actions is presented to them, unless it is such as is governed exclusively by the rules of Canon Law.[1a]

188. Since the limitations of the American Law are established according to the classes of action known to that system, rather than according to those known to the Canonical and Civil system, it seems advisable to explain briefly for the use of Canonists the meaning of some of the more commonly mentioned classes of action to be found in the American Law, in order that they may the more readily explain to the American lawyer the type of action regarding which they are consulting him when they seek to learn what limitation applies thereon in their state.

ARTICLE 2. RECOVERY OF REAL PROPERTY

189. Actions at law for recovery or possession of real property [2] differ in the various jurisdictions as to the time within which they must be brought. An action of this type means: 1—an action of

[1] Cf. 37 *C.J.*, 737-807.

[1a] Cf. *supra*, Chap. II, art. 2, and Chap. VI, art. 2.

[2] Cf. canon 1693.

ejectment; [3] 2—an action of trespass to try title; [4] 3—an action to recover the land itself.[5] "Land" in this connection includes houses and other buildings on the land,[6] but is not referable to an action in which the right to an incorporeal hereditament is involved.[7] As a matter of pleading, in the American Law, the statute does not apply to an action at law to recover land, for the lapse of time is only an aid to any prescriptive title which the defendant may set up.[8]

An action for deceit inducing the purchase of real estate of much less value than the price paid,[9] in which plaintiff sought to recover a part of the purchase price in proportion to a deficiency in acreage, and nowhere alleged that any specific tract or part of the tract was omitted from the deed, was held not an action to recover land, as respected limitations.[10]

190. By analogy a court of equity usually adopts the limitation at law on recovery of lands when it hears a case of: 1—recovery of an equitable estate; 2—enforcement of a right cognizable only in equity,[11] or when a statutory provision as to limitation of actions, express or implied, exists.[12] In case of concurrent jurisdiction between equity and law, equity follows the statute of limitations as a statute, not by analogy.[13]

[3] A form of action which lies to regain the possession of real property, with damages for the unlawful detention. It lies for corporeal hereditaments only, Carmalt v. Platt, 7 Watts (Pa.) 318; People v. Mauran, 5 Denio (N.Y.) 389.

[4] An action used sometimes for the recovery of the possession of real property and of damages for any trespass committed upon the same by the defendant.

[5] Lott v. Van Zandt, 107 S.W. 2nd 761.

[6] Fidelity Cotton Oil, etc., Co. v. Martin (Tex. Civ. A.) 136 S.W. 533.

[7] Lehigh Valley R. Co. v. McFarland, 43 N.J.L. 605 (quot. Martin v. Burr, 111 Tex. 57, 228 S.W. 543).

[8] Hughes v. Purcell, 135 Ga. 174, 68 S.E. 1111; Fuller v. Calhoun Nat'l Bank, 1 S.E. 2nd 86; i. e., a traverse is in order, not a demurrer.

[9] Cf. canon 1684, § 2; also *supra*, n. 165.

[10] Phipps v. Wright, 28 Ga. A. 164, 110 S.E. 511.

[11] John v. Smith, 91 Fed. 827 (aff. 102 Fed. 218, 42 C.C.A. 275).

[12] Tilton v. Bader, 181 Ia. 473, 164 N.W. 871 (quot. Richland Tp. School Dist. v. Hanson, 186 Ia. 1314, 173 N.W. 873).

[13] Godden v. Kimmell, 99 U.S. 201, 25 L. Ed. 431; Wagner v. Baird, 7 How. 234, 12 L. Ed. 681.

191. When a suit to enforce a vendor's lien is brought, if the statute does not fix the time,[14] the limitation is usually that which applies to an action to recover the debt.[15] If, however, the vendor has retained the legal title in himself, the limitation applicable in actions of ejectment or for possession is applied by analogy in the absence of statutory provisions.[16]

192. Actions or proceedings for the partition of land have been held not covered by limitations applicable to actions for recovery of real property.[17] These are, then, governed by general statutes (residuary clause explained below) unless specific provisions are made.[18] In case the right to partition is no longer an equitable one[19] the limitations relating to real actions may be pleaded against a bill for partition by one cotenant against another.[20] A widow's action for partition against strangers claiming the entire title and estate under a deed from the husband, and under which they have been in actual possession for the statutory period, is barred by the statute concerning recovery of land.[21]

193. A mortgagor, it is held, may redeem at any time within the period set by the statute for limitation of the rights of entry and actions for recovery of land,[22] unless the statute expressly provides another period,[23] or the courts have construed it to provide otherwise.[24] An action to redeem is usually[25] regarded as an action to

[14] Day v. Baldwin, 34 Ia. 380; Hitt v. Pickett, 91 Ky. 644, 11 S.W. 9, 12 Ky. L. 51.

[15] Borst v. Corey, 15 N.Y. 505 (foll. Fuller v. Morian, 85 Misc. 529, 147 N.Y.S. 650).

[16] McGehee v. Blackwell, 28 Ark. 27.

[17] Frakes v. Elliott, 102 Ind. 47, 1 N.E. 195.

[18] McCray v. Humes, 116 Ind. 103, 18 N.E. 500; Nutter v. Hawkins, 93 Ind. 260.

[19] Haig v. Haig, 20 Ont. 61.

[20] Stout v. Rigney, 107 Fed. 545; 44 C.C.A. 459 (Missouri).

[21] Britt v. Gordon, 132 Ia. 431, 439, 108 N.W. 319, 11 Ann. Cas. 407.

[22] Helton v. Martin, 52 Ind. 529; McNair v. Lot, 34 Mo. 285, 84 Am. Dec. 78, 25 Mo. 182.

[23] Raynor v. Drew, 72 Cal. 307, 13 Pac. 866.

[24] Hubbell v. Sibley, 50 N. Y. 468 (aff. 5 Lans. 51).

[25] Miner v. Beekman, 50 N.Y. 337, 14 Abb. Pr. (N.S.) 1 (rev. 33 N.Y. Sup. 67, 11 Abb. Pr. [N.S.] 147, 42 How. Pr. 33).

recover land.[26] When an action to redeem by the mortgagor is barred, a similar action by anyone claiming under him will also be barred.[27] If any part of the debt for which the security was given remains unpaid and enforceable, it is held that the limitation does not run against an action for an accounting and to redeem.[28]

194. Aside from special statutes in some jurisdictions,[29] the limitation applicable to actions for the recovery of real property, or for the recovery of possession thereof, is, as a general rule, applicable to actions to test title to lands under public grant or patent, or to recover possession under such title.[30]

195. Statutes providing that all actions against purchasers for the recovery of land sold at judicial or execution sales or at sales by executors and the like shall be brought within a specified period after the date of such sale, and not thereafter,[31] are intended to apply when the purchaser went into possession within the statutory period,[32] and are binding both in equity and at law.[33] They apply likewise to actions to set aside sales on the ground of fraud.[34] The weight of authority is that a purchaser at a void judicial sale who

[26] Campbell v. Imperial Loan Co., 18 Man. 144; Smith v. Darling, 36 Ont. L. 587, 10 Ont. W.N. 161, 32 Dom. L.R. 307.

[27] Tucker v. White, 22 N.C. 289.

[28] Salinger v. McAllister, 165 Ia. 508, 146 N.W. 8; cf. *supra*, n. 167, note 35.

[29] Jodd v. Mehrtens, 262 Mo. 391, 171 S.W. 322; Collins v. Pease, 146 Mo. 135, 47 S.W. 925.

[30] Curtner v. U.S., 149 U.S. 662, 13 Sup. Ct. 985, 1041, 37 L. Ed. 890; Manning v. San Jacinto Tin Co., 9 Fed. 726, 7 Sawy. 418.

[31] Johnson v. Taylor, 140 Ark. 100, 215 S.W. 162; Hunt v. Stevens, 174 Mich. 501, 140 N.W. 992; West Michigan Park Assoc. v. Pere Marquette R. Co., 172 Mich. 179, 137 N.W. 799.

[32] Cunningham v. Dellmon (Ark.), 237 S.W. 450.

[33] Bland v. Fleeman, 58 Ark. 84, 23 S.W. 4.

[34] Hindman v. O'Connor, 54 Ark. 627, 16 S.W. 1052, 13 L.R.A. 490; but cf. Williams v. Allison, 33 Ia. 278 (applying limitation applicable to the action for the recovery of real property).

enters into and holds possession of the property for the period set by the statute is protected thereby.[35]

Foreclosure sales have been held judicial sales within the statute,[36] and a statute limiting actions for recovery of real property sold on execution applies to sales under foreclosure proceedings.[37]

196. The rule regarding limitation on the action against a purchaser at a judicial sale or at a sale by an executor does not apply when: 1—the executor, guardian, or administrator had no legal authority to act as such; [38] 2—the sale was made by order of a court which had no jurisdiction to make it; [39] 3—the suit is upon a right in no wise connected with, or dependent upon, the validity or invalidity of the judicial sale.[40]

Article 3. Recovery of Personal Property

197. In the different jurisdictions one finds different statutes regarding the limitation on actions for the taking, detention, or recovery of personalty.[41] Where the statute is a bar, peaceful possession for the statutory time defeats a suit for recovery by the former owner.[42] If title was not lost by the lapse of time, an action to recover will lie.[43]

[35] Van Gilder v. Warfield's Unknown Heirs and devisees, 120 Pac. 2nd 243; cf. *supra*, n. 98, note 13.

[36] Holloway v. Eagle, 135 Ark. 206, 205 S.W. 113; Johnson v. Umsted, 64 Fed. 2nd 316.

[37] Sinclair v. Gunzenhauser, 179 Ind. 78, 98 N.E. 37, 100 N.E. 376; Moore v. Ross, 139 Ind. 200, 38 N.E. 817.

[38] Harrison v. Miller, 87 Kan. 48, 123 Pac. 854.

[39] Indiana, etc., Lumber, etc., Co. v. Brinkley, 164 Fed. 963; 91 C.C.A. 91 (Arkansas).

[40] Byerly v. Eadie, 95 Kan. 400, 148 Pac. 757, 96 Kan. 137, 150 Pac. 523.

[41] Bresnahan v. Nugent, 92 Mich. 76, 52 N.W. 736; cf. also canon 1693.

[42] Rees v. Rees, 82 W. Va. 598, 96 S.E. 1019; cf. *supra*, nn. 4, 159, 161.

[43] Manka v. Martin Metal Mfg. Co., 153 Kan. 811, 113 Pac. 2nd 1041; Lightfoot v. Davis, 198 N.Y. 261, 91 N.E. 582, 139 Am. St. Rep. 817, 29 L.R.A. (N.S.) 119, 19 Ann. Cas. 747.

Replevin [44] and detinue [45] are within the statutory limitation for "actions for taking or injuring any goods or chattels." [46]

Article 4. Actions or Contracts

a. In General

198. By express wording of the statutes or by judicial construction, practically all simple contracts are held to be governed by these statutes.[47] The action of assumpsit [48] is here included by construction,[49] or by express words.[50]

Examples of contract actions thus limited are: 1—an action at law to recover a dividend declared by a corporation; [51] 2—an action against a telegraph company for delay in delivering a telegram; [52] 3—an action for breach of contract by means of a tort; [53] 4—an action on a contract of employment; [54] 5—an action on a contract for professional services; [55] 6—an action on a contract of safe car-

[44] Pickens v. Sparks, 44 Ark. 29. This is a form of action which lies to regain the possession of chattels which have been taken from the plaintiff unlawfully. It may be brought in some states wherever a person wishes to recover specific goods to which he alleges title.

[45] Sullivan v. Hadley, 16 Ark. 129. This is a form of action which lies for the recovery, in specie, of chattels from the one who acquired possession of them lawfully but retains it without right, together with damages for the detention. The judgment is in the alternative that the plaintiff recover the goods, or the value thereof if he cannot have the property itself. 3 Blackstone's *Commentaries on the Law*, c. 26, p. 718.

[46] Cf. Pickens v. Sparks, 44 Ark. 29; Sullivan v. Hadley, 16 Ark. 129.

[47] Cf. Topsham v. Blondell, 82 Me. 152, 19 Atl. 93.

[48] This is a form of action which lies for the recovery of damages for the non-performance of a parol or simple contract. It differs from debt, since the amount claimed need not be liquidated, and from covenant, since it does not require a contract under seal to support it.

[49] Washington, etc., R. Co. v. District of Columbia, 136 U.S. 653, 10 Sup. Ct. 1075, 34 L. Ed. 549.

[50] Cf. statute of the particular state.

[51] Baille v. Columbia Gold Min. Co., 86 Or. 1, 166 Pac. 1167.

[52] Western Union Tel. Co. v. Witt, 110 S.W. 889, 33 Ky. L. 685.

[53] Sellers v. Noah, 209 Ala. 103, 95 South. 167.

[54] McCurley v. National Sav., etc., Co., 258 Fed. 154, 49 App. (D.C.) 10.

[55] Consaul v. Rawlins, 130 Ga. 726, 61 S.E. 704.

riage, whether of goods [56] or of passengers; [57] 7—an action on a contract of a warehouseman; [58] 8—an action by a corporation,[59] its trustee in bankruptcy,[60] its receiver,[61] or its creditors,[62] on a subscription to its stock, or by its stockholders against the directors for losses due to their negligence,[63] or by creditors against stockholders,[64] or against stockholders and directors,[65] of an insolvent corporation,[66] though some hold otherwise as to an action by creditors against stockholders or by stockholders against directors.[67]

Collateral security given may [68] or may not [69] affect the running of the limitation on a simple contract debt.

199. The difference in the length of the time within which a suit must be brought on the various classes of contracts to be explained below is determined by the type of the evidence which must be used to establish the existence of the contract.[70]

b. Sealed Instruments or Specialties

200. In most jurisdictions [71] the actions on these specialties constitute a special class.[72] Whether the action is or is not of this

[56] Yazoo, etc., R. Co. v. Zemurray, 238 Fed. 789, 151 C.C.A. 639.

[57] Patterson v. Augusta, etc., R. Co., 94 Ga. 140, 21 S.E. 283; Blakely v. Le Duc, 22 Minn. 476.

[58] Western R. Co. v. Hart, 160 Ala. 599, 49 South. 371.

[59] Pittsburgh, etc., R. Co. v. Graham, 36 Pa. 77, 2 Grant 259.

[60] Sweet v. Barnard, 66 Col. 526, 182 Pac. 22.

[61] Bourne v. Baer, 107 Neb. 255, 185 N.W. 408; Hoffman v. Geiger, 281 N.W. 625.

[62] Brown v. Union Ins. Co., 3 La. Ann. 177.

[63] Percy v. Millaudon, 3 La. 568, 591.

[64] South Carolina Mfg. Co. v. Bank, 6 Rich. (S.C.) Eq. 227.

[65] Lindsay v. Hyatt, 4 Edw. (N.Y.) 97.

[66] Little v. Kohn, 185 Fed. 295 (Pennsylvania).

[67] Andrews v. Bacon, 38 Fed. 777; Bullard v. Bell, 4 Fed. Cas. No. 2,121; 1 Mas. 243; Blythe v. Enslen, 209 Ala. 96, 95 South. 479.

[68] Hargraves v. Igo, 64 N.H. 619, 15 Atl. 137.

[69] Low v. Allen, 26 Cal. 141.

[70] Homire v. Stratton, etc., Co. 157 Ky. 822, 827, 164 S.W. 67.

[71] Pittsburgh, etc., R. Co. v. Alleghany County, 63 Pa. 126; Duffy v. McHale, 35 R.I. 16, 85 Atl. 36; Alexander v. Byrd, 85 Va. 690, 8 S.E. 577.

[72] Near v. Lowe, 49 Mich. 482, 13 N.W. 825; Fellows v. National Can Co., 276 Fed. 309 (aff. 290 Fed. 201).

class is determined by the use made of the instrument, i. e., whether or not it is the basis and immediate foundation of the suit, not an ultimate source of the obligation sought to be enforced.[73]

201. The following have been held not an action on a specialty: 1—an action to enforce payment of a legacy made a charge on land; [74] 2—an action on an implied promise not contained in the specialty itself; [75] 3—an action on a written acknowledgment under seal but containing no promise to pay; [76] 4—an action on a note merely because it is secured by a mortgage; [77] 5—an action to have property or a right assigned because this is provided in a specialty; [78] 6—an action for specific performance of a contract under seal; [79] 7—an action to set aside a deed of land; [80] 8—an action on an agreement by a grantee in a deed of mortgaged premises to assume the mortgage by a clause in the deed.[81]

202. County or town warrants, if under seal, are specialties; [82] if not, they are merely instruments for payment of money,[83] unless some other provision is made.[84]

203. A note under seal is likewise a specialty,[85] but an action against a surety or indorser thereon or an anomalous indorser of a

[73] Clark v. Iowa City, 20 Wall. 583, 22 L. Ed. 427; Lexington v. Butler, 14 Wall. 282, 20 L. Ed. 809; Near v. Lowe, 49 Mich. 482, 13 N.W. 825.

[74] Loder v. Hatfield, 71 N.Y. 92.

[75] Pierce v. Stitt, 126 Wis. 62, 105 N.W. 479.

[76] Harding v. Covell, 217 Mass. 120, 104 N.E. 452; cf. *infra,* n. 247.

[77] Seymour v. Street, 5 Neb. 85.

[78] McKenzie v. Matthews, 153 Ala. 437, 44 South. 958; cf. Grist v. Carswell, 165 South. 102.

[79] Peters v. Delaplaine, 49 N.Y. 362, 372.

[80] O'Donohue v. Smith, 57 Misc. 448, 109 N.Y.S. 929.

[81] Hollister v. Strahon, 23 S.D. 570, 122 N.W. 604, 21 Ann. Cas. 677 (dist. Hill v. Huron, 39 S.D. 530, 165 N.W. 534).

[82] Heffleman v. Pennington County, 3 S.D. 162, 54 N.W. 851.

[83] King Iron Bridge, etc., Co. v. Otoe County, 27 Fed. 800 (rev. on other grounds, 120 U.S. 225, 7 Sup. Ct. 552, 30 L. Ed. 623).

[84] Knox County v. Morton, 68 Fed. 787, 15 C.C.A. 671 (aff. 65 Fed. 369).

[85] Rawsom v. Davidson, 49 Mich. 607, 14 N.W. 565; Goodrich v. Leland, 18 Mich. 110; Clarke v. Pierce, 215 Mass. 552, 102 N.E. 1094, Ann. Cas. 1914D 421.

promissory note [86] executed under seal by a corporation [87] is one of simple contract debt.

A corporation's negotiable certificate of indebtedness under the corporate seal and payable to bearer is a specialty,[88] and so is a written instrument executed on behalf of a copartnership and signed and sealed by an individual partner in the firm name, but only as to such partner,[89] so as to found an action on a sealed instrument.

204. These limitations on sealed instruments generally cover all classes of bonds,[90] e. g., those of officials or of persons acting in a fiduciary capacity,[91] those of clerks of court,[92] those for payment of money,[93] those for title,[94] those authorized by statute for railroad aid,[95] those for an appeal,[96] unless otherwise provided.[97] Coupons detached from bonds [98] are, as a rule, governed by the statute on sealed instruments.[99]

205. Actions on covenants of warranty [100] or of seizin [101] in a deed, where not otherwise provided by statute,[102] are actions on

[86] I. e., one who signs for the accommodation of the payee, Neg. Instr. Act, § 64.

[87] Somers v. Florida Pebble Phosphate Co., 50 Fla. 275, 280, 39 South. 61; Spragins v. McCaleb, 188 South. 251.

[88] Conowingo Land Co. v. McGaw, 124 Md. 543, 93 Atl. 222.

[89] Aycock Supply Co., v. Windley, 176 N.C. 18, 19, 96 S.E. 664.

[90] Bovo v. Norton, 10 Ohio St. 514.

[91] Owen v. State, 25 Ind. 107.

[92] Farmers' Bank v. Raugust, 42 N.D. 503, 173 N.W. 793.

[93] Mattocks v. Bellamy, 8 Vt. 463.

[94] Bedell v. Smith, 23 Ala. 619; Day v. Baldwin, 34 Ia. 380.

[95] Smythe v. New Providence, 263 Fed. 481 (aff. 253 Fed. 824).

[96] Young v. Daley, 185 Fed. 209.

[97] Richardson v. Chanslor, 103 Ky. 425, 45 S.W. 774, 20 Ky. L. 121.

[98] Amy v. Dubuque, 98 U.S. 470, 25 L. Ed. 228.

[99] Koshkonong v. Burton, 104 U.S. 668, 26 L. Ed. 886 (mod. 4 Fed. 373); Clark v. Iowa City, 20 Wall. (U.S.) 583, 22 L. Ed. 427.

[100] Johnson v. Hesser, 61 Neb. 631, 85 N.W. 894.

[101] Matter of Boylan, 119 Misc. 545, 197 N.Y.S. 710.

[102] Priest v. Capitain (Mo.), 197 S.W. 83.

a specialty,[103] as is an action against the grantee on covenants in a deed accepted by him,[104] provided the deed is under seal.[105]

c. Written Contracts

206. Whether or not a time different from that for writings under seal is provided depends upon the jurisdiction. Where no limitation is specifically provided they are governed by the residuary clause explained below.[106] Such an action presupposes a writing evidencing an acknowledgement of indebtedness or promising to pay in such terms as to render any supplemental evidence unnecessary.[107] Written propositions accepted in writing constitute a contract in writing within this statute,[108] though the plaintiff may have to go beyond the terms of the writing to show performance on his part and breach on the part of the defendant.[109] Ratification of the act of an agent in making a written contract constitutes a written contract by the party ratifying.[110]

207. In some states it will be found that the period limited for an action not founded upon an instrument in writing is expressly extended to an action founded upon an instrument in writing executed out of the state.[111]

[103] Cf. Thomas v. Bland, 91 Ky. 1, 14 S.W. 955, 12 Ky. L. 640, 11 L.R.A. 240; Johnson v. Hesser, 61 Neb. 631, 85 N.W. 894.

[104] Anguish v. Blair, 160 App. Div. 52, 145 N.Y.S. 392 (aff. 216 N.Y. 746 mem., 111 N.E. 1084 mem.).

[105] Atlanta, etc., R. Co. v. McKinney, 124 Ga. 929, 53 S.E. 701, 110 Am. St. Rep. 215, 6 L.R.A. (N.S.) 436; Alropa Corp. v. Pomerance, 8 S.E. 2nd 62.

[106] Fowlkes v. Lea, 84 Miss. 509, 36 South. 1036, 2 Ann. Cas. 466, 68 L.R.A. 925 (foll. Washington v. Soria, 73 Miss. 665, 19 South. 485, 56 Am. St. Rep. 555; Rather v. Moore, 173 South. 664).

[107] Foote v. Farmer, 71 Miss. 148, 14 South. 445; Blount v. Miller, 160 South. 598.

[108] Patten v. Iroquois Furnace Co., 124 Ill. A. 1; Bayer v. Hindley, 222 Ill. 319, 78 N.E. 626.

[109] Curtis v. Sexton, 201 Mo. 217, 100 S.W. 17 (dist. Menefee v. Arnold, 51 Mo. 536, and Brady v. St. Joseph, 84 Mo. A. 399).

[110] Richardson v. Louisville, etc., R. Co., 129 Ky. 449, 111 S.W. 343, 33 Ky. L. 916, 112 S.W. 582, 33 Ky. L. 972.

[111] Sanford v. Bergin, 156 Cal. 43, 103 Pac. 333.

208. Examples of actions on written contracts are: 1—an action for specific performance of a written contract to sell or convey; [112] 2—an action to recover damages for breach of a written contract to sell or convey; [113] 3—an action to enforce a vendor's lien reserved in a deed of land; [114] 4—an action by a payee or indorsee of a check to recover thereon.[115]

209. When the statute provides a limitation for actions on bills of exchange, negotiable notes, orders, etc., it is not applicable to notes not transferable by indorsement or delivery, which are under the longer period established for written instruments and evidences of indebtedness.[116]

210. Attested notes, i. e., such as were signed in the presence of an attesting witness,[117] are in some states provided for specifically in the statute of limitations.

211. A receipt or written contract acknowledging the receipt of money and promising to repay it is within the limitation prescribed by statute for actions on instruments for the payment of money generally.[118]

d. Unwritten Contracts

212. The limitation on the actions on these contracts is usually shorter than on those regarding instruments in writing [119] and those regarding specialties.[120] Within this shorter period one must usually bring also an action on an obligation created or implied by law,

[112] Luco v. Toro, 91 Cal. 405, 18 Pac. 866, 27 Pac. 1082.

[113] Ames v. Moir, 130 Ill. 582, 22 N.E. 535 (aff. 27 Ill. A. 88).

[114] Elliott v. Saufley, 89 Ky. 52, 11 S.W. 200, 10 Ky. L. 958; First Nat'l Bank of Berwin v. Raymer, 71 Pac. 2nd 485.

[115] Connor v. Becker, 56 Neb. 343, 76 N.W. 893 (dist. Platt v. Black, 10 O. Cir. Ct. 499, 6 Oh. Circ. Dec. 817).

[116] New Orleans v. Warner, 175 U.S. 120, 20 Sup. Ct. 44, 44 L. Ed. 96 (mod. 81 Fed. 645, 26 C.C.A. 508); Goodall v. Tucker, 13 How. (U.S.) 469, 14 L. Ed. 227.

[117] Daggett v. Daggett, 124 Mass. 149.

[118] Moorman v. Sharp, 35 Mo. 283; Reyburn v. Casey, 29 Mo. 129.

[119] Baker v. Bundy, 55 Ind. A. 272, 103 N.E. 668.

[120] Matter of Hibbard, 89 Misc. 707, 153 N.Y.S. 1097, 14 Mills Surr. 124.

which is often termed a "quasi contract." [121] A claim for contribution is likewise subject to this limitation.[122]

e. Accounts

213. The Statute 21 James I provided that all actions of account other than such as concern the trade of merchandise between merchant and merchant, etc., should be brought within six years next after the cause of such action, and not after.[123] Statutes have been adopted in the various states providing after this pattern a limitation for actions on accounts,[124] and providing that actions on open, unliquidated, mutual accounts shall be barred within a designated period from the accrual of the last item therein.[125]

214. An "account," while not easy of definition, may be said to imply a dealing between parties involving reciprocal debits and credits or in which the debt is increased from time to time, or in which goods are sold on credit, or something similar.[126] Hence, charges arising by statute, not from contract, are not within this provision of the statute.[127]

An "open account" may be said to be one in which some term of the contract is not settled by the parties,[128] or in which there are current dealings and the account is kept open because of some contemplated future dealings, whether the account consists of one or more items.[129] This account must be mutual,[130] open and current between the parties to come within this provision of the statute,[131]

[121] Tietjen v. Heberlein, 54 Mont. 486, 171 Pac. 928.

[122] Hinshaw v. Warren, 167 Mo. A. 365, 151 S.W. 497; Fairies v. Cockerell, 88 Tex. 428, 31 S.W. 190, 639, 28 L.R.A. 528; Gregg v. Carroll, 201 Mo. A. 473, 211 S.W. 824; Mann v. Bradshaw, 136 Va. 351, 377, 118 S.E. 326.

[123] Cottam v. Partridge, 4 M. & G. 271, 43 Eng. C. L. 146, 134 Reprint 111, 16 Eng. R. C. 179.

[124] Cf. various statutes.

[125] Courson v. Courson, 19 Oh. St. 454.

[126] Illinois Cent. R. Co. v. Segari, 205 Fed. 998.

[127] Hildebrand v. Kinney, 172 Ind. 447, 87 N.E. 832, 19 Ann. Cas. 788; *In re* Beaseley's Estate, 11 N.E. 2nd 60.

[128] National Lumber Co. v. Tejunga Valley Rock Co., 22 Cal. A. 726, 730, 136 Pac. 508.

[129] New Orleans, etc., R. Co. v. Lindsay, 4 Wall. (U.S.) 650, 18 L. Ed. 328.

[130] Todd v. Todd, 15 Ala. 743, 745.

[131] Hebinger v. Ross, 175 Mich. 241, 141 N.W. 629.

and transactions treated by the parties as distinct from each other do not constitute such an open account.[132] It is not the same as the statutory account between "merchant and merchant."[133] Money lent or advanced may constitute part of such an account.[134]

A "book account" within the meaning of the statute is not a series of book entries of charges against, and credits in favor of, one party alone.[135]

An "open book account" mentioned in a statute does not include an account upon which no money payment has been made.[136]

A "merchant's account" is sometimes distinguished in the statutes from an account "between merchant and merchant."[137]

A "store account" when mentioned in a statute is not confined to that of a keeper of a retail store, but may include sales by a wholesaler to a retailer.[138]

"Accounts between merchants" which were expressly excepted from the limitation in 21 James I are in this country either excepted or specifically provided for.[139] The business which constitutes this type of account must be not only between two merchants, but they must be the plaintiff and defendant in the case in which this issue is raised.[140]

An "account stated," where it is provided for in a statute, means an agreement between persons who have had previous transactions fixing the amount due in respect of such transactions. The period depends on whether the statement is written or verbal.[141]

132 Houghton v. Keveney, 230 Mass. 49, 119 N.E. 447.

133 Russell v. Robertson, 1 U.C. Q.B. 235.

134 Moreland v. Dickerson, etc., Lumber Co., 12 Ala. A. 576, 68 South. 526.

135 Wright v. Loaiza, 177 Cal. 605, 171 Pac. 311 (rev. [A.] 166 Pac. 369, and quot. Furlow Pressed Brick Co. v. Balboa Land, etc., Co., 186 Cal. 754, 200 Pac. 625, 627).

136 Merchants' Collection Agency v. Levi, 32 Cal. A. 595, 163 Pac. 870.

137 Hetterman v. Oil Well Supply Co., 185 Ky. 290, 214 S.W. 923.

138 Salomon v. Pioneer Co-op. Co., 21 Fla. 374, 384, 58 Am. Rep. 667.

139 Hearn v. Van Ingen, 7 Bush (Ky.) 426.

140 Blair v. Drew, 6 N.H. 235; Bradford v. Spyker, 32 Ala. 134; Mattern v. McDivitt, 113 Pa. 402, 6 Atl. 83; Spring v. Gray, 6 Pet. (U.S.) 151, 8 L. Ed. 352 (aff. 22 Fed. Cas. No. 13,259, 5 Mas. 305) (under the Maine statute).

141 Thompson v. Fisher, 13 Pa. 310.

Article 5. Torts

215. Though "tort" is sometimes expressly mentioned, generally the statutes include these actions in some specified descriptions of causes of action. When the tort may be waived and suit brought in assumpsit, this will lie even though the limitation on the action sounding in tort may have run.[142] The nature of the grievance, not the form of action, determines whether the action is *ex delicto* or *ex contractu*.[143]

The statute 21 James I limited actions on the case,[144] other than slander, to six years from the time the cause of action accrued.[145] This remains in some of our states,[146] but usually the statutes describe these actions differently with different periods of limitation provided.

216. "Offenses" or "quasi-offenses" limited in Louisiana to one year [147] are such as arise from the infringement of some right personal to the individual,[148] or relating to his property,[149] or the violation of some duty imposed by law.[150]

217. An action on a "liability" not founded upon a writing [151] is in some states applied to actions for various torts not otherwise

[142] Frankfort Land Co. v. Hughett, 137 Tenn. 32, 191 S.W. 530; cf. canon 1704, 1°.

[143] Ft. Smith, etc., R. Co. v. Ford, 34 Okl. 575, 126 Pac. 745, 41 L.R.A. (N.S.) 745 (foll. Herron v. Miller, 96 Okl. 59, 220 Pac. 36).

[144] This is a form of action which lies to recover damages for injuries for which the more ancient forms of action will not lie. It is distinguished from assumpsit and covenant, in that it is not founded upon any contract, express or implied; from trover, which lies only for unlawful conversion; from detinue and replevin, in that it lies for injuries committed without force; and from trespass because it lies for forcible injuries which damage the plaintiff consequentially only, and in other respects.

[145] Lamb v. Walker, 3 Q.B.D. 389.

[146] Cf. various statutes; Shippen v. Tankersley, 13 Fed. 537, 4 McCrary 259 (Colorado statute).

[147] Goodwin v. Bodcaw Lumber Co., 109 La. 1050, 34 South. 74.

[148] Sims v. New Orleans R., etc., Co., 134 La. 897, 64 South. 823.

[149] Sims v. New Orleans R., etc., Co., 134 La. 897, 64 South. 823.

[150] Sims v. New Orleans R., etc., Co., 134 La. 897, 64 South. 823.

[151] Cf. various statutes.

specifically limited.[152] Usually, however, this term designates a contractual liability, not one arising from a negligent act.[153]

218. In Texas "debt" may embrace demands for unliquidated damages, though the cause of action for such damages does not rest in contract.[154]

219. An action for injuries to the person, if not specifically mentioned, is covered by the limitation applicable to actions for injury to the rights of another not arising from contract,[155] or by the residuary section of the statute. The period is usually shorter than that for an action on a contract.[156] Ordinarily the statute applies only to an action by the one whose person suffered the injury.[157]

Included under the action for injuries to the person are: 1—an action by a husband for a hurt to his wife; [158] 2—an action for seduction brought by the woman seduced,[159] or by a father for the seduction of his daughter.[160]

[152] St. Louis, etc., R. Co. v. Mynott, 83 Ark. 6, 102 S.W. 380; Kansas City Southern R. Co. v. Akin, 138 Ark. 10, 210 S.W. 350; Enrich v. Little Rock Tract., etc., Co., 71 Ark. 71, 70 S.W. 1035; Lowe v. Ozmun, 137 Cal. 257, 70 Pac. 87; Wood v. Currey, 57 Cal. 208; McCusker v. Walker, 77 Cal. 208, 119 Pac. 382 (foll. Sharp v. Miller, 57 Cal. 431); Taylor v. Bidwell, 65 Cal. 489, 4 Pac. 491; Daneri v. Southern California R. Co., 122 Cal. 507, 55 Pac. 243; Bonam v. Southern Menhaden Corp., 284 Fed. 362 (Florida).

[153] Northern Grain, etc., Co. v. Holst, 95 Wash. 312, 163 Pac. 775.

[154] Gordon v. Rhodes, 102 Tex. 300, 301, 116 S.W. 40.

[155] Cf. various statutes.

[156] The reason is clearly stated in Borchert v. Bash, 97 Neb. 593, 595, 150 N.W. 830, Ann. Cas. 1917A 116: "It is significant that libel, slander, assault and battery, malicious prosecution, and false imprisonment—all personal wrongs—are included in the one year statute. The legislature evidently thought that the public interest requires a prompt prosecution of such actions. Charges of this nature are easily made and difficult to defend against, and the lapse of more than one year after the alleged occurrence of the wrong allows time for the dispersion of witnesses, and makes the difficulty of defending such actions much greater."

[157] Sherman House Hotel Co. v. Butler St. Fdy., etc., Co., 168 Ill. A. 549.

[158] Mullen v. New Castle, 180 Ind. 386, 103 N.E. 1.

[159] May v. Wilson, 164 Mich. 26, 28, 128 N.W. 1084, Ann. Cas. 1912B 654.

[160] Hutcherson v. Durden, 113 Ga. 987, 39 S.E. 495, 54 L.R.A. 811.

"Assault and battery" is confined to an injury intentionally administered to the person.[161]

220. If the action on grounds of fraud and deceit is not specifically provided for, or covered by the phrase "injury to the rights of another," [162] it is governed by the residuary clause.

221. An action of trover has been held to be governed by the limitation applying to "actions for taking or injuring" personal property; [163] on the other hand it has been said that the wrongful conversion of personal property does not necessarily cause injury to the property.[164] The tort in the conversion of property may be waived and an action *ex contractu* maintained for its value, in some jurisdictions, and then the limitation on that type of contract action applies,[165] even if the limitation has run on the tort action and in that jurisdiction the title to the property has vested in the tortfeasor before suit is brought.[166]

222. When the statute provides a limitation for actions for "injury to property" this means: 1—an action for even a single trespass upon land where physical injury is done; [167] 2—an action to abate a private nuisance; [168] 3—an action for fraud and deceit whereby plaintiff incurred financial loss; [169] 4—an action for overflowing land.[170]

[161] Donner v. Graap, 134 Wis. 523, 115 N.W. 125.

[162] Cf. various statutes.

[163] Lowe v. Ozmun, 137 Cal. 257, 70 Pac. 87.

[164] Hicks v. Moyer, 10 Ga. A. 488, 489, 73 S.E. 754.

[165] Kirchner v. Smith, 28 Oh. Cir. Ct. 45.

[166] McCombs v. Guild, 9 Lea (Tenn.) 81.

[167] Kauha v. Palolo Land, etc., Co., Ltd., 20 Hawaii 237.

[168] McClusker v. Wile, 70 Misc. 135, 128 N.Y.S. 190 (rev. on other grounds 144 App. Div. 470, 129 N.Y.S. 455); cf. canon 1678.

[169] Crawford v. Crawford, 134 Ga. 114, 67 S.E. 673, 28 L.R.A. (N.S.) 353, 19 Ann. Cas. 932. This is more usually an action for injury to "property," not to the person.

[170] Lucas v. Marine, 40 Ind. 289. When this does not result in absolute destruction of any part of the plaintiff's land—Hill v. Empire State-Idaho Min., etc., Co., 158 Fed. 881 (dist. Atkinson v. Amador, etc., Canal Co., 53 Cal. 102)—it may be included under the limitation on an action upon a "liability," etc.—Daneri v. Southern California R. Co., 122 Cal. 507, 55 Pac. 243—or that for "injury to rights of another"—Eagle, etc., Mfg. Co. v. Gibson, 62 Ala. 369.

223. When the statute provides a limitation on an action for taking personal property it includes under this description an action against a judgment creditor for directing a levy and sale under execution of exempt personal property.[171]

224. When the statute limits actions for "trespass upon real property" or "trespass to real or personal property" this usually means "trespass" as understood at Common Law.[172] This statute does not cover: 1—an exclusively statutory proceeding; [173] 2—an action for consequential damages; [174] 3—an action which at Common Law was on the case.[175]

225. A provision concerning "taking or injuring property without compensation" applies also to the taking of property by eminent domain without condemnation, and when adverse possession of the property in question is complete it bars a constitutional right to demand such compensation,[176] as a rule,[177] though the authorities are in conflict.

226. Actions against persons in their official capacity are frequently treated as *ex delicto*, and governed by the limitation applicable to other actions on the case,[178] unless some other limitation is provided specifically. Actions against such an official on his bond may likewise be considered *ex contractu* for misfeasance, malfeasance, or nonfeasance of office, in which case they are limited as are contract actions.[179] They may likewise be treated as actions upon liabilities created by statute and the limitation for such actions then applies.

[171] Snow v. West, 35 Utah 206, 99 Pac. 674, 136 Am. St. Rep. 1047; cf. canon 1923.

[172] O'Neill v. San Pedro, etc., R. Co., 38 Utah 375, 114 Pac. 127.

[173] Delaware, etc., R. Co. v. Burson, 61 Pa. 369.

[174] Hill v. Empire State-Idaho Min., etc., Co., 158 Fed. 881 (Idaho statute).

[175] Roundtree v. Grantley, 34 Ala. 544, 73 Am. Dec. 470.

[176] Johnson v. Hawthorne Ditch Co., 32 S.D. 499, 143 N.W. 959.

[177] Cf. Aylmore v. Seattle, 99 Wash. 515, 171 Pac. 659, L.R.A. 1918E 127.

[178] Cockrill v. Cooper, 86 Fed. 7, 29 C.C.A. 529 (rev. 78 Fed. 679).

[179] Cf. canons 1521-1528, 1534-1536.

ARTICLE 6. LIABILITIES CREATED BY STATUTE

227. There are liabilities which would not exist but for the statute,[180] e. g., statutory duty of a railroad to give shippers equality of switch track connections,[181] action to collect an ordinary tax,[182] action against a county based on injuries due to a defective bridge.[183]

In the absence of an express provision this action has sometimes [184] been held to be included under the limitation of actions on specialties.[185]

228. Other actions on "liabilities" sometimes included here are: 1—an action against a public officer; [186] 2—an action on the bond of a guardian, executor, or administrator; [187] 3—an action for official salaries or statutory fees; [188] 4—an action against a stockholder for a debt of a corporation; [189] 5—an action for injury to property, when the liability is created by statute; [190] 6—an action upon a statute for penalty or forfeiture.[191]

ARTICLE 7. EQUITABLE ACTIONS AND REMEDIES

229. Equity in the past has by analogy applied the limitations existing at law,[192] though not too rigorously.[193] Nowadays, many

180 Hocking Valley R. Co. v. New York Coal Co., 217 Fed. 727, 132 C.C.A. 387.

181 Hocking Valley R. Co. v. New York Coal Co., 217 Fed. 727, 132 C.C.A. 387.

182 Bristol v. Washington County, 177 U.S. 153, 20 Sup. Ct. 585, 44 L. Ed. 701 (foll. Redwood County v. Winona, etc., Land Co., 40 Minn. 512, 41 N.W. 465, 42 N.W. 473 [aff. 159 U.S. 526, 16 Sup. Ct. 83, 40 L. Ed. 247]).

183 Hollinger v. Dickinson County, 115 Kan. 92, 222 Pac. 136.

184 Little v. Kohn, 185 Fed. 295.

185 Watson v. Jersey City, 84 N.J.L. 422, 86 Atl. 402, L.R.A. 1916C 1106.

186 Graham County v. Van Slyck, 52 Kan. 622, 35 Pac. 299; People v. Van Ness, 76 Cal. 121, 18 Pac. 139.

187 Hawk v. Sayler, 83 Kan. 775, 112 Pac. 602, (foll. Davis v. Clark, 58 Kan. 454, 49 Pac. 665).

188 Outwater v. Passaic, 51 N.J.L. 345, 18 Atl. 164.

189 Davis v. Drury, 105 Kan. 69, 181 Pac. 559.

190 Cf. various statutes.

191 Frizell Grain, etc., Co. v. Atchison, etc., R. Co., (Mo.), 201 S.W. 78; Fuson v. Stewart, 137 Ky. 748, 126 S.W. 1097.

192 Hotchkin v. McNaught-Collins Impr. Co., 102 Wash. 161, 172 Pac. 864, 865 (ct. Cyc.); Nichols v. Nichols, 79 Conn. 644, 66 Atl. 161.

193 Smith v. Griswold, 161 Ill. A. 483.

states have by statute made limitations to suits at law equally applicable to those in equity,[194] or made special limitations for such suits,[195] or included them in the residuary section.

230. Where Law and Equity have concurrent jurisdiction some states hold equity is bound to apply the limitations as at law.[196] The limitation is not here applied by analogy but in obedience to the statute itself.[197]

231. Frequently the statutes provide a special period of limitation [198] for an "action for relief on the ground of fraud or mistake," and provide that the cause of action shall not be deemed to have accrued until the discovery of the fraud, though it is sometimes provided that in no event shall the action be maintained after the lapse of a prescribed period.

232. Such a statute as was mentioned above applies: (a) to suits in equity such as: 1—an action to cancel a deed for fraud; [199] 2—an action to cancel securities fraudulently issued by a corporation to its promoters; [200] 3—an action to set aside a fraudulent conveyance; [201] 4—an action to enforce a trust *ex maleficio;* [202] (b) to suits at law such as: 1—an action for a money judgment on the grounds of fraud,[203] at least when fraud must be proved to support recovery in any form of action; [204] 2—an action to recover money obtained by duress; [205] 3—an action on grounds of undue influence.[206]

[194] Cf. various statutes.

[195] Williams v. Thrall, 167 Wis. 410, 167 N.W. 825.

[196] Sullivan v. Portland, etc., R. Co., 94 U.S. 806, 24 L. Ed. 324 (aff. 23 Fed. Cas. No. 13,596, 4 Cliff. 212).

[197] Carrol v. Green, 92 U. S. 509, 23 L. Ed. 728.

[198] Cf. various statutes.

[199] Tucker v. Tucker, 201 Ky. 383, 257 S.W. 46.

[200] Beal v. Smith, 46 Cal. A. 271, 189 Pac. 341.

[201] Davey v. Dodge, 213 Fed. 722, 130 C.C.A. 236 (Nebraska statute).

[202] Kissane v. Brewer, 208 Mo. A. 244, 232 S.W. 1106.

[203] Johnson v. Equitable L. Assur. Soc., 137 Ky. 437, 125 S.W. 1074.

[204] Orozem v. McNeill, 103 Kan. 429, 175 Pac. 633, 3 A.L.R. 1598.

[205] Jett v. Jett, 171 Ky. 548, 188 S.W. 669.

[206] Jett v. Jett, 171 Ky. 548, 188 S.W. 669.

This statute also applies to an action to reform an instrument on grounds of mistake.[207] It does not, however, apply when the relief on grounds of mistake is merely incidental to,[208] or involved in,[209] another and real cause of action.

233. The statute in question does not, however, apply: 1—when no relief of any kind is asked against the defendant because of his fraud; [210] 2—when the case is not dependent upon proof of fraud; [211] 3—when the action is for mere breach of warranty; [212] 4—when the action affects real estate,[213] and is not a personal action; 5—when fraud was perpetrated by one in a fiduciary relationship to the one defrauded; [214] 6—When the action for relief is on the ground of duress by threats.[215]

234. Trusts which are direct, technical, and continuing,[216] and which are in no way cognizable at law cannot be reached or affected by the statute of limitations.[217] It is sometimes expressly provided that the statute shall not apply to a case of technical and subsisting trusts.[218] Nevertheless, the rule that the limitations at law apply to equity wherever there is a concurrent remedy at law is very generally held applicable in favor of a cestui que trust [219] seeking equitable relief against a trustee in the case of a trust not falling within the peculiar and exclusive jurisdiction of the courts of equity.[220]

[207] Hart v. Walton, 9 Cal. A. 502, 99 Pac. 719.

[208] Banks v. Stockton, 149 Cal. 599, 87 Pac. 83.

[209] Taylor v. McCowen, 154 Cal. 798, 99 Pac. 351.

[210] Boyer v. Barrows, 166 Cal. 757, 138 Pac. 354.

[211] Barlow v. Hitzler, 40 Col. 109, 90 Pac. 90.

[212] Murphy v. Stelling, 8 Cal. A. 702, 97 Pac. 672.

[213] Empire Ranch, etc., Co. v. Zehr, 54 Col. 185, 129 Pac. 828.

[214] Ballard v. Golob, 34 Col. 417, 83 Pac. 376.

[215] Eureka Bank v. Bay, 90 Kan. 506, 135 Pac. 584.

[216] Thomas v. Brinsfield, 7 Ga. 154, 158.

[217] Harris v. Doyle, 9 Ky. Ap. 327, because a cause of action does not accrue while there is a continuing trust; cf. *supra*, n. 19.

[218] Cf. various statutes.

[219] Beneficiary.

[220] This distinction will be treated by writers on the American Law regarding Trusts, q.v.

235. Specific performance in some jurisdictions is not covered by the general statute of limitations,[221] but in others it is held that, if the analogous claim is barred at law, a bill for specific performance will be dismissed.[222] At other times it is held that actions for specific performance are governed by the residuary section of the statute.[223] Actions for specific performance of contracts of conveyance of real estate are sometimes expressly limited by the statute.[224]

236. Reformation of an instrument will be barred, even where the statute of limitations is looked upon merely as a guide to the discretion of the court, if between the filing of the bill and discovery of the mistake, or when by the use of due diligence it should have been discovered, the time has run.[225]

237. A limitation of actions "for the nullity or rescission [226] of contracts, testaments or other acts" applies only to: 1—contracts having a real existence; [227] 2—an action to rescind a contract for causes patent on the face of the record and where there is no actual fraud; [228] 3—an action to annul and cancel a dation en paiement except as to allegations of fraud and simulation.[229] This "dation en paiement" is a giving by the debtor and receipt by the creditor of something in payment of a debt instead of a sum of money. It is a Civil Law term.

It does not apply to: 1—contracts absolutely void [230] and not susceptible of ratification; [231] 2—public sales or judicial transfers.[232]

In some states an equitable action for rescission of a contract on

[221] Swan v. Shanahan, 1 Oh. Circ. Ct. 216, 1 Oh. Cir. Dec. 119.

[222] Castner v. Walrod, 83 Ill. 171, 25 Am. Rep. 369.

[223] Amundson v. Severson, 41 S.D. 337, 170 N.W. 633.

[224] Cubit v. Jackson (Tex. Civ. A.) 194 S.W. 594.

[225] Oakes v. Howell, 27 How. Pr. (N.Y.) 145.

[226] Cf. canon 1684, § 1.

[227] Welch v. Forest Lumber Co., 151 La. 960, 92 South. 400.

[228] Strong v. Haynes, 152 La. 695, 94 South. 322.

[229] Lewis v. Lewis, 129 La. 638, 56 South. 621.

[230] Cf. canons 1679-1680.

[231] Welch v. Forest Lumber Co., 151 La. 960, 92 South. 400.

[232] Brewer v. Brewer, 145 La. 835, 83 South. 30.

the ground of fraud,[233] is governed by the residuary clause or section of the statute of limitation.[234]

238. A limitation of actions "for the reduction of excessive donations" applies to the action of forced heirs to reduce a donation that trenches on their legitime,[235] and to an action in reduction of the donation made by a father in favor of his concubine and his bastard children, in fraud of the rights of his forced heirs.[236] "Forced heirs," in Louisiana, are those persons whom the testator or donor cannot deprive of the portion of his estate reserved for them by law, except in cases in which he has a just cause to disinherit them.[236a] Louisiana Civil Code, 1493-5, 1502.

239. Bills filed to establish a lost deed, or will, have been held not included in the statute of limitation.[237]

A vendor's lien for the unpaid purchase money, despite the fact that an action at law is barred by the statute, is not lost or destroyed.[238]

240. Some states hold that when the mortgagee's right of action on the debt is barred his right to foreclose in equity is likewise barred, while others hold that the bar of the suit at law is no defense to a suit in equity to enforce the lien.[239]

241. As a rule courts of equity seem to follow the limitations at law as to the right to redeem mortgaged property,[240] though some have held that the limitation does not run in favor of the mortgagee.[241]

[233] Cf. canon 1684, § 1.

[234] Cf. various statutes.

[235] Meisner's Succ., 121 La. 863, 46 South. 889.

[236] Malbrough v. Roundtree, 128 La. 39, 54 South. 463.

[236a] Louisiana Civil Code, 1493-5, 1502.

[237] Rockwell v. Servant, 54 Ill. 251.

[238] Randall v. Jaques, 20 Fed. Cas. No. 11,553.

[239] Stringer v. Stevens, 146 Mich. 181, 109 N.W. 269, 117 Am. St. Rep. 620, 8 L.R.A. (N.S.) 393, 10 Ann. Cas. 337 (obiter); Weber v. Ryan, 54 Mich. 70, 19 N.W. 751.

[240] Dexter v. Arnold, 7 Fed. Cas. No. 3,859, 3 Sumn. (U.S.) 152.

[241] Wood v. Jones, Meigs (Tenn.) 513.

242. A bill in equity for an accounting may be limited by the limitations at law on accounts, by judicial precedent,[242] or by express statute.[243]

ARTICLE 8. RESIDUARY CLAUSE

243. Most jurisdictions have in their statute of limitations a residuary clause covering actions or proceedings not specifically provided for. The scope of such a clause varies according to the number of provisions specifically excluded by the terms of the section.[244] It has been held to apply to: 1—an action for rescission of a contract on the ground of fraud; [245] 2—an action for the reformation of an instrument on the ground of mistake; [246] 3—an action to set aside a deed on the ground of infancy; [247] 4—an action of account or for an accounting [248] when there was a trust relationship between the parties; [249] 5—an action for the establishment or enforcement of a trust [250] not based on actual fraud,[251] and even though an accounting is asked for as merely incidental to the action; [252] 6—an action or proceeding for the partition of land; [253] 7—a creditors' bill [254] or a bill in the nature of a creditors' bill; [255] 8—an action to redeem from a tax sale; [256] 9—an action to vacate a judgment; [257] 10—an action of creditors to charge a decedent's estate or the de-

[242] Livingston v. Story, 11 Pet. (U.S.) 351, 9 L. Ed. 746.

[243] Cf. various statutes.

[244] Cf. various statutes.

[245] Wolf v. Schmidt, 15 Daly 107, 2 N.Y.S. 705.

[246] Pierce v. Vansell, 35 Ind. A. 525, 74 N.E. 554.

[247] Henson v. Culp, 157 Ky. 442, 163 S.W. 455.

[248] Big Sespe Oil Co. v. Cochran, 276 Fed. 216 (California statute).

[249] McArthur v. Blaisdell, 159 Cal. 604, 115 Pac. 52.

[250] Taylor v. Calvert, 138 Ind. 67, 37 N.E. 531.

[251] Finnegan v. McGuffog, 139 App. Div. 899, 123 N.Y.S. 539 (aff. 203 N.Y. 342, 96 N.E. 1015).

[252] Hannah v. Canty, 175 Cal. 763, 167 Pac. 373.

[253] McCray v. Humes, 116 Ind. 103, 18 N.E. 500.

[254] Sherman v. S.K.D. Oil Co., 185 Cal. 534, 197 Pac. 799 (obiter).

[255] Sherman v. S.K.D. Oil Co., 185 Cal. 534, 197 Pac. 799.

[256] Gibson v. Bernstein, 72 Ind. A. 681, 126 N.E. 491.

[257] Hynes v. M.J. & M.M. Consolidated, 168 Cal. 651, 144 Pac. 144.

visee; [258] 11—an action (statutory) against a devisee to enforce his liability as a stockholder of an insolvent bank; [259] 12—an action (statutory) to charge the defendant's property on an unpaid judgment against him and a joint debtor; [260] 13—an action in equity to subject the estate of a married woman to satisfaction of her indebtedness; [261] 14—an action by the state to set aside the purchase by executors or trustees of land sought to be condemned; [262] 15—an equitable action to abate or enjoin a nuisance; [263] 16—an action to compel issuance of a new bond in place of a lost original; [264] 17—proceedings by mandamus for the enforcement of a substantial right; [265] 18—an action for separation on ground of cruelty; [266] 19—an action for consequential damages to real property as distinguished from an action of trespass; [267] 20—a statutory remedy by writ for assessment of damages for a right of way taken by a railroad company; [268] 21—an action by a passenger against a carrier for personal injuries caused by negligence; [269] 22—a proceeding to probate a will,[270] although the contrary has been held.[271] In some jurisdictions it has been held applicable to all purely equitable actions,[272] including those concerning the right to possession of land.[273]

Where special proceedings are not considered an "action" they

[258] Mortimer v. Chambers, 63 Hun (N.Y.) 335, 17 N.Y.S. 874.

[259] Richards v. Gill, 138 App. Div. 75, 122 N.Y.S. 620.

[260] Hofferberth v. Nash, 191 N.Y. 446, 84 N.E. 400 (aff. 117 App. Div. 284, 102 N.Y.S. 317, 38 N.Y. Civ. Proc. 259).

[261] Mathers v. Hewitt, 8 Oh. Dec. (Reprint) 616, 9 Cin. L. Bul. 63.

[262] New York Cent., etc., R. Co. v. Cottle, 102 Misc. 30, 168 N.Y.S. 463 (aff. 187 App. Div. 131, 175 N.Y.S. 178).

[263] Thornton v. Webb, 13 Minn. 498.

[264] Pensacola, etc., R. Co. v. Hilton, 147 Ky. 553, 144 S.W. 1077.

[265] State v. Ralston, 182 Ind. 150, 105 N.E. 54.

[266] Sturm v. Sturm, 80 Misc. 277, 141 N.Y.S. 61.

[267] Boise Dev. Co. v. Boise City, 30 Ida. 675, 167 Pac. 1032.

[268] Shortle v. Terre Haute, etc., R. Co., 131 Ind. 338, 30 N.E. 1084.

[269] Thomas v. Union Pac. R. Co., 1 Utah 235.

[270] Combs v. Jent, 164 Ky. 536, 175 S.W. 1031.

[271] *In re* Hume, 179 Cal. 338, 176 Pac. 681.

[272] Piller v. Southern Pac. R. Co., 52 Cal. 42, 44 (foll. Dore v. Thornburgh, 90 Cal. 64, 27 Pac. 30, 25 Am. St. Rep. 100).

[273] Hubbell v. Sibley, 50 N.Y. 468.

are likewise not considered to be within the residuary section,[274] but some states have special provisions for special remedies and proceedings,[275] while others do not.

Article 9. Defenses

244. Pure defenses [276] are not barred by the statute of limitations,[277] including a defense to a counter-claim for affirmative relief.[278] The defense of reduction or recoupment which arises out of the same transaction [279] as the note or claim survives as long as the cause of action upon the note or claim exists, although an affirmative action upon the subject of it may be barred by the statute of limitations.[280] On the other hand, in the absence of statutory provisions to the contrary, a set-off [281] or a counter-claim not available as a defense in any other way than by counter-claim [282] may be barred by the statute of limitations.

Article 10. Different Limitations on the Same Action or Proceeding

245. In the event that different limitations are applicable on the same action or proceeding it is held under the American Law that the limitation should be based on the longest term given by

[274] Thomas v. Williams, 80 Kan. 632, 103 Pac. 772, 25 L.R.A. (N.S.) 1304.

[275] Cf. various statutes.

[276] If a defendant pleads not a defense but a cause of action it may be barred under the statute—Ft. Smith v. Fairbanks, 101 Tex. 24, 102 S.W. 908.

[277] Robinson v. Glass, 94 Ind. 211; cf. canon 1667.

[278] Pinkham v. Pinkham, 61 Neb. 336, 85 N.W. 285.

[279] Recoupment as now understood under the American Law seems to correspond to the reconvention of the Civil Law. Cf. canon 1670, § 2.

[280] Williams v. Neely, 134 Fed. 1, 67 C.C.A. 171.

[281] Kincade v. Peck, 193 Mich. 207, 159 N.W. 480.

[282] Muckenthaler v. Noller, 104 Kan. 551, 180 Pac. 453; Wonnacott v. Kootenai County, 32 Ida. 342, 182 Pac. 353; Nelson v. Gulf, etc., R. Co., (Tex. Civ. A.), 214 S.W. 366; Utah Commercial, etc., Bank v. Fox, 44 Utah 323, 140 Pac. 660.

statute to bring the suit.[283] If, however, the court is satisfied that the shorter period should be applied, it may do so.[284] In any event, when the longest limitation has run, the suit is certainly barred.[285]

[283] Adelbert College v. Toledo, etc., R. Co., 13 Oh. Cir. Ct. 590, 591, 5 Oh. Cir. Dec. 240.

[284] Sonoma County v. Hall, 132 Cal. 589, 62 Pac. 257, 312, 65 Pac. 12, 459.

[285] Waymire v. Waymire, 144 Ind. 329, 43 N.E. 267.

TABLE OF PERIODS REQUIRED

	ADVERSE POSSESSION			LIMITATION OF ACTIONS														
	Realty	*Personalty*	*Prescription*	*Specialties*	*Written Contracts*	*Prom. Notes (Unsecd.)*	*Oral Contracts*	*Accounts*	*Fraud and Deceit*	*Taking Personalty*	*Trespass*	*Nonfeas., Malfeas., Misfeas. Officer*	*Stat. Liability*	*Personal Inj.*	*Crim. con.; A & B, etc.*	*Judgment (dom.)*	*Judgment (for.)*	*Residuary Cl.*
Alabama	10[1]			10	6	6	6	3[2]			6[3]	10	1	2[4]	1	20[5]	20	1[6]
Alaska	7[7]	6		10	6	6	6	6		6	6	3[8]	6[9]	2	2	10	10	10[10]
Arizona	10[11]			6[12]	6	6	3	4[13]	3	2[14]	2[15]	5[16]	1	2		5	4	4
Arkansas	7[17]	3		5[18]	5	5	3	3		3	3	4[19]		3	1	10	10	5
California	5[20]	3		10[21]	4	4	2	4	3	3	3	2[22]	3[23]	1[24]		5	5	4
Colorado	18[25]	6		6	6	6	6[26]	6	3	6	6	1	2[27]	2	1	20[28]	6	5[29]
Connecticut	15	6	15	17[30]	6	6[31]	3	6	3	3	3	2[32]		1[33]	3	20[34]		3[35]
Delaware	20	3		20	6	6	3	3[36]		3	3	6[37]	3	1		5	5	
Dist. of Col.	15	3	15	12[38]	3	3	3	3			3[39]			1	1	12	20[40]	3
Florida	7[41]	3		20	5	5	3	3[42]	3[43]	3	3		3[44]		2	20	7	4
Georgia	20[45]	4		20	6	6	4	4			4[46]			2		10	5	4[47]
Hawaii	10			6	6	6	6	6			2			2		10[48]	6	
Idaho	5[49]	3		5	5	5	4	4	3[50]	3	3	2	3	2	2	6	6[51]	4
Illinois	20[52]	5		10	10	10	5	5	5[53]	5[54]	5[55]	3[56]	2[57]	1[58]	2	20[59]	5	5[60]
Indiana	20[61]	6		10[62]	10[62]	10	6	6	6	6[63]	6[63]	5	2[64]	2		20[65]	20	15
Iowa	10	5	10[66]	10	10	10	5	5	5[67]	5[68]	5[68]	3	2	2		20[69]	20	5
Kansas	15[70]	2		5	5	5	3	3	2[71]	2	2	5	3	2[72]	1	5	5	5
Kentucky	15[73]	5		15	15	15[74]	5	5[75]	10[76]	5[77]	5[77]	15	5[78]	1		15	10	10
Louisiana	10[79]	3[80]			10	5	1[81]	3								10	10[82]	1[83]
Maine	20[84]	6	20	20	6	6[85]	6	6		6[86]	6				2	20[87]	20	20[88]
Maryland	20[89]	3		12	3	3	3	3[90]		3[91]	3[91]	5	3	3[92]	1	12	12	3[93]
Massachusetts	20	6	20	20	6	6[94]	6	6				4[95]		2[96]	2	20[97]	20	20[98]
Michigan	15[99]	3		10	6	6	6	6		3	3	2	2[100]	3	2	10	10	
Minnesota	15	6	15	6	6	6	6	6	6	6	6	3	6[101]	6[102]	6[103]	10	10	
Mississippi	10[104]	3		6	6	6	3	3		6[105]	6[105]			1[106]	1	7	7[107]	6[108]
Missouri	10[109]	5		10	10	10	5	5	5[110]	5	5	3	5[111]	5	2	10	10	10[112]

TABLE OF PERIODS REQUIRED

	ADVERSE POSSESSION			LIMITATION OF ACTIONS														
	Realty	*Personalty*	*Prescription*	*Specialties*	*Written Contracts*	*Prom. Notes (Unsecd.)*	*Oral Contracts*	*Accounts*	*Fraud and Deceit*	*Taking Personalty*	*Trespass*	*Nonfeas., Malfeas. Misfeas. Officer*	*Stat. Liability*	*Personal Inj.*	*Crim. con.; A & B, etc.*	*Judgment (dom.)*	*Judgment (for.)*	*Residuary Cl.*
Montana	[113] 10	2		8	8	8	[114] 5	5	2	2	2	3		2	2	[115] 10	10	5
Nebraska	10	4		5	[116] 5	5	4	4	[117] 4	4	4	[118] 10	[119] 4	[120] 4	1	5	5	4
Nevada	[121] 5	3		6	6	6	4	4	[122] 3	3	3	2	[123] 3	[124] 2	2	6	6	4
New Hampshire .	20	6		20	6	[125] 6	6	6	6	6	6	6		2	2	20	20	6
New Jersey	20	6		16	6	6	6	6		6	6			2	2	20	[126] 6	
New Mexico	[127] 10	4		[128] 6	6	6	4	4	4	[129] 4	[129] 4	3		1		[130] 7	7	4
New York	[131] 15	6		6	6	6	6	6	[132] 6	3	[133] 3	3	6	[134] 6	2	[135] 20	20	10
North Carolina ..	[136] 20	3		10	3	3	3	3	[137] 3	3	[138] 3	[139] 6	3	3	[140] 1	[141] 10	10	10
North Dakota ..	[142] 20	6		[143] 6	6	6	6	6	[144] 6	6	6	3	[145] 6	[146] 6	2	10	[147] 10	[148] 6
Ohio	21	4		15	15	15	6	6	4	[149] 4	4	[150] 10	[151] 6	[152] 2	1	21	15	10
Oklahoma	15	2		5	5	5	3	3	[153] 2	2	2	5	[154] 3	[155] 2	1	5	1	[156] 5
Oregon	[157] 10	6		10	[158] 6	6	6	6	2	[159] 6	[159] 6	3	[160] 6	2		10	10	[161] 10
Pennsylvania ...	[162] 21	6	21	20	6	6	6	6		[163] 6	[163] 6			[164] 2		[165] 20	20	[166] 6
Puerto Rico	[167] 30	[168] 6																[169] 15
Rhode Island ...	10	6		20	6	6	6	[170] 6			4			2		20	20	
South Carolina .	[171] 10	6	[172] 20	[173] 20	6	6	6	6	[174] 6	6	6	3	[175] 6		[176] 6	20	20	10
South Dakota ..	[177] 10	6		20	6	6	6	6	[178] 6	6	6	3	[179] 6	3	[180] 6	20	10	10
Tennessee	[181] 7	10		6	6	6	6	6		[182] 3	[182] 3	[183] 10	[184] 1	1	1	10	10	10
Texas	[185] 25	4		4	4	4	2	[186] 4		2	2	[187] 5		2		10	[188] 10	4
Utah	[189] 7	3		6	6	6	4	[190] 4	[191] 3	3	3	2	[192] 3	[193] 4	1	8	8	4
Vermont	[194] 15	6		8	6	[195] 6	6	6			6				3	8	8	[196] 6
Virginia	[197] 15	5	20	[198] 10	5	[199] 5	3	[200] 3		[201] 5	[201] 5	[202] 10	[203] 2	[204] 1		10	10	[205] 5
Washington	[206] 7	3		6	6	6	3	3	[207] 3	3	3	3	[208] 3	3	2	6	6	[209] 2
West Virginia ...	10	5		10	10	10	5	5		[210] 5	[210] 5			[211] 2		10	[212] 10	[213,] 1
Wisconsin	[214] 10	6		[215] 20	6	6	6	6	[216] 6	6	6	3	[217] 6	[218] 6	2	[219] 20	10	[220,] 10
Wyoming	10	4	10	10	[221] 10	10	8			4	4	[222] 10	[223] 8	[224] 2	1	5	[225] 5	10

NOTES TO TABLE

1—This requires: (1) a deed or other color of title, recorded with the judge of probate for ten years before the action is commenced; (2) annual listing for ten years for taxation by the claimant or his predecessor; or (3) acquisition of title by descent cast or devise from a predecessor in title who was in possession. Adverse possession for three years entitles defendant in ejectment to the allowance of the value of permanent improvements in excess of the value of use and occupation. If the occupation was under color of title he will not be liable for damages nor for rent for more than one year.

2—This is for open, unliquidated, accounts. If they are stated, liquidated, the period is six years.

3—Includes trespass to persons or to personal or real property.

4—This covers actions by representatives to recover damages for wrongful act, omission, or negligence, resulting in death of the decedent.

5—This is true as to judgments in a court of record. In a court not of record or of a justice of the peace judgments are limited to a period of six years.

6—This is for any *tort* not specifically provided for.

7—An *action to recover* realty or possession thereof is limited to ten years.

8—This covers an action for escape.

9—Under a statute for penalty or forfeiture the period is three years, where the action is given to the party aggrieved and the United States. Where the action is given to the United States or to the Territory of Alaska, the period is two years. Where it is given in whole or in part to the person prosecuting, the period is one year.

10—Any action for any injury to the person or rights of another not arising on contract and not specifically enumerated is limited to two years.

11—Two years with claim of right of possession establishes the right against a suit to recover. Three years after the cause of action accrues with color of title suffices; five years after the cause of action accrued by person claiming under a recorded deed, except a forged deed, defeats an action for the property if the possession was peaceable, the land cultivated, the taxes paid. Ten years is the period if the possessor cultivated the land or used it, but this will not be good for more than 160 acres, or the number actually enclosed. If there is a written memorandum of title, other than a deed, it will be good for all the land within the boundaries, if fixed, and duly recorded. In the matter of city lots it is sufficient if there is claim of title under a recorded deed and the taxes were paid for five years next preceding the action.

12—In case of a written instrument, sealed or unsealed, executed out of the state the period is four years.

13—On accounts other than mutual and current accounts concerning trade between merchants, the period is three years.

14—I. e., injury to personal property as well as wrongful taking or detention.

15—I. e., injury to real property or trespass.

16—Against a sheriff or sureties for not returning execution.

17—Minors and insane persons have three years to act after removal of the disability.

18—On bonds of executors or administrators the period is eight years.

19—"Actions on official bonds."

20—This requires substantial enclosure, cultivation, payment of taxes. On an action by the state the period is ten years, by others, five.

21—On bonds or coupons issued by the State of California. Action on bonds, notes or debentures and their coupons by any corporation issued on a permit of the Commissioner of Corporations issued to or held by the public, excluding those of a public district or corporation is limited to six years.

22—On bond of a public official, if the cause of action is based on fraud or embezzlement, the period is three years. Two years is the period on liability of a sheriff, coroner, or constable, for acts or omissions in his official capacity, except for escape for which the period is one year.

23—I. e., other than penalty or forfeiture.

24—I. e., for most injuries to person or character.

25—Actual possession and payment of taxes for seven years under color of title, or payment of taxes alone for that period in case of vacant and unoccupied land, gives legal ownership according to paper title.

26—Action on contract not otherwise covered is limited to three years.

27—Other than forfeiture or penalty (one year), or if created by federal statute which prescribes no limitation.

28—Presumption of satisfaction after twenty years. Court not of record, judgment limited to six years.

29—1939, c. 125. Actions not otherwise provided for, three years. Escape against sheriff, six months. *Tort*, except as otherwise provided, six years.

30—Same for non-negotiable promissory note, though unsealed.

31—Same for implied contract.

32—I. e., in case of sheriff's, constable's, or deputy's negligence.

33—I. e., negligent injury to person or property.

34—*Prima facie* presumption of payment, cf. 74 Conn. 652.

35—I. e., for *torts* not otherwise specified.

36—If account is mutual and running, statute does not run while account is open and current.

37—I. e., on recognizance of sheriff, testamentary or administration bonds. Rec-

ognizance in orphan's court, guardian and official bonds (other than sheriff's) are limited to three years.
38—Executor's or administrator's bond, limited to five years.
39—On action to recover damages to real or personal property.
40—Presumption, cf. 26 D. C. App. 449.
41—Must pay taxes and special improvement liens.
42—If mutual account, runs from date of last item.
43—Runs from discovery.
44—If by another than the state for penalty or forfeiture, limit is two years.
45—Seven years under written evidence of title not known to be forged or fraudulent, gives title then by prescription.
46—Also for injury to personalty.
47—Action *ex contractu* for which no other period is prescribed.
48—Courts not of record, six years.
49—Payment of taxes required. Claim founded on written instrument, usual cultivation or improvement of all or a portion is required; not so founded, substantial enclosure, or that it be cultivated or improved is required.
50—Runs from discovery.
51—Provision also for four-year limitation on judgment of a foreign court.
52—Possession by actual residence for seven years under grant of public authority is sufficient. If holder gets title after possession the period runs from the day he got title. A *bona fide* claim with color of title and possession and payment of taxes for seven successive years will be good to the extent of paper title. If it is *bona fide* with color of title to vacant land and payment of taxes for seven years, it will be good to the extent of paper title.
53—I. e., cause of action fraudulently concealed, runs from discovery.
54—I. e., injury, detention or conversion.
55—I. e., injury to realty.
56—I. e., for damages in replevin matters.
57—I. e., statutory *penalty*.
58—I. e., against an incorporated city, village, town, in which case statement is to be filed with city attorney and city clerk in six months from date of injury.
59—If not court of record, ten years. Judgment of justice' court cannot be brought in court of like jurisdiction in same county within seven years.
60—I. e., civil actions not otherwise provided for.
61—Proof is required that all taxes and assessments have been paid.
62—I. e., if for payment of money. If for conveyance of land, fifteen years. If for other purposes, twenty years.
63—I. e., for injuries to real or personal property.
64—I. e., for statutory penalties or forfeiture.
65—If court not of record, fifteen years.
66—Must be established by evidence distinct from and independent of its use.
67—Runs from discovery.
68—I. e., injury to real or personal property.
69—If not of record—ten years.
70—Color of title not necessary.
71—From discovery.
72—I. e., injury to rights of another, not arising on contract and not otherwise enumerated.
73—Seven years under patent from state is sufficient.
74—If actually negotiated, limit is five years.
75—I. e., open or stated, any item more than five years old, counting from January 1st following date of purchase, is barred.
76—Regardless of time of discovery. In case of fraud or mistake, limit is five years from discovery, but not over ten years from event.
77—I. e., injury to real or personal property.
78—If no different limitation is fixed.
79—Requires good faith and just title, but thirty years establishes ownership without need for title, and regardless of good faith.
80—Requires good faith and just title, not sufficient if movable was lost or stolen (*res vitiosa* of Canon and Roman Law). Ten years gives ownership without need of title or good faith.
81—I. e., certain classes of oral contracts.
82—I. e., unless prescribed earlier by law of state where rendered.
83—I. e., as to all *tort* actions. All personal actions not specifically enumerated are limited to ten years.
84—Extensions for disability will not go beyond forty years.
85—If witnessed, twenty years.
86—I. e., "injury to chattels."
87—In court not of record, except municipal, police or justice' court, six years.
88—I. e., all contracts not otherwise limited.
89—Oyster grounds, twelve months, for residents.
90—Except between merchants and merchants, their factors and servants not residents of Maryland.
91—"Injury to real or personal property."
92—"Negligent personal injury."
93—*Tort* not otherwise limited.
94—If witnessed, twenty years.
95—I. e., for misconduct or negligence of deputy. For taking or conversion of personalty, two years.
96—If due to automobile may be one year limitation.
97—Presumption of payment. Courts not of record, six years.
98—As to contracts not limited by any other statutory provision.
99—All except real action when defendant claims title through deed made on certain sales, in which case five years; ten years when deed made by some officer of state or United States on sale for taxes; vendor, against vendee in possession and claiming title by the contract, may bring suit any time within twenty years.
100—I. e., penalty or forfeiture on penal statute.
101—If for penalty or forfeiture, three years.

102—I. e., injury to person or rights of another and not arising on obligation and not otherwise enumerated.
103—Libel, slander, assault and battery, false imprisonment, other *tort* resulting in personal injury, two years.
104—Even allowing for disabilities, period never over thirty-five years.
105—I. e., injury to realty or personalty.
106—Action for death, six years.
107—If party defeated in foreign judgment was resident of this state at the time, limit is three years.
108—Trust not cognizable at law and not otherwise provided for, ten years.
109—Even allowing for disabilities, period is never over 24 years. If owner is out of possession for thirty years and paid no taxes, he is barred one year after the occupation.
110—From discovery, at any time within ten years of facts, action may be begun.
111—For penalty or forfeiture, three years.
112—Injury to person or rights of another not arising on contract and not otherwise enumerated, five years.
113—Payment of taxes necessary.
114—In case of action on obligation or liability, not founded on an instrument in writing, other than contract or promise, limit is three years.
115—Court not of record, five years.
116—If on damages arising out of failure of consideration, or to recover money paid on contract consideration for which failed in whole or in part, limit is four years.
117—From discovery.
118—I. e., action on his official bond.
119—I. e., other than forfeiture or penalty, if created by federal statute, three years.
120—Action for death, two years.
121—If the holder cannot show a written instrument on which he bases his claim he must show sufficient enclosure, and cultivation and payment of taxes. If he can show such a written instrument, he must also show cultivation, or substantial enclosure, or that he used the land to supply fuel, pasturage, etc. Possession of one lot is not good for the rest. The holder must have paid all taxes.
122—From discovery.
123—For penalty or forfeiture, two years.
124—I. e., action for damages for death by wrongful act.
125—If secured by mortgage of real estate lasts as long as mortgage.
126—Cf. 55 N. J. L. 383.
127—Requires color of title and claim of right and payment of taxes. Land granted by Spain, Mexico, or United States, no requirement of taxes paid.
128—On municipal bonds, ten years.
129—Injuries to realty or personalty.
130—Courts not of record, six years.
131—Possession of one lot will not be good for another. One is deemed to have possessed when he has cultivated or improved the property, substantially enclosed it; if it was not enclosed it must have been used for fuel, fencing timber, husbandry or ordinary use of occupant. State has' forty years to recover realty.
132—From discovery.
133—I. e., injury to property.
134—Personal injury from negligence, three years.
135—Court not of record, unless judgment docketed in county clerk's office in this state, six years, if docketed same as if of record.
136—I. e., by known and visible boundaries, if under color of title, seven years. State is barred by thirty years possession by known and visible boundaries, twenty-one if under colorable title.
137—From discovery in cases heretofore solely cognizable by courts of equity.
138—If continuing trespass, three years from *original* trespass.
139—I. e., action on his official bond.
140—Criminal conversation, three years.
141—Judgment by justice of peace, seven years.
142—Actual occupation under claim of title. With payment of taxes and assessments, ten years. State barred from recovery of realty after forty years, others after twenty (bar extends to defense or counter-claim).
143—On contract contained in conveyance or instrument affecting title to realty, ten years.
144—From discovery.
145—Penalty or forfeiture, three years.
146—I. e., injury to person or rights not based on contract.
147—"On judgment of any domestic, federal or sister state court" (Comp. Stat. 1913, 7374); but six years also provided on foreign judgment (Comp. Stat. 1913, 7375).
148—I. e., on contract, obligation, liability not otherwise provided for. Other actions not otherwise provided for, ten years.
149—For injury to personalty, two years.
150—I. e., on his official bond.
151—Penalty or forfeiture, one year.
152—I. e., bodily injury. Injury to rights of plaintiff not arising on contract and not otherwise enumerated, four years.
153—From discovery.
154—Penalty or forfeiture, not otherwise specified, one year.
155—Injury not arising from contract.
156—*Torts* not otherwise specified, two years.
157—No adverse possession of registered land so as to give title.
158—Contracts for sale of realty, five years.
159—I. e., injury to real or personal property.
160—Penalty or forfeiture, one year; if private person does not sue by then, district attorney may in behalf of state within two-year period.
161—Suit in equity must be commenced within limit applicable to action at law.
162—Claimant by adverse possession must file and have recorded in the office for recording deeds in that county a statement of claim which will then have effect of deed or conveyance from former owner. Failure so to record leaves one out of possession without title

available against a purchaser or mortgagee from owner for value and without notice or against a judgment creditor of owner.

163—I. e., trespass to real or personal property.

164—If trespass to person results in death, one year.

165—Presumption of payment, may be rebutted by positive proof of non-payment, Cf. 282 Pa. 536.

166—I. e., actions for *torts* for which trespass would lie at Common Law and for which no other limitation is provided. Actions for specific performance of a contract for sale of realty, unless a longer time is expressed in the contract, or there has been subsequent performance, or an acknowledgment in writing in this period, in which case the period is five years. Actions to enforce any right or easement in a vacated private street, five years. Actions on an implied trust arising from the relation of attorney and client, no limitation.

167—I. e., even without need of title or good faith. Against persons living in the country the period is ten years, twenty against persons residing outside, in which case one must possess in good faith, under lawful title, in the character of owner, publicly and quietly, without interruption (cf. Canon Law of Adverse Possession).

168—I. e., with no other condition; with good faith three years are sufficient. Stolen property can be acquired by guilty parties only after the time for criminal action expires.

169—I. e., ordinary personal actions for which no other period is specified.

170—Except concerning merchandise or trade between merchants.

171—To bring an action against one in possession on claim of title by virtue of a written instrument, claimant or ancestor must have been actually in possession of the premises or of part thereof within forty years of commencement of the action. State is barred after twenty years. If grant by state was declared void by court, state or subsequent grantee may sue within ten years of such declaration, other persons only if they were in possession thereof within ten years before the commencement of the action.

172—Adverse possession as to land only. Rights in land not acquired by deed or will must be founded on prescription or presumption of grant. Person holding himself or through a predecessor in title for twenty years establishes prescription.

173—I. e., on bonds or other contracts in writing secured by mortgage of real property and sealed instrument other than sealed note or personal bond for payment of money only.

174—I. e., in cases heretofore solely cognizable by a court of chancery; runs from discovery.

175—Forfeiture or penalty, two years.

176—I. e., criminal conversation; assault and battery, two years.

177—Claim and color of title in good faith with payment of all taxes causes to be deemed owner to extent of paper title. Color of title to vacant and unoccupied land and payment of all taxes causes to be deemed legal owner according to the paper title. Possession of one lot is not good for another. If there is no written instrument, property must be enclosed substantially or occupied as is usual, or improved. These provisions do not extend to school lands, land belonging to the United States or to South Dakota, or to religious or charitable societies, or lands held for public purpose, nor to lands or tenements to which there is adverse title, holder of which is at expiration of said ten years under twenty-one, insane, imprisoned for less than life (S. D. Code 1939, 33.02,30). Actions to recover realty, except in certain special cases, are limited to twenty years.

178—I. e., on *equitable* action for fraud; runs from discovery.

179—Penalty or forfeiture to party aggrieved, three years; penalty or forfeiture to state, two years.

180—I. e., as to criminal conversation, other injury to rights not arising on contract and not otherwise provided for. Assault and battery, two years.

181—If there is some assurance of title, recorded, it vests good title after seven years' adverse possession; same if property is held under grant of North Carolina or Tennessee, recorded and possessed for seven years and no claim in law or equity has been effectually prosecuted against the holder. An action to recover realty is limited to seven years. A grant or deed will be presumed after twenty years.

182—I. e., injury to realty or personalty, and for detention or conversion of personalty.

183—I. e., on his bond.

184—I. e., statutory *penalty*.

185—After this period no action, regardless of coverture, minority or other disability, will be allowed against one in peaceable adverse possesssion under a claim of right, in good faith, and under a deed or deeds or instrument purporting to convey the same and recorded in the county. In case of peaceable adverse possession, three years suffice under title (regular back to the sovereignty) or color of title (back to sovereignty but irregular) to bar action to recover. Peaceable adverse possession for five years under a deed duly registered (unless forged or executed under a forged power of attorney) and cultivation, use or enjoyment, and payment of taxes for this period, bars an action to recover. Peaceable adverse possession for ten years with use, cultivation or enjoyment, without other evidence of title bars recovery as to 160 acres and more if actually occupied.

186—Other than between merchants, two years.

187—I. e., on his bond for failure to make return of execution.

188—Unless barred sooner where rendered.

189—Must have paid all taxes during this period. If there is no written instrument, judgment, or decree, possessor must show substantial enclosure, usual cultivation or improvement or expenditure of money or labor up to $5.00 per acre for irrigation. If registered under Torrens Act, adverse possession will not give title or interest therein in derogation of title of true owner. Action to recover realty held by another under tax deed limited to four years, otherwise, even by state, seven years.

190—If stated and in writing, six years.

191—From discovery.

192—Penalty or forfeiture, one year, unless otherwise provided.

193—Action for death limited to two years.

194—Action against a grantee under tax sale deed, five years.

195—Signed in presence of attesting witness, fourteen years. If note is under seal, eight years.

196—I. e., on *tort* for which no other limitation is prescribed.

197—Land west of Allegheny Mountains (Carroll County is deemed west), ten years.

198—Action against an estate of a decedent, five years from the qualification of representatives, or from the accrual if accrued after death.

199—If under seal and seal is referred to in body of note, ten years.

200—Accounts between partners or merchant and merchant, five years.

201—I. e., injury to real or personal property.

202—I. e., against officer or his sureties for failure to return execution.

203—I. e., of directors of a corporation.

204—I. e., action for wrongful death, except against a carrier for death of an employee.

205—I. e., personal actions which would survive; unless otherwise prescribed.

206—No adverse possession against public lands. Possession, good faith, connected title, claim and color of title, payment of all taxes make legal owner to the extent of paper title in this period. If color of title and payment of taxes on vacant or unoccupied lands for seven years, one becomes owner to the extent of the paper title. Ten-year possession, actual, open, notorious, hostile, defeats any claim other than that of the occupant.

207—From discovery.

208—Unless some other period is prescribed. Forfeiture or penalty to state, two years.

209—I. e., any relief not otherwise provided for. Injury to person or rights of another not specifically enumerated, three years.

210—I. e., injury to real or personal property.

211—I. e., action for death.

212—Unless barred sooner where rendered.

213—I. e., personal actions, not otherwise limited, which would not survive to be brought by personal representative; if they would so survive, five years.

214—Action to recover realty, generally this period. Action by state, forty years. Action by one entitled to make entry, twenty years, but if adverse possession was under a written instrument, ten years. Action to enforce an easement or covenant restricting use of real estate in a recorded instrument, sixty years from date of record. Action affecting possession or title to real estate founded on an instrument executed or recorded more than thirty years prior to action, thirty years unless in meantime notice was filed with register of deeds in such place, or unless right is barred by another statute, or unless action is brought by a person in possession as owner.

215—If cause of action accrued without the state, ten years.

216—From discovery.

217—Penalty or forfeiture, two years, if no other period is prescribed.

218—I. e., any injury to person or rights of another not arising on contract, unless some other period is prescribed.

219—Court not of record, six years.

220—I. e., action cognizable in court of chancery on February 28, 1858, if no other limitation is prescribed; action in favor of state when no other limitation is prescribed; personal actions on contract not otherwise provided for.

221—On foreign contract, incurred or contracted before debtor became resident of this state, five years from time became resident.

222—I. e., on his official bond.

223—I. e., on liability created by federal statute providing no limitation.

224—I. e., for death of decedent.

225—I. e., incurred before debtor became resident of this state, runs from time became resident.

CHAPTER VIII

NEW PROMISE, ACKNOWLEDGMENT, AND PART PAYMENT [1]

ARTICLE 1. NEW PROMISE AND ACKNOWLEDGMENT

246. The American Law recognizes an important class of exceptions to the operation of the statute of limitations made not by 21 James I, c. 16, but by the courts, wherein, although the statutory limitation may have expired, parties bringing themselves within the exception are allowed to act. In actions of assumpsit, and in these alone,[2] a new express [3] promise to pay, or an acknowledgment of existing indebtedness made under such circumstances as to be equivalent to a new promise,[4] and within the period of limitation on the revived action will, whether at law or in equity,[5] take the case out of the operation of the statute, although the original cause of action is barred at the time of suit.[6] The reason for this rule is that the statutory limitation is held merely to bar the remedy and not to discharge the debt, so the promise is supported not by a merely moral obligation, but by a pre-existent debt, which is a sufficient consideration for the new promise.[7] The new promise upon this sufficient consideration constitutes a new cause of action.[8]

[1] Cf. 2 Bouvier 2010-2015.

[2] Nelson v. Petterson, 229 Ill. 240, 82 N.E. 229, 13 L.R.A. (N.S.) 912, 11 Ann. Cas. 178; Von Hemert v. Porter, 11 Metc. (Mass.) 210, Lord v. Shaler, 3 Conn. 131, 8 Am. Dec. 160; Barwick v. Barwick, 21 Grant Ch. (Ont.) 39.

[3] Alexandria Bank v. Clarke, 2 Fed. Cas. No. 844, 2 Cranch (U.S.) C.C. 464; Bell v. Morrison, 1 Pet. (U.S.) 351, 7 L. Ed. 174; Quaker Oats v. North, 102 Misc. 108, 168 N.Y.S. 145; Welles-Kahn Co. v. Klein, 81 Fla. 524, 88 South. 315.

[4] Kirk v. Williams, 24 Fed. 437; Lamkin v. Cambron, 194 Ky. 246, 238 S.W. 766.

[5] Harris v. Mills, 28 Ill. 44, 81 Am. Dec. 259.

[6] O'Hara v. Murphy, 196 Ill. 599, 63 N.E. 1081.

[7] Johnson v. Evans, 8 Gill (Md.) 155, 50 Am. Dec. 669; Phelps v. Williamson, 26 Vt. 230; Fries v. Boisselet, 9 S. & R. (Pa.) 128, 11 Am. Dec. 683; Jordan v. Jordan, 85 Tenn. 561, 3 S.W. 896; Samuel Williston & George J. Thompson, *A Treatise on the Law of Contracts* (rev. ed. 8 vol., New York: Baker, Voorhis & Co., 1936), § 143, hereinafter cited, Williston, *Contracts*.

[8] 4 East. 399; 6 Taunt. 210; Bell v. Morrison, 1 Pet. (U.S.) 351, 7 L. Ed. 174; Williston, *Contracts*, § 143.

The Canon Law did not know of this precise provision, for it considered that when the time had run title had passed, or in the case of obligations, which is the case here, one was free from the obligation. Subsequent bad faith, as was seen,[9] did not prevent the one for whom "*praescriptio*" had run from making use of the benefits accruing therefrom. One may, however, find in this provision of the American Law some similarity with the Canon Law on obligations remaining in the internal forum though outlawed in the external.[10]

247. This construction, under the American Law, of the statute is very liberal, but it was early adopted and has maintained itself, despite much adverse criticism, to the present time. In the early period there was an inclination on the part of the courts to accept the slightest and most ambiguous expressions as evidence of a new promise. The tendency of modern decisions, however, is towards a greater strictness, and seems to be fairly expressed in the learned judgment of Mr. Justice Story, in the case of Bell v. Morrison.[11]

"It has often been matter of regret, in modern times, that in the construction of the statute of limitations, the decisions had not proceeded upon principles better adapted to carry into effect the real objects of the statute; that, instead of being viewed in an unfavorable light, as an unjust and discreditable defense[12] it had not received such support as would have made it, what it was intended to be, emphatically a statute of repose. It is a wise and beneficial law not designed merely to raise a presumption of payment of a just debt from lapse of time, but to afford security against stale demands after the true state of the transactions may have been forgotten, or be incapable of explanation, by reason of the death or removal of witnesses.[13] It has a manifest tendency to produce speedy settle-

[9] Cf. *supra*, n. 92.

[10] Cf. *supra*, n. 54, note 11.

[11] 1 Pet. (U.S.) 351, 7 L. Ed. 174.

[12] Cf. Rubeus, *Annotationes*, in *Decisiones Recentiores*, Part. 3, dec. 20, nn. 13-18; Rubeus, *Annotationes*, in *Decisiones Recentiores*, Part. 3, dec. 3, nn. 31-32; *S.R.R. in causa Interamnen., Fideicommissi, coram Taia* (1676)—*Decisiones Recentiores*, Part. 18, tom. 2, dec. 666, n. 12.

[13] Cf. *supra*, nn. 1-2.

ment of accounts, and to suppress those prejudices which may rise up at a distance of time and baffle every honest effort to counteract or overcome them. Parol evidence may be offered of confessions (a species of evidence which, it has been often observed, it is hard to disprove and easy to fabricate) applicable to such remote times as may leave no means to trace the nature, extent, or origin of the claim, and thus open the way to the most oppressive charges. If we proceed one step further, and admit, that loose and general expressions, from which a probable or possible inference may be deduced of the acknowledgment of a debt by a court or jury, that, as the language of some cases has been, any acknowledgment, however slight, or any statement not amounting to a denial of the debt, that any admission of the existence of an unsettled account, without any specification of amount or balance, and however indeterminate and casual, are yet sufficient to take the case out of the statute of limitations, and let in evidence, *aliunde,* to establish any debt, however large and at whatever distance of time; it is easy to perceive that the wholesome objects of the statute must be in a great measure defeated, and the statute virtually repealed. . . . If the bar is sought to be removed by the proof of a new promise, that promise, as a new cause of action, ought to be proved in a clear and explicit manner, and be in its terms unequivocal and determinate; and, if any conditions are annexed, they ought to be shown to be performed."

248. To be sufficient, the promise must be made to the party in interest or his agent, i. e., in order to toll the statute.[14] A promise to pay will, however, be implied from an acknowledgment of a debt as an existing debt.[15] If a mortgage be delivered it will be a sufficient acknowledgment to exempt the debt secured thereby from the operation of the statute,[16] and so will the answer to a bill in chancery which expressly sets forth the existence of such a debt.[17] Even

[14] Spangler v. Spangler, 122 Pa. 358, 15 Atl. 436, 9 Am. St. Rep. 114.

[15] Barlow v. Barner, 2 Fed. Cas. No. 998, 1 Dill. (U.S.) 418.

[16] Balch v. Onion, 4 Cush. (Mass.) 559; Merrils v. Swift, 18 Conn. 257, 46 Am. Dec. 315; Grayson v. Taylor, 14 Tex. 672.

[17] Bloodgood v. Bruen, 4 Sandf. (N.Y.) 427; Allender v. Vestry of Trinity Church, 3 Gill (Md.) 166.

under a statute requiring a new promise to be in writing [18] it was held that where a receiver of a bank orally promised a creditor that he would not plead the statute if the creditor would refrain from bringing suit, the running of the statute of limitation was prevented, since the defendant was estopped from pleading it.[19] An indorsement on a note dated the day before it would outlaw, that "the within note shall not be outlawed," written and signed by the party thereto, will take it out of the statute.[20]

249. Further examples of a sufficient promise or acknowledgment are: 1—a promise to the known [21] agent or attorney of the creditor, [22] although he is only authorized to collect the demand; [23] 2—an acknowledgment made to: (a) a surviving partner,[24] (b) a managing partner,[25] (c) a bankrupt creditor acting in behalf of his assignees,[26] (d) the widow of the creditor,[27] (e) an heir who inherits the claim, even when the promise is made prior to his appointment as administrator,[28] (f) an executor who is the guardian of a legatee of the claim,[29] (g) an executor of a devisee of the claim,[30] (h) an administrator while acting as such,[31] or one entitled to take out letters of administration and who afterward does so,[32] (i) one of several administrators, although made to him individually and not in his representative capacity; [33] 3—an offer to pay part of an acknowl-

[18] Cf. various statutes, most do.

[19] Bridges v. Stephens, 132 Mo. 524, 34 S.W. 555.

[20] *In re* Estate of King, 94 Mich. 411, 54 N.W. 178; Bacchus v. Peters, 85 Tenn. 678, 4 S.W. 833.

[21] Wesner v. Stein, 97 Pa. 322, 326 (quot. Bahny v. Levy, 236 Pa. 348, 350, 84 Atl. 835).

[22] Wetz v. Greffe, 71 Ill. A. 313.

[23] Emerson v. Miller, 27 Pa. 278.

[24] Barney v. Smith, 4 Harr. & J. (Md.) 485, 7 Am. Dec. 679.

[25] Yarbrough v. Gilland, 77 Miss. 139, 24 South. 170.

[26] Leach v. Coyle, 15 Fed. Cas. No. 8,156.

[27] Hodnett v. Gault, 64 App. Div. 163, 71 N.Y.S. 831.

[28] Drawbaugh v. Drawbaugh, 7 Pa. Super. 349.

[29] Melton v. Beasley, 56 Tex. Civ. A. 537, 121 S.W. 574.

[30] Croman v. Stull, 119 Pa. 91, 12 Atl. 812.

[31] Farrell v. Palmer, 36 Cal. 187.

[32] Robertson v. Burrill, 22 Ont. A. 356, 362.

[33] Hill v. Hill, 51 S.C. 134, 28 S.E. 309.

edged debt, which renews the entire debt; [34] 4—an unqualified admission or acknowledgment,[35] which will not be destroyed by an offer to arbitrate.

By some courts an offer or promise to pay the principal or debt exclusive of the interest is held to revive no part of the debt,[36] by others it is held to revive the debt as to the principal only,[37] while by others the whole debt is held to be revived.[38]

250. Under other conditions a promise or acknowledgment is considered not sufficient. Thus, an acknowledgment to a third person not intended to be communicated to the creditor will not suffice.[39] Further examples of an insufficient promise or acknowledgment are: 1—an agreement to refer; [40] 2—an offer to refer to arbitration,[41] especially if the offer is refused by the creditor; [42] 3—an offer of a compromise,[43] particularly: (a) when the debtor declares he will not pay more; [44] (b) when his offer indicates that he regards the indebtedness as paid; [45] (c) when the offer is not accepted,[46] especially if it is coupled with an unmistakable determination to pay nothing in case the offer is not accepted; [47] 4—an admission contained in a writing the purpose of which is to procure a compromise of a barred claim; [48] 5—an insertion by an insolvent debtor of an outlawed claim in a schedule of his creditors required by law; [49] 6—an agreement

[34] Austin v. Bostwick, 9 Conn. 496, 25 Am. Dec. 42.

[35] Cheslyn v. Dalby, 4 Y. & C. Exch. 238, 160 Reprint 993.

[36] Pearson v. Darrington, 32 Ala. 227.

[37] McDonald v. Underhill, 10 Bush (Ky.) 584.

[38] Foster v. Smith, 52 Conn. 449.

[39] Cunkle v. Heald, 6 Mackey (D.C.) 485.

[40] Broddie v. Johnson, 1 Sneed (Tenn.) 464.

[41] Read v. Wilkinson, 20 Fed. Cas. No. 11,611, 2 Wash. C.C. 514.

[42] Rossiter v. Colby, 71 N.H. 386, 52 Atl. 927.

[43] Bell v. Morrison, 1 Pet. (U.S.) 351, 7 L. Ed. 174.

[44] Lackey v. Macmurdo, 9 La. Ann. 15.

[45] Marcum v. Terry, 146 Ky. 145, 142 S.W. 209, 37 L.R.A. (N.S.) 885.

[46] Stewart v. McFarland, 84 Ia. 55, 50 N.W. 221.

[47] Creuse v. Defiganiere, 23 N.Y. Super. 122.

[48] Philp v. Hicks, 112 Miss. 581, 72 South. 931, 73 South. 610.

[49] Christy v. Flemington, 10 Pa. 129, 49 Am. Dec. 590; Roscoe v. Hale, 7 Gray (Mass.) 274; Woodbridge v. Allen, 12 Metc. (Mass.) 470; not so in Louisiana, Morgan's Ex'rs v. Metayer, 14 La. Ann. 612.

not to take advantage of the statute; [50] 7—a devise of property to pay exempt debts upon which the statute has run prior to the testator's death; [51] 8—in general, any statement of debt, made officially, in pursuance of a special legal requirement, or with another purpose than to recognize it as an existing debt; [52] 9—a deed of assignment made by the debtor for the payment of certain debts, and of his debts generally, and a partial payment by the assignor to a creditor; [53] 10—an assignment for the benefit of creditors made to a third party; [54] 11—a listing of the claim in the schedule of liabilities; [55] 12—an acknowledgment by the debtor made after the assignment that the debt was one of those on which payment was to be made; [56] 13—an entry of a debt in an unsigned schedule of the debtor's liabilities, made for his own use; [57] 14—an undelivered mortgage to secure a debt against which the statute has run, though duly executed, acknowledged and recorded.[58]

251. If there is anything said to repel the inference of a promise, or inconsistent therewith, the statute will not be avoided,[59] and it is held that a mere acknowledgment is insufficient.[60] A promise pre-

[50] Hodgdon v. Chase, 29 Me. 47; Maitland v. Wilcox, 17 Pa. 232; Stockett v. Sasscer, 8 Md. 374; Sutton v. Burruss, 9 Leigh (Va.) 381, 33 Am. Dec. 246; if such an agreement were valid, it might be made part of the contract, and thus the object of the law would be defeated, Hodgdon v. Chase, 32 Me. 169.

[51] Carrington v. Manning's Heirs, 13 Ala. 611; Agnew's Adm'x v. Fetterman's Ex'r, 4 Pa. 56, 45 Am. Dec. 671; Tazewell's Ex'r v. Whittle's Adm'r, 13 Gratt. (Va.) 329; Bloodgood v. Bruen, 4 Sandf. (N.Y.) 427.

[52] 12 E. L. & Eq. 191; Wellman v. Southard, 30 Me. 425; Bradford v. Spyker's Adm'r, 32 Ala. 134.

[53] Reed v. Johnson, 1 R.I. 81; 6 E.L. & Eq. 520.

[54] Niblack v. Goodman, 67 Ind. 174.

[55] Georgia Ins., etc., Co. v. Ellicott, 10 Fed. Cas. No. 5,354, Taney 130; though the contrary has been held, Van Patten v. Bedow, 75 Ia. 589, 39 N.W. 907.

[56] Pickett v. King, 34 Barb. (N.Y.) 193 (aff. 34 N.Y. 175).

[57] Wellman v. Southard, 30 Me. 425.

[58] Merriam v. Leonard, 6 Cush. (Mass.) 151.

[59] Moore v. Bank, 6 Pet. (U.S.) 86, 8 L. Ed. 329; Thayer v. Mills, 14 Me. 300.

[60] Wood v. Merrietta, 66 Kan. 748, 71 Pac. 579; Lambert v. Doyle, 117 Ga. 81, 43 S.E. 416; Hanson v. Towle, 19 Kan. 273, 281; Gragg v. Barnes, 32 Kan. 301, 4 Pac. 276; Pritchard v. Howell, 1 Wis. 131, 138, 60 Am. Dec. 363.

venting or repelling the bar of the statute of limitations may be implied from a clear, unconditional admission of the existence of the debt at the time of such admission,[61] if it is unaccompanied by any circumstances which rebut such implication.[62]

252. Examples of statements which are justly inferred to rebut the idea of a promise are: 1—a refusal to pay; [63] 2—expressions indicating a mere willingness to pay at a future time; [64] 3—expressions indicating inability to pay; [65] 4—circumstances indicating an intention not to pay; [66] 5—a denial of liability; [67] 6—a statement that one will pay if he owes, but denies that he owes; [68] 7—a declaration of exoneration from liability; [69] 8—a denial of the justness of a debt; [70] 9—an admission that the claim was once due, but claiming that it is paid by an account against the claimant; [71] 10—declarations indicative of an intent to insist upon the statute of limitations as a bar,[72] although the rule is sometimes limited by confining the qualifications which will rebut the implication to those which, if true, would exempt the party from a moral obligation to discharge the debt.[73]

253. In many of the earlier cases it was often stated that there must be an acknowledgment of willingness and liability to pay [74] or

[61] Bell v. Morrison, 1 Pet. (U.S.) 351, 7 L. Ed. 174.

[62] Ft. Scott v. Hickman, 112 U.S. 150, 5 Sup. Ct. 56, 28 L. Ed. 636.

[63] Jenkins v. Boyle, 13 Fed. Cas. No. 7,262, 2 Cra. (U.S.) C.C. 120.

[64] Lawson v. McCartney, 104 Pa. 356.

[65] Barnard v. Bartholomew, 22 Pick. (Mass.) 291; Manning v. Wheeler, 13 N.H. 486.

[66] Rumsey v. Settle, 120 Mich. 372, 79 N.W. 579.

[67] Ennis v. Pullman Palace-Car Co., 165 Ill. 161, 46 N.E. 439 (aff. 60 Ill. A. 398).

[68] Perley v. Little, 3 Greenl. (Me.) 97; Bangs v. Hall, 2 Pick. (Mass.) 368, 13 Am. Dec. 437; Meyer v. Andrews, 70 Tex. 327, 7 S.W. 814.

[69] Miller v. Lancaster, 4 Me. 159.

[70] Goodwin v. Buzzell, 35 Vt. 9.

[71] Marshall v. Dalliber, 5 Conn. 480; Belknap v. Gleason, 11 Conn. 160, 27 Am. Dec. 721.

[72] Penley v. Waterhouse, 3 Ia. 418.

[73] Felty v. Young, 18 Md. 163; at Canon Law this is preferable, cf. *supra*, n. 54, note 11.

[74] Shepherd v. Thompson, 122 U.S. 231, 7 Sup. Ct. 1229, 30 L. Ed. 1156.

to remain liable; [75] but it is not now considered necessary, save in those jurisdictions where an express promise is necessary to revive a barred debt,[76] that such ackowledgment be express.[77] Intention to pay need not be expressed in the acknowledgment.[78] Under the statutes of some jurisdictions an acknowledgment alone may be sufficient, although insufficient to raise an implication of a promise,[79] or even if accompanied by a refusal, upon insufficient grounds, to pay the debt,[80] although the generally accepted doctrine is that an acknowledgment of the existence of a debt is allowed to remove the bar of the statute because such acknowledgment or admission carries with it an implied promise to pay.[81] An implication of a promise cannot, however, be found if there is express language of the debtor to the contrary.[82] An acknowledgment can operate only to remove the bar of the statute and cannot validate a void promise or obligation unless it in itself amounts to a promise upon which an action may be based.[83] An acknowledgment tainted by a fraud will not sustain an inference of a new promise,[84] nor an admission of the debt made only *modo et forma,* i.e., in an accounting of debts required by statute.[85] Letters which merely acknowledge an indebtedness, but do not refer to any particular account, or mention the amount of the debt, and which are not written to serve as an acknowledgment, are not sufficient.[86]

254. If the new promise is subject to conditions or qualifications, is indefinite as to time or amount, or as to the debt referred to, or in

[75] Robinson v. Larabee, 58 Vt. 652, 5 Atl. 512.

[76] Cf. various jurisdictions.

[77] Chidsey v. Powell, 91 Mo. 622, 4 S.W. 446, 60 Am. Rep. 267.

[78] Morris v. Carr, 77 Ark. 228, 91 S.W. 187.

[79] Cleland v. Hostetter, 13 N.M. 43, 79 Pac. 801.

[80] Ellicott v. Nichols, 7 Gill (Md.) 85, 48 Am. Dec. 546.

[81] Kleis v. McGrath, 127 Ia. 459, 103 N.W. 371, 109 Am. St. Rep. 396, 69 L.R.A. 260.

[82] Cosio v. Guerra, 67 Fla. 331, 65 South. 5.

[83] Simrell v. Miller, 169 Pa. 326, 32 Atl. 548.

[84] Ellicott v. Nichols, 7 Gill (Md.) 85, 48 Am. Dec. 546.

[85] Ex p. Topping, 4 De G. J. & S. 551, 69 Eng. Ch. 423, 46 Reprint 1033 (foll. Cockshutt Plow Co. v. Young, 10 Sask. L. 68).

[86] Allen v. Hillman, 69 Miss. 225, 13 South. 871.

any other way limited or contingent, the plaintiff must bring himself strictly within the terms of the promise, and show that the condition has been performed, or that the contingency happened, and that he is not excluded by any limitation, qualification, or uncertainty.[87] If the original promise was conditional, and the new promise absolute, the latter will not alter the former.[88] The offer must be accepted altogether or rejected altogether. The liability of the defendant is to be tried by the test he has himself prescribed.[89] It must appear clearly that the promise is made with reference to the particular demand in suit,[90] though a general admission would show that there were other demands between the parties.[91] If the admission be broad enough to cover the debt in suit, according to some authorities, the plaintiff can prove the amount really due, *aliunde,* but the authorities are not at one on this point.[92]

255. Examples of a conditional promise such as is discussed above are: 1—if the promise be to pay when able, the ability then being required to be proved by the plaintiff; [93] 2—if it be to pay as soon as convenient, the convenience then being required to be proved by the plaintiff; [94] 3—if there was a promise to pay in specific articles, the plaintiff then being held to show that he offered to accept them; [95] 4—if a town was to vote that a committee be appointed to "settle the dispute" this was a conditional promise, requiring, to give it force

[87] Wetzell v. Bussard, 11 Wheat. (U.S.) 309, 6 L. Ed. 481; Sands v. Gelston, 15 Johns. (N.Y.) 511; Shown v. Hawkins, 85 Tenn. 214, 2 S.W. 34.

[88] Lonsdale v. Brown, 3 Wash. C.C. 404, 15 Fed. Cas. No. 8,492.

[89] Dean v. Pitts, 10 Johns. (N.Y.) 35.

[90] Moore v. Bank, 6 Pet. (U.S.) 86, 8 L. Ed. 329; Martin v. Broach, 6 Ga. 21, 50 Am. Dec. 306; Arey v. Stephenson, 33 N.C. 86.

[91] Gibson v. Grosvenor, 4 Gray (Mass.) 606; Huff v. Richardson, 12 Pa. 388; Buckingham v. Smith, 23 Conn. 453.

[92] 12 C. & P. 104; Eastman v. Walker, 6 N.H. 367; Barnard v. Wyllis, 22 Pick. (Mass.) 291; Bell v. Morrison, 1 Pet. (U.S.) 351, 7 L. Ed. 174; Sutton v. Burruss, 9 Leigh (Va.) 381, 33 Am. Dec. 246; Shitler v. Bremer, 23 Pa. 413.

[93] 4 Esp. 36; Manning v. Wheeler, 13 N.H. 486; cf. Cummings v. Gassett, 19 Vt. 308; Sennott v. Horner, 30 Ill. 429; Cocks v. Weeks, 7 Hill (N.Y.) 45; Bulloch v. Smith, 15 Ga. 395; Shown v. Hawkins, 85 Tenn. 214, 2 S.W. 34; Lange v. Caruthers, 70 Tex. 718, 8 S.W. 604.

[94] Edmunds v. Downes, 2 Cr. & M. 459.

[95] Bush v. Barnard, 8 Johns. (N.Y.) 407.

as against the statute, proof that the committee reported something due; [96] 5—if the promise by A was to pay if the debtor could not prove that B had paid it, it was held that the onus was upon A to prove that B had paid it.[97]

Article 2. Part Payment

256. Part payment of a debt made voluntarily is *prima facie* evidence [98] of a new promise to pay the remainder,[99] provided it is voluntary and made with the intent that it should be applied upon the debt.[100] Payment of the interest has the same effect as payment of part of the principal.[101]

257. Further examples of part payment are: 1—the giving of a note for part of a debt;[102] 2—the giving of a note for accrued interest; [103] 3—the giving of a second mortgage as payment of interest on the first mortgage;[104] 4—the credit of interest in an account stated; [105] 5—the delivery of goods on account; [106] 6—part payment upon a mortgage debt, which will extend the limitation period for actions upon the mortgage as well as upon the debt; [107]

[96] Fiske v. Inhabitants of Needham, 11 Mass. 452.

[97] Richmond v. Fugua, 33 N.C. 445.

[98] Aldrich v. Morse, 28 Vt. 642; White v. Jordan, 27 Me. 370; Jewett v. Petit, 4 Mich. 508; L.R. 7 Q.B. 493; U.S. v. Wilder, 13 Wall. (U.S.) 254, 20 L. Ed. 681; Harper v. Fairley, 53 N.Y. 442; Davidson v. Harrisson, 33 Miss. 41.

[99] Carshore v. Huyck, 6 Barb. (N.Y.) 583; Blaskower v. Steel, 23 Or. 106, 31 Pac. 253.

[100] Austin v. McClure, 60 Vt. 453, 15 Atl. 161.

[101] Barron v. Kennedy, 17 Cal. 574; Town of Huntington v. Chesmore, 60 Vt. 566, 15 Atl. 173.

[102] Isley v. Jewett, 2 Metc. (Mass.) 168; Pracht v. McNee, 40 Kan. 1, 18 Pac. 925.

[103] Wenman v. Ins. Co., 13 Wend. (N.Y.) 267, 28 Am. Dec. 464; Sigourney v. Wetherell, 6 Metc. (Mass.) 553.

[104] Blair v. Carpenter, 75 Mich. 167, 42 N.W. 790.

[105] Smith v. Ludlow, 6 Johns. (N.Y.) 267.

[106] 4 Ad. & E. 71; Sibley v. Lumbert, 30 Me. 253; Randon v. Toby, 11 How. (U.S.) 493, 13 L. Ed. 784.

[107] Hughes v. Thomas, 131 Wis. 315, 111 N.W. 474, 11 L.R.A. (N.S.) 744, 11 Ann. Cas. 673.

7—dividends on stock assigned as collateral security to a payee of a note, applied as payments on the debt.[108]

258. Examples of what is not considered "part payment" in this sense are: 1—the payment of a dividend by the assignee of an insolvent debtor; [109] 2—the payment of part of the sum sued for when the evidence does not show that at the time of such payment the party knew that he owed the sum in suit, and the payment was apparently made on account of bills that accrued after the accrual of the debt in suit; [110] 3—a payment intended to cover the whole amount due; [111] 4—the payment of taxes on a mortgage.[112]

A general payment on account of a debt for which several notes were given, without direction as to the application of the payment, may be applied by the creditor to either of the notes, so as to take the note to which the payment is applied out of the statute; but the payment cannot be apportioned to the several notes with the same effect.[113] With respect to promissory notes and bonds, the general proof of part payment or of payment of interest is the indorsement of that fact thereon.[114] It must, however, be made *bona fide,* and with the privity of the debtor.[115]

259. Part payment may be made by various persons. Thus, part payment by a surety in the presence of his principal, and without dissent, is payment by the principal,[116] but part payment by the surety after the statute has barred the debt is not a new promise to pay the other part.[117] A payment by the maker of a note cannot, furthermore, be relied on to take the note out of the statute as to the

[108] Bosler v. McShane, 78 Neb. 86, 110 N.W. 726, 12 L.R.A. (N.S.) 1032.

[109] Stoddard v. Doane, 7 Gray (Mass.) 287; 6 E.L. & Eq. 520.

[110] Crow v. Gleason, 141 N.Y. 489, 36 N.E. 497.

[111] Compton v. Bowns, 5 Misc. 213, 25 N.Y.S. 465.

[112] Snyder v. Miller, 71 Kan. 410, 80 Pac. 970, 69 L.R.A. 250, 114 Am. St. Rep. 489.

[113] Ayer v. Hawkins, 19 Vt. 26; 31 E.L. & Eq. 55; Pond v. Williams, 1 Gray (Mass.) 630.

[114] 1 Ad. & E. 102; Hathaway v. Haskell, 9 Pick. (Mass.) 42; Roseboom v. Billington, 17 Johns. (N.Y.) 182.

[115] 2 Campb. 321; Read v. Hurd, 7 Wend. (N.Y.) 408; President, etc., of Village Bank v. Arnold, 4 Metc. (Mass.) 587.

[116] Whipple v. Stevens, 22 N.H. 219.

[117] Emmons v. Overton, 18 B. Monr. (Ky.) 643.

surety.[118] An acknowledgment or part payment by one of several joint-contractors does not take the claim out of the statute as to the other joint-contractors,[119] unless made with their acquiescence, consent, or ratification. An acknowledgment or part payment made by an agent acting within the scope of his authority is an acknowledgment or part payment by the principal; [120] hence, if a partner has been appointed specially to settle the affairs of a dissolved partnership, his acknowledgment or part payment by virtue of his authority as such agent will take the claim out of the statute,[121] as will part payment by a partner without special authority.[122] A wife may be such an agent as to a claim for goods sold to her during the absence of her husband,[123] but a wife, during coverture, not made specially or by implication of law an agent, cannot make a new promise effectual to take a claim to which she was a party *dum sola* out of the statute,[124] even though the coverture be removed before the expiration of six years after the alleged promise.[125] The husband is likewise not an agent for the wife for such a purpose.[126] The weight of authority seems to be in favor of the binding force of a promise or part payment made by an executor or administrator,[127] particularly if the promise be express.[128] A promise by the life tenant to pay

[118] Davis v. Mann, 43 Ill. App. 301.

[119] Clinton v. Clinton, 148 Mich. 496, 111 N.W. 1087.

[120] John Henry Wigmore, *A Treatise on the Anglo-American Law of Evidence in Trials at Common Law* (3. ed. Boston: Little, Brown & Co., 1940), § 1078.

[121] Smith v. Ludlow, 6 Johns. (N.Y.) 267; Bell v. Morrison, 1 Pet. (U.S.) 351, 7 L. Ed. 174.

[122] Harding v. Butler, 156 Mass. 34, 30 N.E. 168.

[123] 3 Bing. 119.

[124] 1 B. & C. 248; Farrar v. Bessey, 24 Vt. 89.

[125] Kline v. Guthart, 2 Pen. & W. (Pa.) 490.

[126] Powers v. Southgate, 15 Vt. 471, 40 Am. Dec. 691.

[127] Foster v. Starkey, 12 Cush. (Mass.) 324; Hall v. Darrington, 9 Ala. 502; Griffin v. Justices of the Inferior Court of Baker County, 17 Ga. 96; Semmes v. Magruder, 10 Md. 242.

[128] Johnson v. Beardslee, 15 Johns. (N.Y.) 3; Oakes v. Mitchell, 15 Me. 360; Shreve v. Joyce, 36 N.J.L. 44, 13 Am. St. Rep. 417. Cf. *contra*, Riser v. Snoddy, 7 Ind. 442, 65 Am. Dec. 740; Miller v. Dorsey, 9 Md. 317; Moore v. Hillebrant, 14 Tex. 312, 65 Am. Dec. 118.

taxes may be relied upon as against a remainderman who pleads the statute, to remove the bar of the statute.[129]

260. Part payment may be made to various persons. Thus it may be made to an agent,[130] as well as to the creditor himself, or even to a stranger erroneously supposed to be authorized to receive it.[131] It is as much an admission of the debt if made to these parties as if made to the principal himself,[132] just as it is in the case of acknowledgments or new promises.[133] A written acknowledgment to take a barred demand out of the statute must be made to the creditor or his agent, and it must be made with knowledge of his agency.[134] A husband is an agent for the wife, payee of a note given to her *dum sola,* to whom a new promise or part payment may be made.[135] A new promise to an executor or administrator is sufficient.[136]

Article 3. Need of a Writing

261. To put an end to all litigation in England as to the effect of a new promise or acknowledgment, it was enacted by stat. 9 Geo. IV, c. 14, commonly known as Lord Tenterden's Act, that the new promise or acknowledgment by words only, in order to be effectual to take the case out of the statute of limitations, had to be in writing, signed by the party chargeable thereby; and this statute has been substantially adopted by most of the states in this country. This statute affects merely the mode of proof. The same effect is to be given to the words reduced to writing as would, before the passage of the statute, have been given to them when proved by oral

129 Duvall v. Perkins, 77 Md. 582, 26 Atl. 1085.

130 Spring v. Perkins, 156 Mich. 327, 120 N.W. 807.

131 Wakeman v. Sherman, 9 N.Y. 85.

132 1 Bing. 480; 10 B. & C. 122.

133 Whitney v. Bigelow, 4 Pick. (Mass.) 110; Howe v. Thompson, 11 Me. 152; Philips v. Peters, 21 Barb. (N.Y.) 351; Palmer v. Butler, 36 Ia. 576; Keener v. Crull, 19 Ill. 189.

134 Williamson v. Williamson, 50 Mo. App. 194.

135 6 Q.B. 937.

136 Baxter v. Penniman, 8 Mass. 134; Peck v. Botsford, 7 Conn. 179, 18 Am. Dec. 92.

testimony.[137] If part payment is alleged, "words only," if they admit the fact of payment, though they be not in writing, are admissible to strengthen the proof of the fact of payment.[138]

262. Examples of a writing such as is required under these statutes are: 1—the return, under citation, by an administrator of the maker of a note, showing the note as one of his intestate's debts; [139] 2—the entry by an insolvent debtor of the debt in his schedule of liabilities.[140]

263. Examples, on the other hand, of what is not such a "writing" are: 1—the making of one note and tendering it in payment of another; [141] not even if the note be delivered, if it be later redelivered to the maker for the purpose of restoring matters between the parties to the state they were in before the note was given; [142] 2—when A and B had an unsettled account, and in 1845 A signed the following: "It is agreed that B, in his general account, shall give credit to A for £10, for books delivered in 1834"; it was no acknowledgment in writing, so as to give B a right to an account against A's estate for a period more than six years before A's death.[143] 3—the signature of the husband's name by the wife, though at his request, has been held not a signing by the party to be charged; [144] 4—the signature by a clerk is not sufficient; [145] 5—a promise in the handwriting of the defendant; for unless it is signed it will not be sufficient; [146] 6—a request by the defendant to get certain moneys due the defendant from third parties, which does not charge the party making

[137] 7 Bing. 163; cf. Pittman v. Elder, 76 Ga. 371.

[138] 2 Gale & D. 59.

[139] 12 Sim. 17.

[140] Woodbridge v. Allen, 12 Metc. (Mass.) 470. It was held in this case that the mere entry was not in itself a sufficient acknowledgment; but being in writing, within the meaning of the statute it could be used with other written evidence to prove a new promise.

[141] Smith v. Eastman, 3 Cush. (Mass.) 355.

[142] Sumner v. Sumner, 1 Metc. (Mass.) 394.

[143] 35 E. L. & Eq. 195.

[144] 2 Bing. (N.C.) 776.

[145] 8 Scott 147.

[146] 12 Ad. & E. 493.

the request, because it is not apparent that the defendant intended to render himself personally liable.[147]

264. The effect, however, of part payment is left by the statute as before,[148] and the fact of part payment, it has been held, contrary to some earlier cases, may be proved by unsigned written evidence,[149] or by oral testimony.[150]

[147] 5 C. & P. 209.
[148] 10 B. & C. 122.
[149] 4 E. L. & Eq. 514.
[150] Williams v. Gridley, 9 Metc. (Mass.) 482.

CHAPTER IX

EFFECTS AND ETHICS OF THE INSTITUTE

ARTICLE 1. EFFECTS

265. At Canon Law, when the adverse possession was complete it prevented the owner from regaining his property despite contrary acts by him, unless a new adverse possession was shown in his favor.[1] The adverse possession was said to be made the equivalent of the truth, and to follow that nature which the thing itself regularly and properly had.[2] By it ownership was acquired.[3] In case there were contrary presumptions the court decided in favor of the one who could show adverse possession.[4] When adverse possession was complete the former owner could not recover the property, and if the new owner through ignorance of the law and by error gave it back he could recover it.[5]

According to its traditional doctrine, therefore, the Canon Law holds that the result of adverse possession, prescription, or of the running of the statute of limitations is, in the one holding, the acquisition of the right of ownership or the quasi-right (in the case of incorporeal things); and in the destruction of the right of the other party either real or personal, and this through the continuation of possession in the time and manner defined by the laws or the Sacred Canons.[6] Further, when the possession is complete and the required

[1] *S.R.R. in causa Romana, Vineae, coram Dunozetto* (1631)—*Decisiones Recentiores,* tom. 6, dec. 46, nn. 1-2; *S.R.R. in causa Cracovien., Iuris respondendi, coram Bichio* (1651)—*Decisiones Recentiores,* tom. 11, dec. 134, n. 17.

[2] *S.R.R. in causa Ianuen., Abbatiae, coram Caprara* (1694), tom. 1, dec. 195, n. 13.

[3] *S.R.R. coram Crescentio,* tom. 4, *de Praescriptionibus,* dec. 156, n. 8.

[4] *S.R.R. in causa Mechoacan., Crediti,* 7 ian. 1913, *coram R.P.D. Michaele Lega,* dec. XXXII, n. 16—*S.R.R. coram Lega,* p. 376; *AAS,* V (1913), 188-201.

[5] Schmalzgrueber, Part. III, tit. 26, nn. 14-15.

[6] Schmalzgrueber, Part. III, tit. 26, nn. 1,126; Reiffenstuel, lib. II, tit. 26, n. 21; and modern commentators generally.

period of time has run it relieves the one favored from the obligation of restitution.[7]

266. Some authors writing on Canon Law held that although full ownership of chattels was acquired by adverse possession, only "*dominium utile*" of realty was acquired, but Schmalzgrueber taught: 1—the law does not distinguish between full ownership and "*dominium utile*"; 2— words are to be taken in the stronger sense when they are doubtful, and full ownership is the stronger sense; 3—if full ownership is not conferred, the object in cutting off suits will not be obtained.[8]

267. Though "*praescriptio*" was referred to in harsh terms, e. g., its subject matter was called prejudicial, most odious, most inequitable, and contrary to justice and equity,[9] and was compared by some authors to catching eels,[10] it was, nevertheless, adopted for public utility lest ownership be always uncertain,[11] and was as a result called by Cassiodorus (ca. 490-583) the patroness of the human race.[12] Since it was an institute of private law, however, it did not affect matters of public law.[13]

268. Under the American Law, title by adverse possession for a period such as is required by statute to bar an action is a fee simple title, and is as effective as any otherwise acquired.[14] Adverse possession of personal property gives title at the expiration of the statutory period after the possession becomes adverse,[15] but one who holds by

[7] Schmalzgrueber, Part. III, tit. 26, n. 126; but cf. *supra*, n. 92.

[8] Schmalzgrueber, Part. III, tit. 26, n. 4; cf. also Pirhing, lib. II, tit. 26, n. 4; Reiffenstuel, lib. II, tit. 26, n. 18 sqq.

[9] Rubeus, *Annotationes*, in *Decisiones Recentiores*, Part. 3, dec. 3, nn. 31-32.

[10] *S.R.R. in causa Interamnen, Fideicommissi, coram Taia* (1676)—*Decisiones Recentiores*, Part. 18, tom. 2, dec. 666, n. 12.

[11] *S.R.R. in causa Bononien., Bonorum, coram Pauluccio* (1676)—*Decisiones Recentiores*, Part. 18, tom. 2, dec. 709, n. 7.

[12] *S.R.R. in causa Bononien., Bonorum, coram Pauluccio* (1676)—*Decisiones Recentiores*, Part. 18, tom. 2, dec. 709, n. 8.

[13] *S.R.R. in causa Mediolanen., Curae animarum*, 23 mart. 1909, *coram R.P.D. Michaele Lega*, Dec. II, n. 11—*S.R.R. Decisiones*, I (1909), 40; *AAS*, I (1909), 314-325.

[14] Cox v. Cox, 7 Mackey (D.C.) 1; cf. Sharon v. Tucker, 144 U.S. 533, 12 Sup. Ct. 720, 36 L. Ed. 532.

[15] Stevens v. Whitcomb, 16 Vt. 124; Mercein v. Burton, 17 Tex. 206.

consent of the true owner is not entitled to have the statute run in his favor until denial of the true owner's claim.[16] Different adverse possessions cannot be linked together to give title.[17] The statute acts upon the title to property, and, when the bar is perfect, transfers it to the adverse possessor; but in contracts for payment of money there is no such thing as adverse possession, the statute simply affects the remedy, and not the debt,[18] hence it is possible for a new promise, acknowledgment, or part payment to revive the obligation and start the statute running all over again.[19]

Article 2. Ethics of the Institute

269. Discussing the question of the ethics of the institute of "*praescriptio*," which includes the Adverse Possession, Prescription, and Limitation of Actions of the American Law, Schmalzgrueber (1663-1735) taught that, while some held it to be contrary to the *ius gentium* to take away ownership in this fashion, the *ius gentium* nevertheless prescribed obedience to the state and to its laws adopted for the common good, thus indicating that the *ius gentium*, far from being contrary to this institute, gave it strength. Another objection offered was that even the Emperor Justinian (527-565) recognized the institute as unjust, calling it "*impium praesidium, et improbam temporis allegationem*," to which Schmalzgrueber replied that Justinian spoke of a time when it ran for those in bad faith as well as for those in good faith. It was further objected "that which is ours cannot be transferred to another without some act on our part,"[20] to which the same author answered that this did not apply to the operation of law, and moreover the law presumed consent in the one neglecting for so long to prosecute his right, and even if he did not know of the affair the law supplied the consent and knowledge. To the further objection that one may not be enriched to the injury of

[16] Lucas v. Daniels, 34 Ala. 188; Baker v. Chase, 55 N.H. 61; Angell, *Limitations*, 304, note; cf. *supra*, n. 14, note 40.

[17] Moffat v. Buchanan, 11 Humphr. (Tenn.) 369, 54 Am. Dec. 41.

[18] Jones v. Jones, 18 Ala. 248.

[19] Cf. *supra*, Chap. VIII.

[20] D (50.17) 11.

another[21] this same author replied that the rule did not apply to the operation of law for a just and public reason. Finally, to the objection that time is not a method of inducing or removing an obligation he countered that time alone is not the reason for the transfer, but possession, time, title, and good faith.[22]

270. It was Schmalzgrueber's opinion that in the final analysis it was eminent domain, in the broad sense of the term, which allowed the transfer from the former to the new owner. To the objection that in the c. *Vigilanti*[23] adverse possession was shown as a punishment for the negligence of the owner who failed to recover in time from a *bona fide* possessor, and that therefore if he was not negligent he should not be deprived of his property, he replied that the correction of the owner's laziness was not the only nor even the principal reason for this law, but the reason was to cut down on the number of suits, and to provide that rights of ownership should not be uncertain, etc., so that even without negligence adverse possession is good. Even if punishment of the owner's negligence were the only and principal reason, the law is universal and for a universal end, and consequently it remains even if in a particular case the reason of the law is not verified. Further, it was objected that the one in ignorance was said to be like one under a disability, but Schmalzgrueber replied that the law supplies consent in the one ignorant. Even if in a particular case the adverse possession is not necessary to the welfare of the community, in general it is and this suffices, as in the case of other laws. When it was objected that the law was founded on a presumption and that if this was false it did not bind in conscience, that the owner was frequently not negligent and consequently was not bound in conscience by this law, this author answered that the law of adverse possession was founded on the public good, so even if the former owner was not negligent, prescription transferred ownership if the other requisites were present.[24]

[21] "*Locupletari non debet aliquis cum alterius iniuria, et iactura*"—Reg. 48, R.J., in VI°.

[22] Schmalzgrueber, Part. III, tit. 26, nn. 8-9; cf. Pirhing, lib. II, tit. 26, nn. 5-7; Reiffenstuel, lib. II, tit. 26, nn. 21-23.

[23] C. 5, X, *de praescriptionibus*, II, 26.

[24] Schmalzgrueber, Part. III, tit. 26, nn. 10-12.

271. As to the question whether one must give back the property if, after the adverse possession is complete, he finds that it did not really belong to him, Schmalzgrueber answered the objection that the natural law says one must restore property to its owner, by pointing out that when the property has been held for the time prescribed by law it is then the property of the new owner, so he then holds it not as the property of another, but as his own.[25] Hence, one need not give back the property if only after the time has run he becomes aware that it belonged of right to some one else.

272. When there is question of liberation from debt through the running of the prescribed period of time it seems that one must consider whether the failure to bring the suit was due to something on the part of the defendant which prevented bringing it, or to something on the part of the plaintiff which prevented him from bringing it. If the failure to bring suit was due to something on the part of the defendant this will presumably be due to his fraud,[26] or his absence,[27] both of which things will prevent the running of the statute of limitations, so that it cannot be pleaded. If the failure to bring suit was due to something on the part of the plaintiff, it could have been due to some disability under which he labored [28] and which prevented the running of the statute so that it could not be pleaded, or it could have been due to his negligence in bringing his suit, which negligence this institute was intended to correct. Since the only case in which the limitation can be successfully pleaded is the one in which the plaintiff is at fault, there seems to be no valid objection to pleading it in the matter of debt.

273. When there is question whether the attorney may ethically advise the defendant to plead the statute of limitations, one must consider, first, that it is the duty of the attorney to advise his client of all the legal safeguards to which he is entitled; second, that it is a matter for the court to decide whether the present defendant has a legal right to plead the defense of limitation of the plaintiff's action. If the defendant has not been able to acquire title because of his bad

[25] Schmalzgrueber, Part. III, tit. 26, nn. 13-16.

[26] Cf. *supra*, n. 80 sqq.

[27] Cf. *supra*, n. 180.

[28] Cf. *supra*, n. 176 sqq.

faith,[29] neither he nor his attorney can plead such title against a title asserted by the plaintiff, since under the circumstances the defendant is a wrongful holder of the property, and on trial the plaintiff would be entitled to judgment. If, however, there is a reasonable doubt as to the defendant's title, he may go to the court and plead his possession for the court to decide which of the two parties is, on the basis of evidence adduced, entitled to judgment in his favor, and in such case the attorney can advise the plea and make it at the direction of the defendant.

If there is question of pleading a limitation of the action in the stricter sense, it seems that the attorney can advise the plea and make it at the direction of the defendant, since in this case the law has provided that neither the courts nor the citizens are to be disturbed by stale claims. The defendant may have been aware all the time of the existence of the claim in question, but may with reason have concluded from the plaintiff's failure to bring suit or to make some other demand that the plaintiff did not intend to collect the amount due. If in reliance upon this fact the defendant has changed his position to his detriment, i. e., granted that he should now be compelled to satisfy it, there would be an even stronger reason for allowing him to plead the limitation of the action. This, indeed, seems to be the more probably tenable doctrine.

To conclude, it seems that the attorney is justified in advising the plea of limitation of actions in any case, and that of adverse possession or of prescription in any case except the one in which the defendant cannot plead it because of his lack of good faith, which has prevented him from acquiring title by his adverse holding.

[29] Cf. *supra*, n. 72 sqq.

CONCLUSIONS

1—Allowing for differences of time and place, as well as of economic conditions, the concept of *"praescriptio"* of the Canon Law is not much different from the Adverse Possession, Prescription, and Limitation of Actions of the American Law.

2—When the period is complete, title to real or personal property is in the one who has held adversely under the required conditions, as is a right of user (e. g., of an easement), under either Law.

3—In the case of money owed, a new promise, acknowledgment, or part payment by the one owing after the period is complete revives the obligation under the American Law, and this seems also to be acceptable in the Canon Law, the more so since such new promise, acknowledgment, or part payment seems to indicate bad faith on the part of the debtor were he not to pay the debt which he has again recognized.

4—Good faith, while not much discussed in the American Law, and usually said not to be required by it, is nonetheless important if one considers the requirements of the holding in adverse possession and prescription and the attitude of the law in the event of fraud.

5—The variations in the provisions of the statutes of the various states as to the classes of action limited and the length of the limitation make it imperative that a court of Canon Law wishing to apply the limitation for the state in which it is sitting shall consult an expert on the law of that state for the latest information regarding that statute.

BIBLIOGRAPHY

Sources

Acta Sanctae Sedis, 41 vols., Romae, 1865-1908.

Codex Iuris Canonici Pii X Pontificis Maximi iussu digestus, Benedicti Papae XV auctoritate promulgatus, Romae: Typis Polyglottis Vaticanis, 1917. Reimpressio, 1930.

Codicis Iuris Canonici Fontes, cura Emi Petri Card. Gasparri Editi, 9 vols., Romae (postea Civitate Vaticana): Typis Polyglottis Vaticanis, 1923-1939. (Vols. VII-IX ed. cura et studio Emi Iustiniani Card. Serédi.)

Corpus Iuris Civilis, ed. stereotypa quinta decima, Vol. I, *Institutiones* recognovit Paulus Krueger, *Digesta* recognovit Theodorus Mommsen, retractavit Paulus Krueger, Berolini: Apud Weidmannos, 1928.

Corpus Iuris Civilis, ed. stereotypa nona, Vol. II, *Codex Iustinianus* recognovit et retractavit Paulus Krueger, Berolini: Apud Weidmannos, 1915.

Corpus Iuris Civilis, ed. stereotypa quinta, Vol. III, *Novellae* recognovit Rudolfus Schoell, absolvit Guglielmus Kroll, Berolini: Apud Weidmannos, 1928.

Decretalium Collectiones, ed. Lipsiensis secunda, post Aemilii Ludovici Richteri curas instruxit Aemilius Friedberg, Lipsiae, 1881. Editio anastatice repetita, Lipsiae, 1922.

Decretales Gregorii Papae IX, suae integritati una cum glossis restitutae cum privilegio Gregorii XIII, Pont. Max. et aliorum Principum, Romae, 1582.

Decretum Gratiani, emendatum et notationibus illustratum una cum glossis restitutae cum privilegio Gregorii XIII, Pont. Max. et aliorum Principum, Romae, 1582.

Decretum Magistri Gratiani, ed. Lipsiensis secunda post Aemilii Ludovici Richteri curas ad librorum manu scriptorum et editionis Romanae fidem recognovit et adnotatione critica instruxit Aemilius Friedberg, Lipsiae, 1879. Editio anastatice repetita, Lipsiae, 1922.

Liber Sextus Decretalium D. Bonifacii Papae VIII suae integritati una cum *Clementinis* et *Extravagantibus* earumque Glossis restitutus, Romae, 1582.

Digesta Pontificum Romanorum ab condita Ecclesia ad annum post Christum natum 1198 edidit Philippus Jaffé, ed. secundam correctam et auctam auspiciis Guglielmi Wattenbach curaverunt S. Loewenfeld, F. Kaltenbrunner, P. Ewald, 2 vols. in 1, Lipsiae, 1885-1888.

Sacrae Rotae Romanae Decisiones:

Decisiones Sacrae Rotae Romanae coram R.P.D. Ansaldo de Ansaldis, 2. ed., 8 vols., Romae, 1711.

Decisiones Sacrae Rotae Romanae coram R.P.D. Clemente de Arostegui, Romae, 1781.

Sacrae Rotae Romanae Decisiones coram R.P.D. Alexandro Caprara, 2 vols., Lucae, 1725.

Decisiones Sacrae Romanae Rotae coram R.P.D. Hercule Consalvi, Romae, 1822.

Decisiones Sacrae Rotae Romanae coram R.P.D. Marcello Crescentio, 5 vols., Romae, 1763.

Decisiones S. Rotae Romanae coram R.P.D. Cosma de Cursiis, 5 vols., Romae, 1855.

Sacrae Romanae Rotae Decisiones seu Sententiae quae iuxta Legem Propriam et Constitutionem "Sapienti Consilio" Pii PP. X prodierunt, cura eiusdem S. Tribunalis editae, 23 vols., ——, Romae, 1912-.

Decisiones Sacrae Rotae Romanae coram R.P.D. Iacobo Emerix de Matthys, 3 vols., Romae, 1701.

Decisiones Sacrae Rotae Romanae coram R.P.D. Alexandro Falconerio, 5 vols., Romae, 1730.

Decisiones Sacrae Rotae Romanae coram R.P.D. Antonio Dominico Gamberini, Romae, 1824.

S. Rotae Romanae Decisiones Recentissimae et Selectissimae D. Ioannis Gutierrez Operae Omnia, 2. ed., *"20 decisionibus aucta,"* Coloniae Allobrogum, 1735.

Decisiones Sacrae Rotae Romanae coram R.P.D. Ioanne de Herrera, Romae, 1731.

Decisiones Sacrae Rotae Romanae coram R.P.D. Francisco Herzan, 3 vols., Romae, 1789.

Decisiones Sacrae Rotae Romanae coram R.P.D. Ioachim Ioanne Xaverio Isoard, 3 vols., Romae, 1829.

Sacrae Rotae Romanae Decisiones coram R.P.D. Francisco Carolo Kaunitz, 2 vols., Romae, 1734.

Sacrae Rotae Romanae Decisiones coram R.P.D. Cyriaco Lancetta, 7 vols., Romae, 1735.

Coram Lega Habitae Sacrae Romanae Rotae Decisiones sive Sententiae annis 1909-1914, 2. ed., Romae, 1926.

Decisiones Sacrae Romanae Rotae coram R.P.D. Alexandro Malvasia, 3 vols., Romae, 1832.

Sacrae Rotae Romanae Decisiones coram R.P.D. Io. Francisco Marco et Catalan, 3 vols., Romae, 1829.

Decisiones Sanctae Romanae Rotae coram Em̃.mo et Rev.m̃o D.ño Cardinali Petro Marini, 3 vols., Romae, 1853.

Decisiones Sacrae Rotae Romanae coram R.P.D. Theodulpho Mertel, Romae, 1853.

Sacrae Rotae Romanae Decisiones Novissimae, in *Decisiones Recentiores,* Part. 5, toms. 1-2.

Sacrae Rotae Romanae Decisiones Nuperrimae, 11 vols. in 10, Romae, 1751-1792.

Decisiones Sacrae Rotae Romanae coram R.P.D. Karolo ex Ducibus Odescalchi, 3 vols., Romae, 1827.

Decisiones Sacrae Rotae Romanae coram R.P.D. Bartholomaeo Olivatio, 8 vols., Romae, 1784.

Decisiones Sacrae Rotae Romanae coram R.P.D. Thoma Ratto, 4 vols., Romae, 1754.

Sacrae Rotae Romanae Decisiones Recentiores, Part. I, Francofurti, 1623; Part. 2, Aurelii, 1623; Part. 3-19, Romae, 1645-1703.

Decisiones Sacrae Rotae Romanae coram R.P.D. Carolo Rezzonico (Clemente XIII), 4 vols. in 3, Romae, 1762.

Decisiones Sacrae Rotae Romanae coram R.P.D. Io. Maria Riminaldo, 8 vols., Romae, 1792.

Decisiones Sacrae Rotae Romanae coram R.P.D. Antonio Rusconi, Romae, 1826.

Decisiones Sacrae Rotae Romanae coram R.P.D. Alexandro Tanario, 2 vols., Romae, 1748.

Decisiones Sacrae Rotae Romanae coram R.P.D. Iosepho Alphonso de Veri, 2 vols., Romae, 1787.

Reference Works

Ames, James Barr, *Lectures on Legal History,* Cambridge, 1913.

Angell, Joseph Kinnicut, *Limitations,* 4. ed. by John Wilder May, Boston, 1861.

Antonii Augustini, *Antiquae Collectiones Decretalium* (?).

Bernardus Papiensis, *Summa Decretalium,* ed. Laspeyres, Ratisbonae, 1860.

Bispham, George Tucker, *The Doctrine of Equity,* 7. Am. ed. by John Adams, Boston, 1881.

Blackstone's *Commentaries on the Law,* ed. Bernard C. Gavit, Washington: Washington Law Book Co., 1941.

Bouvier's *Law Dictionary* (Unabridged), 3. ed. by Francis Rawle, 2 vols., Kansas City, Missouri, and St. Paul, Minnesota, 1914.

Broom, Herbert, *Selection of Legal Maxims,* 7. Am. ed., Philadelphia, 1868.

Cruise, William, *A Digest of the Law of Real Property* (rev. H. Hopeley), Boston, 1849-50.

Cyclopaedia of Law and Procedure, 40 vols., New York, 1901-1912.

Gaius, *Institutiones,* ed. Johannes Baviera, in *Fontes Iuris Romani Antejustiniani,* Florentiae, 1909.

Hostiensis (Cardinalis) (Henricus de Segusio), *Summa Aurea,* Lugduni, 1568.

Pirhing, Emricus, S.J., *Jus Canonicum,* ed. noviss., 5 vols. in 4, Dilingae, 1722.

Pruemmer, Dominicus M., O.Pr., *Manuale Iuris Canonici,* 5. ed., Friburgi Brisgoviae: Herder, 1927.

Reiffenstuel, Anacletus, O.F.M., *Ius Canonicum Universum,* ed. noviss., 6 vols. in 5, Romae, 1831-1834.

Ricardus Anglicus, *Summa de Ordine Iudiciario,* in Quellen zur Geschichte des Roemisch-Kanonischen Processes im Mittelalter, herausgegeben von Dr. Ludwig Wahrmund, II Band, III Heft, Innsbruck, 1915.

Rubeus, Paulus, *Annotationes* in *Decisiones Recentiores.*

Rufinus, *Summa Decretorum,* ed. Singer, Paderborn, 1902.

Raymundi de Peñafort, Sti. *Summa,* Veronae, 1744.

Schmalzgrueber, Franciscus, S.J., *Ius Ecclesiasticum Universum,* 5 vols. in 12, Romae, 1843-1845.

Story, Joseph, *Conflict of Laws,* 5. ed., Boston, 1857.

———, *Equity Jurisprudence,* 12. ed. by Jairus W. Perry, Boston, 1877.

Vermeersch, Arthurus, S.J.-Creusen, Joseph, S.J., *Epitome Iuris Canonici,* 5. ed., 3 vols., Mechliniae-Romae: Dessain, 1934-1937.

Wait, William, *Actions and Defense,* Albany, 1885.

Wernz, Franciscus Xaverius, S.J., *Ius Decretalium,* 2. ed., 6 vols. in 10. toms., Romae et Prati, 1905-1913.

Wernz, Franciscus Xaverius, S.J.-Vidal, Petrus, S.J., *Ius Canonicum ad Codicis Normam Exactum,* 7 toms. in 9 vols., Romae: Apud Aedes Universitatis Gregorianae, 1923-1938.

Wigmore, John Henry, *A Treatise on the Anglo-American Law of Evidence in Trials at Common Law,* 3. ed., Boston: Little, Brown & Co., 1940.

Williston, Samuel and Thompson, George J., *A Treatise on the Law of Contracts,* rev. ed., 8 vols., New York: Baker, Voorhis & Co., 1936.

Wooddeson, Richard, *Lectures on the Laws of England,* (Notes by W. R. Williams), Philadelphia, 1842.

ABBREVIATIONS

AAS—*Acta Apostolicae Sedis.*
Abb. Pr. (N.S.)—Abbott's New York Practice Reports (New Series).
Ad. & E.—Adolphus & Ellis' English King's Bench Reports.
Aik.—Aikens' Vermont Reports.
A. K. Marsh. (Ky.)—A. K. Marshall's Reports, Kentucky.
Ala.—Alabama Reports.
Ala. A.—Alabama Appeals.
Allen (Mass.)—Allen's Massachusetts Reports.
A.L.R.—American Law Reports Annotated.
Am. Dec.—American Decisions.
Am. Rep.—American Reports (Selected Cases).
Am. St. Rep.—American State Reports.
Ann. Cas.—American and English Annotated Cases.
App. Div.—Appellate Division, New York.
Ark.—Arkansas Reports.
ASS—*Acta Sanctae Sedis.*
Atl.—Atlantic Reporter.
B. & Ald.—Barnewall & Alderson's English King's Bench Reports.
B. & C.—Barnewall & Cresswell's English King's Bench Reports.
Barb. (N.Y.)—Barbour's Supreme Court Reports, New York.
Barr. Ch.—Barr's Reports Chancery (England).
Bibb (Ky.)—Bibb's Reports, Kentucky.
Bing.—Bingham's Reports, English Common Pleas.
Blackf. (Ind.)—Blackford's Reports, Indiana.
Bosw. (N.Y.)—Bosworth's New York City Superior Court Reports, Vols. 14-23.
Brock.—Brockenbrough's Reports of Marshall's Decisions, United States Circuit Court.
Brod. & B.—Broderip & Bingham's English Common Pleas Reports.
Burr.—Burrow's Reports English King's Bench, *temp.* Mansfield.
Bush. (Ky.)—Bush's Reports, Kentucky.
C. & P.—Craig & Philips' English Chancery Reports.
C.C.A.—U.S. Circuit Court of Appeals Reports.
Cr. & M.—Crompton & Meeson's English Exchequer Reports.
Cai. (N.Y.)—Caines' Reports, Supreme Court, New York.
Cal.—California Reports.
Cal. A.—California Appeals.
Cal. Unrep. Cas.—California Unreported Cases.
Campb.—Campbell's Reports of Taney's Decisions, United States Circuit Court.
Ch.—English Chancery Cases; Law Reports, 1st series (1891).
Cheves (S.C.)—Cheves' Law Reports, South Carolina.

C.J.—Corpus Juris.
Cin. L. Bul.—Cincinnati Law Bulletin, Cincinnati, Ohio.
Cl. & F.—Clark & Finnelly's Reports, English House of Lords.
Cliff.—Clifford's Reports, United States First Circuit.
Col.—Colorado Reports.
Conn.—Connecticut Reports.
Cow. (N.Y.)—Cowen's New York Reports.
Cra. (U.S.)—Cranch's Reports, United States Supreme Court.
Cro. Car.—Croke's Reports, *temp.* Charles I (3 Cro.).
Ct. Cl.—Court of Claims, United States.
Cush. (Mass.)—Cushing's Massachusetts Reports.
Cyc.—Cyclopaedia of Law and Procedure.
D. & B.—Dearsly & Bell's English Crown Cases, Reserved.
Daly—Daly's Reports, New York Common Pleas.
Day (Conn.)—Day's Connecticut Reports.
De G. J. & S.—De Gex, Jones & Smith's Reports, English Chancery.
Denio (N.Y.)—Denio's New York Reports.
Dill. (U.S.)—Dillon's United States Circuit Court Reports.
Dom. L.R.—Dominion Law Reports, Canada.
E.L. & Eq.—English Law & Equity Reports.
East—East's King's Bench Reports.
Edw. Ch. (N.Y.)—Edwards' New York Chancery Reports.
Eng. C.L.—English Common Law Reports.
Eng. Ch.—English Chancery Reports.
Eng. R.C.—English Ruling Cases.
Esp.—Espinasse's English Nisi Prius Reports.
Fed.—Federal Reporter.
Fed. Cas. No.—Federal Case Number.
G. & D.—Gale & Davison's Reports, English Exchequer.
Ga.—Georgia Reports.
Ga. A.—Georgia Appeals.
Gale & D.—Gale & Davison's Queen's Bench Reports.
Gild. (N.M.)—Gildersleeve's New Mexico Reports.
Gill & J. (Md.)—Gill & Johnson's Reports, Maryland.
Grant Ch. (Ont.)—Grant's Upper Canada Chancery Reports, Ontario.
Gratt. (Va.)—Grattan's Virginia Reports.
Gray (Mass.)—Gray's Massachusetts Reports.
G. Greene (Ia.)—G. Greene's Iowa Reports.
Greenl. (Me.)—Greenleaf's Reports, Vols. 1-9 Maine.
H. & J.—Harris & Johnson's Maryland Reports.
H. & McH.—Harris & McHenry's Maryland Reports.
Hare—Hare's Reports, English Chancery.
Hawaii—Hawaii (Sandwich Islands) Reports.
Head (Tenn.)—Head's Reports, Tennessee.
Hill (N.Y.)—Hill's New York Reports.

Houst. (Del.)—Houston's Reports, Delaware.
How. (U.S.)—Howard's United States Supreme Court Reports.
How. Pr. (N.Y.)—Howard's New York Practice Reports.
Hughes—Hughes United States Circuit Court Reports.
Humphr. (Tenn.)—Humphrey's Reports, Tennessee.
Hun (N.Y.)—Hun's New York Supreme Court Reports.
Ia.—Iowa Reports.
Ill.—Illinois Reports.
Ill. A.—Illinois Appellate Court Reports.
Ind.—Indiana Reports.
Ind. A.—Indiana Appeals.
Jac. & W.—Jacob & Walker's English Chancery Reports.
Johns. (N.Y.)—Johnson's Reports, New York Supreme Court.
Johns. Cas. (N.Y.)—Johnson's Cases, New York Supreme Court.
Johns. Ch. (N.Y.)—Johnson's New York Chancery Reports.
Kan.—Kansas Reports.
Kan. App.—Kansas Appeals Reports.
Kay & J.—Kay & Johnson's Reports, English Chancery.
Ky.—Kentucky Reports.
Ky. L. Rep.—Kentucky Law Reporter.
L. Ed.—Lawyers' Edition Supreme Court Reports.
L.R.A.—Lawyers' Reports Annotated.
L.R.A. (N.S.)—Lawyers' Reports Annotated (New Series).
L.R.Q.B.—Law Reports, Queen's Bench (1866-1875).
La.—Louisiana Reports.
La. Ann.—Louisiana Annual Reports.
Lans.—Lansing's Reports, New York Supreme Court Reports, Vols. 1-7.
Ld. Raym.—Lord Raymond's English King's Bench Reports.
Lea—Lea's Tennessee Reports.
Leigh (Va.)—Leigh's Reports, Virginia.
M. & G.—Manning & Granger's English Common Pleas Reports.
M. & W.—Meeson & Welsby's Reports, English Exchequer.
Mackey (D.C.)—Mackey's Supreme Court Reports, District of Columbia.
Man.—Manning's Reports (English Court of Revision).
Mas.—Mason's United States Circuit Court Reports.
Mass.—Massachusetts Reports.
McCord (S.C.)—McCord's Law Reports, South Carolina.
McCrary—McCrary, United States Circuit Court Reports.
Md.—Maryland Reports.
Me.—Maine Reports.
Meigs (Tenn.)—Meigs' Reports, Tennessee.
Metc. (Mass.)—Metcalf's Reports, Massachusetts Reports, Vols. 42-54.
Mich.—Michigan Reports.
Mills Surr.—Mills Reports, New York.
Minn.—Minnesota Reports.

Misc.—Miscellaneous Reports, New York.
Miss.—Mississippi Reports.
Mo.—Missouri Reports.
Mo. A.—Missouri Appeals Reports.
Mod.—Modern Reports, English King's Bench, etc.
Molloy—Molloy's Irish Chancery Reports.
Monr., B. (Ky.)—Ben Monroe's Kentucky Reports.
Mont.—Montana Reports.
N.C.—North Carolina Reports.
N.E.—Northeastern Reporter.
Neb.—Nebraska Reports.
Neb. (Unoff.)—Nebraska Unofficial Reports.
Neg. Instr. Act.—Uniform Negotiable Instruments Act.
Nev.—Nevada Reports.
N.H.—New Hampshire Reports.
N.J. Ch.—New Jersey Equity Reports.
N.J. Eq.—New Jersey Equity Reports.
N.J.L.—New Jersey Law Reports.
N.M.—New Mexico Reports.
N.W.—Northwestern Reporter.
N.Y.—New York Court of Appeals Reports.
N.Y. Civ. Proc.—New York Civil Procedure Reports.
N.Y.S.—New York Supplement.
N.Y. Sup.—New York Supreme Court Reports.
N.Y. Super.—New York Superior Court Reports.
N.Y. Super. Ct.—New York Superior Court Reports.
O. Cir. Ct.—Ohio Circuit Court Reports.
Ohio—Ohio Reports.
Oh. Circ. Dec.—Ohio Circuit Decisions.
Oh. Dec. (Reprint)—Ohio Decisions (Reprint).
Ohio St.—Ohio State Reports.
Okl.—Oklahoma Territorial Reports.
Old.—Oldright's Reports, Nova Scotia.
Ont.—Ontario Reports.
Ont. A.—Ontario Appeal Reports, Canada.
Ont. App. Rep.—Ontario Appeal Reports, Canada.
Ont. L.—Ontario Law Reports.
Ont. W.N.—Ontario Weekly Notes.
Or.—Oregon Reports.
Pa.—Pennsylvania State Reports.
Pa. Super.—Pennsylvania Superior Court.
Pac.—Pacific Reporter.
Paine—Paine's United States Circuit Court Reports.
Pars. Eq. Cas.—Parson's Select Equity Cases, Pennsylvania.
Pen. & W. (Pa.)—Penrose & Watts' Pennsylvania Reports.

Pet. (U.S.)—Peters' United States Supreme Court Reports.
Pick. (Mass.)—Pickering's Reports, Massachusetts.
Plowd.—Plowden's English King's Bench Commentaries or Reports.
Q.B.—Queen's Bench Reports.
Q.B.D.—Queen's Bench Division, English Law Reports (1876-1890).
Rawle (Pa.)—Rawle's Pennsylvania Reports.
Reprint—English Cases Reprint.
Rice (S.C.)—Rice's Law Reports, South Carolina.
Rich. (S.C.)—Richardson's South Carolina Law Reports.
Rich. (S.C.) Eq.—Richardson's South Carolina Equity Reports.
Salk.—Salkeld's Reports, English Courts.
Sandf. (N.Y.)—Sandford's New York Superior Court Reports.
Sandf. Ch. (N.Y.)—Sandford's Chancery Reports, New York.
Sask.—Saskatchewan Law Reports, Canada.
Saund.—Saunders' Reports, English King's Bench.
Sawy.—Sawyer's United States Circuit Court Reports.
Scam. (Ill.)—Scammon's Reports, Vols. 2-5 Illinois.
S.C.C.—Sacra Congregatio Concilii (Sacred Congregation of the Council, i.e., of Trent).
S.C. Ep. et Reg.—Sacra Congregatio Episcoporum et Regularium (Sacred Congregation of Bishops and Regulars).
S.C. EE. et RR.—Sacra Congregatio Episcoporum et Regularium (Sacred Congregation of Bishops and Regulars).
S.C. Ca.—Supreme Court Cases (Cameron's) (Canada).
Sch. & L.—Schoals & Lefroy's Reports, Irish Chancery.
S.C.L.—South Carolina Law Reports.
Scott.—Scott's English Common Pleas Reports.
S.D.—South Dakota Reports.
S.E.—Southeastern Reporter.
Sim.—Simons' English Vice-Chancery Reports.
Sm. & M. (Miss.)—Smedes & Marshall's Mississippi Reports.
Sneed (Tenn).—Sneed's Tennessee Reports.
South.—Southern Reporter.
S. & R. (Pa.)—Sergeant & Rawle's Reports, Pennsylvania.
S.R.R.—Sacra Romana Rota (Sacred Roman Rota).
Sup. Ct.—Supreme Court Reporter of Decisions of United States Supreme Court.
S.W.—Southwestern Reporter.
Taney—Taney's Decisions, by Campbell, United States Circuit Court, 4th Circuit.
Taunt.—Taunton's English Common Pleas Reports.
Tenn.—Tennessee Reports.
Term—Term Reports, English King's Bench.
Tex.—Texas Reports.
Tex. Civ. A.—Texas Civil Appeals Reports.
U.C.Q.B.—Upper Canada Queen's Bench Reports.

U.S.—United States Reports.
U.S.App.—United States Appeals, Circuit Courts of Appeals.
U.S.C.C.—United States Circuit Court, United States Court of Claims.
Utah—Utah Reports.
Va.—Virginia Reports.
Vern.—Vernon's Reports, English Chancery.
Ves. Ch.—Vesey's Reports, English Chancery.
Vt.—Vermont Reports.
Wall.—Wallace' United States Supreme Court Reports.
Wash.—Washington State Reports.
Wash. C.C.—Washington's United States Circuit Court Reports.
Watts (Pa.)—Watts' Pennsylvania Reports.
Watts & S.—Watts & Sergeant's Pennsylvania Reports.
Wend. (N.Y.)—Wendell's Reports, New York Supreme Court.
Whart. (Pa.)—Wharton's Reports, Pennsylvania.
Wheat. (U.S.)—Wheaton's United States Supreme Court Reports.
Wis.—Wisconsin Reports.
Wkly Law Bul.—Weekly Law Bulletin (Ohio).
W.N.C. (Pa.)—Weekly Notes of Cases, Philadelphia.
W. Va.—West Virginia Reports.
Y. & C. Exch.—Younge & Collyer's English Chancery or Exchequer Reports.

INDEX OF ANGLO-AMERICAN CASES CITED

(Numbers refer to marginal numbers)

A

B

C

I

J

K

L

ALPHABETICAL INDEX

BIOGRAPHICAL NOTE

THOMAS OWEN MARTIN was born February 26, 1910, in Grand Rapids, Michigan. After receiving his primary education in the schools of Wayland, St. Louis, and Grand Rapids, Michigan, he entered St. Joseph's Seminary in Grand Rapids, Michigan, for the Preparatory Seminary course. Entering the *Pontificio Seminario Romano Maggiore,* Rome, in the fall of 1928, he received from the Athenaeum of that institution the degree of Doctor of Philosophy in 1930. At the same Athenaeum he received the degree of Doctor of Sacred Theology in 1935. He was ordained to the Priesthood on December 7, 1933. He entered The Catholic University of America in the fall of 1941 and obtained the degree of Baccalaureate in Canon Law in 1942, and the degree of Licentiate in Canon Law in 1943.

CANON LAW STUDIES *

1. FRERIKS, REV. CELESTINE A., C.PP.S., J.C.D., Religious Congregations in Their External Relations, 121 pp., 1916.
2. GALLIHER, REV. DANIEL M., O.P., J.C.D., Canonical Elections, 117 pp., 1917.
3. BORKOWSKI, REV. AURELIUS L., O.F.M., J.C.D., De Confraternitatibus Ecclesiasticis, 136 pp., 1918.
4. CASTILLO, REV. CAYO, J.C.D., Disertacion Historico-Canonica sobre la Potestad del Cabildo en Sede Vacante o Impedida del Vicario Capitular, 99 pp., 1919 (1918).
5. KUBELBECK, REV. WILLIAM J., S.T.B., J.C.D., The Sacred Penitentiaria and Its Relation to Faculties of Ordinaries and Priests, 129 pp., 1918.
6. PETROVITS, REV. JOSEPH, J.C., S.T.D., J.C.D., The New Church Law on Matrimony, X-461 pp., 1919.
7. HICKEY, REV. JOHN J., S.T.B., J.C.D., Irregularities and Simple Impediments in the New Code of Canon Law, 100 pp., 1920.
8. KLEKOTKA, REV. PETER J., S.T.B., J.C.D., Diocesan Consultors, 179 pp., 1920.
9. WANENMACHER, REV. FRANCIS, J.C.D., The Evidence in Ecclesiastical Procedure Affecting the Marriage Bond, 1920 (Printed 1935).
10. GOLDEN, REV. HENRY FRANCIS, J.C.D., Parochial Benefices in the New Code, IV-119 pp., 1921 (Printed 1925).
11. KOUDELKA, REV. CHARLES J., J.C.D., Pastors, Their Rights and Duties According to the New Code of Canon Law, 211 pp., 1921.
12. MELO, REV. ANTONIUS, O.F.M., J.C.D., De Exemptione Regularium, X-188 pp., 1921.
13. SCHAAF, REV. VALENTINE THEODORE, O.F.M., S.T.B., J.C.D., The Cloister, X-180 pp., 1921.
14. BURKE, REV. THOMAS JOSEPH, S.T.D., J.C.D., Competence in Ecclesiastical Tribunals, IV-117 pp., 1922.
15. LEECH, REV. GEORGE LEO, J.C.D., A Comparative Study of the Constitution "Apostolicae Sedis" and the "Codex Juris Canonici," 179 pp., 1922.
16. MOTRY, REV. HUBERT LOUIS, S.T.D., J.C.D., Diocesan Faculties According to the Code of Canon Law, II-167 pp., 1922.
17. MURPHY, REV. GEORGE LAWRENCE, J.C.D., Delinquencies and Penalties in the Administration and the Reception of the Sacraments, IV-121 pp., 1923.
18. O'REILLY, REV. JOHN ANTHONY, S.T.B., J.C.D., Ecclesiastical Sepulture in the New Code of Canon Law, II-129 pp., 1923.

* Below n. 100 only the following numbers are still available: Nn. 3, 4, 9, 25, 34, 57 and 75. Beginning with n. 100 only the following are unavailable: Nn. 100-111 inclusive, and n. 113.

19. MICHALICKA, REV. WENCESLAS CYRILL, O.S.B., J.C.D., Judicial Procedure in Dismissal of Clerical Exempt Religious, 107 pp., 1923.
20. DARGIN, REV. EDWARD VINCENT, S.T.B., J.C.D., Reserved Cases According to the Code of Canon Law, IV-103 pp., 1924.
21. GODFREY, REV. JOHN A., S.T.B., J.C.D., The Right of Patronage According to the Code of Canon Law, 153 pp., 1924.
22. HAGEDORN, REV. FRANCIS EDWARD, J.C.D., General Legislation on Indulgences, II-154 pp., 1924.
23. KING, REV. JAMES IGNATIUS, J.C.D., The Administration of the Sacraments to Dying Non-Catholics, V-141 pp., 1924.
24. WINSLOW, REV. FRANCIS JOSEPH, O.F.M., J.C.D., Vicars and Prefects Apostolic, IV-149 pp., 1924.
25. CORREA, REV. JOSE SERVELION, S.T.L., J.C.D., La Potestad Legislativa de la Iglesia Catolica, IV-127 pp., 1925.
26. DUGAN, REV. HENRY FRANCIS, A.M., J.C.D., The Judiciary Department of the Diocesan Curia, 87 pp., 1925.
27. KELLER, REV. CHARLES FREDERICK, S.T.B., J.C.D., Mass Stipends, 167 pp., 1925.
28. PASCHANG, REV. JOHN LINUS, J.C.D., The Sacramentals According to the Code of Canon Law, 129 pp., 1925.
29. PIONTEK, REV. CYRILLUS, O.F.M., S.T.B., J.C.D., De Indulto Exclaustrationis necnon Saecularizationis, XIII-289 pp., 1925.
30. KEARNEY, REV. RICHARD JOSEPH, S.T.B., J.C.D., Sponsors at Baptism According to the Code of Canon Law, IV-127 pp., 1925.
31. BARTLETT, REV. CHESTER JOSEPH, A.M., LL.B., J.C.D., The Tenure of Parochial Property in the United States of America, V-108 pp., 1926.
32. KILKER, REV. ADRIAN JEROME, J.C.D., Extreme Unction, V-425 pp., 1926.
33. MCCORMICK, REV. ROBERT EMMETT, J.C.D., Confessors of Religious, VIII-266 pp., 1926.
34. MILLER, REV. NEWTON THOMAS, J.C.D., Founded Masses According to the Code of Canon Law, VII-93 pp., 1926.
35. ROELKER, REV. EDWARD G., S.T.D., J.C.D., Principles of Privilege According to the Code of Canon Law, XI-166 pp., 1926.
36. BAKALARCZYK, REV. RICHARDUS, M.I.C., J.U.D., De Novitiatu, VIII-208 pp., 1927.
37. PIZZUTI, REV. LAWRENCE, O.F.M., J.U.L., De Parochis Religiosis, 1927. (Not Printed.)
38. BLILEY, REV. NICHOLAS MARTIN, O.S.B., J.C.D., Altars According to the Code of Canon Law, XIX-132 pp., 1927.
39. BROWN, MR. BRENDAN FRANCIS, A.B., LL.M., J.U.D., The Canonical Juristic Personality with Special Reference to its Status in the United States of America, V-212 pp., 1927.
40. CAVANAUGH, REV. WILLIAM THOMAS, C.P., J.U.D., The Reservation of the Blessed Sacrament, VIII-101 pp., 1927.

41. Doheny, Rev. William J., C.S.C., A.B., J.U.D., Church Property: Modes of Acquisition, X-118 pp., 1927.
42. Feldhaus, Rev. Aloysius H., C.PP.S., J.C.D., Oratories, IX-141 pp., 1927.
43. Kelly, Rev. James Patrick, A.B., J.C.D., The Jurisdiction of the Simple Confessor, X-208 pp., 1927.
44. Neuberger, Rev. Nicholas J., J.C.D., Canon 6 or the Relation of the Codex Juris Canonici to the Preceding Legislation, V-95 pp., 1927.
45. O'Keefe, Rev. Gerald Michael, J.C.D., Matrimonial Dispensations, Powers of Bishops, Priests, and Confessors, VIII-232 pp., 1927.
46. Quigley, Rev. Joseph A. M., A.B., J.C.D., Condemned Societies, 139 pp., 1927.
47. Zaplotnik, Rev. Johannes Leo, J.C.D., De Vicariis Foraneis, X-142 pp., 1927.
48. Duskie, Rev. John Aloysius, A.B., J.C.D., The Canonical Status of the Orientals in the United States, VIII-196 pp., 1928.
49. Hyland, Rev. Francis Edward, J.C.D., Excommunication, Its Nature, Historical Development and Effects, VIII-181 pp., 1928.
50. Reinmann, Rev. Gerald Joseph, O.M.C., J.C.D., The Third Order Secular of Saint Francis, 201 pp., 1928.
51. Schenk, Rev. Francis J., J.C.D., The Matrimonial Impediments of Mixed Religion and Disparity of Cult, XVI-318 pp., 1929.
52. Coady, Rev. John Joseph, S.T.D., J.U.D., A.M., The Appointment of Pastors, VIII-150 pp., 1929.
53. Kay, Rev. Thomas Henry, J.C.D., Competence in Matrimonial Procedure, VIII-164 pp., 1929.
54. Turner, Rev. Sidney Joseph, C.P., J.U.D., The Vow of Poverty, XLIX-217 pp., 1929.
55. Kearney, Rev. Raymond A., A.B., S.T.D., J.C.D., The Principles of Delegation, VII-149 pp., 1929.
56. Conran, Rev. Edward James, A.B., J.C.D., The Interdict, V-163 pp., 1930.
57. O'Neill, Rev. William H., J.C.D., Papal Rescripts of Favor, VII-218 pp., 1930.
58. Bastnagel, Rev. Clement Vincent, J.U.D., The Appointment of Parochial Adjutants and Assistants, XV-257 pp., 1930.
59. Ferry, Rev. William A., A.B., J.C.D., Stole Fees, V-136 pp., 1930.
60. Costello, Rev. John Michael, A.B., J.C.D., Domicile and Quasi-Domicile, VII-201 pp., 1930.
61. Kremer, Rev. Michael Nicholas, A.B., S.T.B., J.C.D., Church Support in the United States, VI-136 pp., 1930.
62. Angulo, Rev. Luis, C.M., J.C.D., Legislation de la Iglesia sobre la intencion en la application de la Santa Misa, VII-104 pp., 1931.
63. Frey, Rev. Wolfgang Norbert, O.S.B., A.B., J.C.D., The Act of Religious Profession, VIII-174 pp., 1931.

64. ROBERTS, REV. JAMES BRENDAN, A.B., J.C.D., The Banns of Marriage, XIV-140 pp., 1931.
65. RYDER, REV. RAYMOND ALOYSIUS, A.B., J.C.D., Simony, IX-151 pp., 1931.
66. CAMPAGNA, REV. ANGELO, PH.D., J.U.D., Il Vicario Generale del Vescovo, VII-205 pp., 1931.
67. COX, REV. JOSEPH GODFREY, A.B., J.C.D., The Administration of Seminaries, VI-124 pp., 1931.
68. GREGORY, REV. DONALD J., J.U.D., The Pauline Privilege, XV-165 pp., 1931.
69. DONOHUE, REV. JOHN F., J.C.D., The Impediment of Crime, VII-110 pp., 1931.
70. DOOLEY, REV. EUGENE A., O.M.I., J.C.D., Church Law on Sacred Relics, IX-143 pp., 1931.
71. ORTH, REV. CLEMENT RAYMOND, O.M.C., J.C.D., The Approbation of Religious Institutes, 171 pp., 1931.
72. PERNICONE, REV. JOSEPH M., A.B., J.C.D., The Ecclesiastical Prohibition of Books, XII-267 pp., 1932.
73. CLINTON, REV. CONNELL, A.B., J.C.D., The Paschal Precept, IX-108 pp., 1932.
74. DONNELLY, REV. FRANCIS B., A.M., S.T.L., J.C.D., The Diocesan Synod, VIII-125 pp., 1932.
75. TORRENTE, REV. CAMILO, C.M.F., J.C.D., Las Procesiones Sagradas, V-145 pp., 1932.
76. MURPHY, REV. EDWIN J., C.PP.S., J.C.D., Suspension Ex Informata Conscientia, XI-122 pp., 1932.
77. MACKENZIE, REV. ERIC F., A.M., S.T.L., J.C.D., The Delict of Heresy in its Commission, Penalization, Absolution, VII-124 pp., 1932.
78. LYONS, REV. AVITUS E., S.T.B., J.C.D., The Collegiate Tribunal of First Instance, XI-147 pp., 1932.
79. CONNOLLY, REV. THOMAS A., J.C.D., Appeals, XI-195, pp., 1932.
80. SANGMEISTER, REV. JOSEPH V., A.B., J.C.D., Force and Fear as Precluding Matrimonial Consent, V-211 pp., 1932.
81. JAEGER, REV. LEO A., A.B., J.C.D., The Administration of Vacant and Quasi-Vacant Episcopal Sees in the United States, IX-229 pp., 1932.
82. RIMLINGER, REV. HERBERT T., J.C.D., Error Invalidating Matrimonial Consent, VII-79, pp. 1932.
83. BARRETT, REV. JOHN D. M., S.S., J.C.D., A Comparative Study of the Third Plenary Council of Baltimore and the Code, IX-221 pp., 1932.
84. CARBERRY, REV. JOHN J., PH.D., S.T.D., J.C.D., The Juridical Form of Marriage, X-177 pp., 1934.
85. DOLAN, REV. JOHN L., A.B., J.C.D., The Defensor Vinculi, XII-157 pp., 1934.
86. HANNAN, REV. JEROME D., A.M., S.T.D., LL.B., J.C.D., The Canon Law of Wills, IX-517 pp., 1934.

87. Lemieux, Rev. Delise A., A.M., J.C.D., The Sentence in Ecclesiastical Procedure, IX-131 pp., 1934.
88. O'Rourke, Rev. James J., A.B., J.C.D., Parish Registers, VII-109 pp., 1934.
89. Timlin, Rev. Bartholomew, O.F.M., A.M., J.C.D., Conditional Matrimonial Consent, X-381 pp., 1934.
90. Wahl, Rev. Francis X., A.B., J.C.D., The Matrimonial Impediments of Consanguinity and Affinity, VI-125 pp., 1934.
91. White, Rev. Robert J., A.B., LL.B., S.T.B., J.C.D., Canonical Ante-Nuptial Promises and the Civil Law, VI-152 pp., 1934.
92. Herrera, Rev. Antonio Parra, O.C.D., J.C.D., Legislacion Ecclesiastica sobra el Ayuno y la Abstinencia, XI-191 pp., 1935.
93. Kennedy, Rev. Edwin J., J.C.D., The Special Matrimonial Process in Cases of Evident Nullity, X-165 pp., 1935.
94. Manning, Rev. John J., A.B., J.C.D., Presumption of Law in Matrimonial Procedure, XI-111 pp., 1935.
95. Moeder, Rev. John M., J.C.D., The Proper Bishop for Ordination and Dimissorial Letters, VII-135 pp., 1935.
96. O'Mara, Rev. William A., A.B., J.C.D., Canonical Causes for Matrimonial Dispensations, IX-155 pp., 1935.
97. Reilly, Rev. Peter, J.C.D., Residence of Pastors, IX-81 pp., 1935.
98. Smith, Rev. Mariner T., O.P., S.T.Lr., J.C.D., The Penal Law for Religious, VIII-169 pp., 1935.
99. Whalen, Rev. Donald W., A.M., J.C.D., The Value of Testimonial Evidence in Matrimonial Procedure, XIII-297 pp., 1935.
100. Cleary, Rev. Joseph F., J.C.D., Canonical Limitations on the Alienation of Church Property, VIII-141 pp., 1936.
101. Glynn, Rev. John C., J.C.D., The Promoter of Justice, XX-337 pp., 1936.
102. Brennan, Rev. James H., S.S., M.A., S.T.B., J.C.D., The Simple Convalidation of Marriage, VI-135 pp., 1937.
103. Brunini, Rev. Joseph Bernard, J.C.D., The Clerical Obligations of Canons 139 and 142, X-121 pp., 1937.
104. Connor, Rev. Maurice, A.B., J.C.D., The Administrative Removal of Pastors, VIII-159 pp., 1937.
105. Guilfoyle, Rev. Merlin Joseph, J.C.D., Custom, XI-144 pp., 1937.
106. Hughes, Rev. James Austin, A.B., A.M., J.C.D., Witnesses in Criminal Trials of Clerics, IX-140 pp., 1937.
107. Jansen, Rev. Raymond J., A.B., S.T.L., J.C.D., Canonical Provisions for Catechetical Instruction, VII-153 pp., 1937.
108. Kealy, Rev. John James, A.B., J.C.D., The Introductory Libellus in Church Court Procedure, XI-121 pp., 1937.
109. McManus, Rev. James Edward, C.SS.R., J.C.D., The Administration of Temporal Goods in Religious Institutes, XVI-196 pp., 1937.

110. Moriarty, Rev. Eugene James, J.C.D., Oaths in Ecclesiastical Courts, X-115 pp., 1937.
111. Rainer, Rev. Eligius George, C.SS.R., J.C.D., Suspension of Clerics, XVII-249 pp., 1937.
112. Reilly, Rev. Thomas F., C.SS.R., J.C.D., Visitation of Religious, VI-195 pp., 1938.
113. Moriarty, Rev. Francis E., C.SS.R., J.C.D., The Extraordinary Absolution from Censures, XV-334 pp., 1938.
114. Connolly, Rev. Nicholas P., J.C.D., The Canonical Erection of Parishes, X-132 pp., 1938.
115. Donovan, Rev. James Joseph, J.C.D., The Pastor's Obligation in Prenuptial Investigation, XII-322 pp., 1938.
116. Harrigan, Rev. Robert J., M.A., S.T.B., J.C.D., The Radical Sanation of Invalid Marriages, VIII-208 pp., 1938.
117. Boffa, Rev. Conrad Humbert, J.C.D., Canonical Provisions for Catholic Schools, VII-211 pp., 1939.
118. Parsons, Rev. Anscar John, O.M.Cap., J.C.D., Canonical Elections, XII-236 pp., 1939.
119. Reilly, Rev. Edward Michael, A.B., J.C.D., The General Norms of Dispensation, XII-156 pp., 1939.
120. Ryan, Rev. Gerald Aloysius, A.B., J.C.D., Principles of Episcopal Jurisdiction, XII-172 pp., 1939.
121. Burton, Rev. Francis James, C.S.C., A.B., J.C.D., A Commentary on Canon 1125, X-222 pp., 1940.
122. Miaskiewicz, Rev. Francis Sigismund, J.C.D., Supplied Jurisdiction According to Canon 209, XII-340 pp., 1940.
123. Rice, Rev. Patrick William, A.B., J.C.D., Proof of Death in Prenuptial Investigation, VIII-156 pp., 1940.
124. Anglin, Rev. Thomas Francis, M.S., J.C.D., The Eucharistic Fast, VIII-183 pp., 1941.
125. Coleman, Rev. John Jerome, J.C.D., The Minister of Confirmation, VI-153 pp., 1941.
126. Downs, Rev. John Emmanuel, A.B., J.C.D., The Concept of Clerical Immunity, XI-163 pp., 1941.
127. Esswein, Rev. Anthony Albert, J.C.D., Extrajudicial Penal Powers of Ecclesiastical Superiors, X-144 pp., 1941.
128. Farrell, Rev. Benjamin Francis, M.A., S.T.L., J.C.D., The Rights and Duties of the Local Ordinary Regarding Congregations of Women Religious of Pontifical Approval, V-195 pp., 1941.
129. Feeney, Rev. Thomas John, A.B., S.T.L., J.C.D., Restitutio in Integrum, VI-1169 pp., 1941.
130. Findlay, Rev. Stephen William, O.S.B., A.B., J.C.D., Canonical Norms Governing the Deposition and Degradation of Clerics, XVII-279 pp., 1941.

131. Goodwine, Rev. John, A.B., S.T.L., J.C.D., The Right of the Church to Acquire Property, VIII-119 pp., 1941.
132. Heston, Rev. Edward Louis, C.S.C., Ph.D., S.T.D., J.C.D., The Alienation of Church Property in the United States, XII-222 pp., 1941.
133. Hogan, Rev. James John, A.B., S.T.L., J.C.D., Judicial Advocates and Procurators, XIII-200 pp., 1941.
134. Kealy, Rev. Thomas M., A.B., Litt.B., J.C.D., Dowry of Women Religious, IX-152 pp., 1941.
135. Keene, Rev. Michael James, O.S.B., J.C.D., Religious Ordinaries and Canon 198, V-164 pp., 1942.
136. Kerin, Rev. Charles A., S.S., M.A., S.T.B., J.C.D., The Privation of Christian Burial, XVI-279 pp., 1941.
137. Louis, Rev. William Francis, M.A., J.C.D., Diocesan Archives, X-101 pp., 1941.
138. McDevitt, Rev. Gilbert Joseph, A.B., J.C.D., Legitimacy and Legitimation, X-247 pp., 1941.
139. McDonough, Rev. Thomas Joseph, A.B., J.C.D., Apostolic Administrators, X-217 pp., 1941.
140. Meier, Rev. Carl Anthony, A.B., J.C.D., Penal Administrative Procedure Against Negligent Pastors, XI-240 pp., 1941.
141. Schmidt, Rev. John Rogg, A.B., J.C.D., The Principles of Authentic Interpretation in Canon 17 of the Code of Canon Law, XII-331 pp., 1941.
142. Slafkosky, Rev. Andrew Leonard, A.B., J.C.D., The Canonical Episcopal Visitation of the Diocese, X-197 pp., 1941.
143. Swoboda, Rev. Innocent Robert, O.F.M., J.C.D., Ignorance in Relation to the Imputability of Delicts, IX-271 pp., 1941.
144. Dubé, Rev. Arthur Joseph, A.B., J.C.D., The General Principles for the Reckoning of Time in Canon Law, VIII-299 pp., 1941.
145. McBride, Rev. James T., A.B., J.C.D., Incardination and Excardination of Seculars, XX-585 pp., 1941.
146. Król, Rev. John T., J.C.D., The Defendant in Ecclesiastical Trials, XII-207 pp., 1942.
147. Comyns, Rev. Joseph J., C.SS.R., A.B., J.C.D., Papal and Episcopal Administration of Church Property, XIV-155 pp., 1942.
148. Barry, Rev. Garrett Francis, O.M.I., J.C.D., Violation of the Cloister, XII-260 pp., 1942.
149. Bolduc, Rev. Gatien, C.S.V., A.B., S.T.L., J.C.D., Les Études dans les Religions Cléricales, VIII-155 pp., 1942.
150. Boyle, Rev. David John, M.A., J.C.D., The Juridic Effects of Moral Certitude on Pre-Nuptial Guarantees, XII-188 pp., 1942.
151. Canavan, Rev. Walter Joseph, M.A., Litt.D., J.C.D., The Profession of Faith, XII-143 pp., 1942.
152. Desrochers, Rev. Bruno, A.B., Ph.L., S.T.B., J.C.D., Le Premier Concile Plénier de Québec et le Code de Droit Canonique, XIV-186 pp., 1942.

153. DILLON, REV. ROBERT EDWARD, A.B., J.C.D., Common Law Marriage, X-148 pp., 1942.
154. DODWELL, REV. EDWARD JOHN, Ph.D., S.T.B., J.C.D., The Time and Place for the Celebration of Marriage, X-156 pp., 1942.
155. DONNELLAN, REV. THOMAS ANDREW, A.B., J.C.D., The Obligation of the Missa pro Populo, VII-131 pp., 1942.
156. ELTZ, REV. LOUIS ANTHONY, A.B., J.C.L., Cooperation in Crime.
157. GASS, REV. SYLVESTER FRANCIS, M.A., J.C.D., Ecclesiastical Pensions, XI-206 pp., 1942.
158. GUINIVEN, REV. JOHN JOSEPH, C.SS.R., J.C.D., The Precept of Hearing Mass, XIV-188 pp., 1942.
159. GULCZYNSKI, REV. JOHN THEOPHILUS, J.C.D., The Desecration and Violation of Churches, X-126 pp., 1942.
10. HAMMILL, REV. JOHN LEO, M.A., J.C.D., The Obligations of the Traveler According to Canon 14, VIII-204 pp., 1942.
161. HAYDT, REV. JOHN JOSEPH, A.B., J.C.D., Reserved Benefices, XI-148 pp., 1942.
162. HUSER, REV. ROGER JOHN, O.F.M., A.B., J.C.D., The Crime of Abortion in Canon Law, XII-187 pp., 1942.
163. KEARNEY, REV. FRANCIS PATRICK, A.B., S.T.L., J.C.L., The Principles of Canon 1127.
164. LINAHEN, REV. LEO JAMES, S.T.L., J.C.D., De Absolutione Complicis In Peccato Turpi, 114 pp., 1942.
165. MCCLOSKEY, REV. JOSEPH ALOYSIUS, A.B., J.C.D., The Subject of Ecclesiastical Law According to Canon 12, XVII-246 pp., 1942.
166. O'NEILL, REV. FRANCIS JOSEPH, C.SS.R., J.C.D., The Dismissal of Religious in Temporary Vows, XIII-220 pp., 1942.
167. PRINCE, REV. JOHN EDWARD, A.B., S.T.B., J.C.D., The Diocesan Chancellor, X-136 pp., 1942.
168. RIESNER, REV. ALBERT JOSEPH, C.SS.R., J.C.D., Apostates and Fugitives from Religious Institutes, IX-168 pp., 1942.
169. STENGER, REV. JOSEPH BERNARD, J.C.D., The Mortgaging of Church Property, 186 pp., 1942.
170. WALDRON, REV. JOSEPH FRANCIS, A.B., J.C.D., The Minister of Baptism, XII-197 pp., 1942.
171. WILLETT, REV. ROBERT ALBERT, J.C.D., The Probative Value of Documents in Ecclesiastical Trials, X-124 pp., 1942.
172. WOEBER, REV. EDWARD MARTIN, M.A., J.C.D., The Interpellations, XII-161 pp., 1942.
173. BENKO, REV. MATTHEW ALOYSIUS, O.S.B., M.A., J.C.L., The Abbot *Nullius.*
174. CHRIST, REV. JOSEPH JAMES, M.A., S.T.L., J.C.L., Dispensation from Vindicative Penalties, XIII-285 pp., 1943.
175. CLANCY, REV. PATRICK M. J., O.P., A.B., S.T.Lr., J.C.D., The Local Religious Superior, X-229 pp., 1943.

176. CLARKE, REV. THOMAS JAMES, J.C.D., Parish Societies, XII-147 pp., 1943.
177. CONNOLLY, REV. JOHN PATRICK, S.T.L., J.C.D., Synodal Examiners and Parish Priest Consultors, X-223 pp., 1943.
178. DRUMM, REV. WILLIAM MARTIN, A.B., J.C.L., Hospital Chaplains, XI-175 pp., 1943.
179. FLANAGAN, REV. BERNARD JOSEPH, A.B., S.T.L., J.C.D., The Canonical Erection of Religious Houses, X-147 pp., 1943.
180. KELLEHER, REV. STEPHEN JOSEPH, A.B., S.T.B., J.C.D., Discussions with Non-Catholics: Canonical Legislation, X-93 pp., 1943.
181. LEWIS, REV. GORDIAN, C.P., J.C.D., Chapters in Religious Institutes, XII-169 pp., 1943.
182. MARX, REV. ADOLPH, J.C.D., The Declaration of Nullity of Marriages Contracted Outside the Church, X-151 pp., 1943.
183. MATULENAS, REV. RAYMOND ANTHONY, O.S.B., A.B., J.C.L., Communication, a Source of Privileges.
184. O'LEARY, REV. CHARLES GERARD, C.SS.R., J.C.L., Religious Dismissed After Perpetual Profession.
185. POWER, REV. CORNELIUS MICHAEL, J.C.L., The Blessing of Cemeteries, XII-231 pp., 1943.
186. SHUHLER, REV. RALPH VINCENT, O.S.A., J.C.D., Privileges of Religious to Absolve and Dispense, XII-195 pp., 1943.
187. ZIOLKOWSKI, REV. THADDEUS STANISLAUS, A.B., J.C.D., The Consecration and Blessing of Churches, XII-151 pp., 1943.
188. HENEGHAN, REV. JOHN JOSEPH, S.T.D., J.C.L., The Marriages of Unworthy Catholics: Canons 1065 and 1066.
189. CARROLL, REV. COLEMAN FRANCIS, M.A., S.T.L., J.C.L., Charitable Institutions.
190. CIESLUK, REV. JOSEPH EDWARD, PH.B., S.T.L., J.C.L., National Parishes in the United States.
191. COBURN, REV. VINCENT PAUL, A.B., J.C.L., Marriages of Conscience.
192. CONNORS, REV. CHARLES PAUL, C.S.SP., A.B., J.C.L., Extra-Judicial Procurators in the Code of Canon Law.
193. COYLE, REV. PAUL RAYMOND, A.B., J.C.L., Judicial Exceptions.
194. FAIR, REV. BARTHOLOMEW FRANCIS, A.B., S.T.L., J.C.L., The Impediment of Abduction.
195. GALLAGHER, REV. THOMAS RAPHAEL, O.P., A.B., S.T.LR., J.C.L., The Examination of the Qualities of the Ordinand.
196. GANNON, REV. JOHN MARK, S.T.L., J.C.L., The Interstices Required for the Promotion to Orders.
197. GOLDSMITH, REV. J. WILLIAM, B.C.S., S.T.L., J.C.L., The Competence of Church and State Over Marriage—Disputed Points.
198. GOODWINE, REV. JOSEPH GERARD, A.B., S.T.B., J.C.L., The Reception of Converts.
199. KOWALSKI, REV. ROMUALD EUGENE, O.F.M., A.B., J.C.L., Sustenence of Religious Houses of Regulars.

200. McCoy, Rev. Alan Edward, O.F.M., J.C.L., Force and Fear in Relation to Delictual Imputability and Penal Responsibility.
201. McDevitt, Rev. Vincent John, Ph.B., S.T.L., J.C.L., Perjury.
202. Martin, Rev. Thomas Owen, Ph.D., S.T.D., J.C.L., Adverse Possession, Prescription and Limitation of Actions: The Canonical "Praescriptio."
203. Miklosovic, Rev. Paul John, A.B., J.C.L., Attempted Marriages and Their Consequent Juridic Effects.
204. Mundy, Rev. Thomas Maurice, A.B., S.T.L., J.C.L., The Union of Parishes.
205. O'Dea, Rev. John Coyle, A.B., J.C.L., The Matrimonial Impediment of Nonage.
206. Olalia, Rev. Alexander Ayson, S.T.L., J.C.L., A Comparative Study of the Christian Constitution of States and the Constitution of the Philippine Commonwealth.
207. Poisson, Rev. Pierre-Marie, C.S.C., A.B., Ph.L., Th.L., J.C.L., Droits Patrimoniaux des Maisons et des Eglises Religieuses.
208. Stadalnikas, Rev. Casimir Joseph, M.I.C., J.C.L., Reservation of Censures.
209. Sullivan, Rev. Eugene Henry, S.T.L., J.C.L., Proof of the Reception of the Sacraments.
210. Vaughan, Rev. William Edward, J.C.L., Constitutions for Diocesan Courts.
211. Lyons, Rev. Joseph Henry, J.C.L., The Joinder of Issue in Canonical Trials.

www.ingramcontent.com/pod-product-compliance
Lightning Source LLC
LaVergne TN
LVHW050244080826
844660LV00012B/594

9780813223902